Rugged Access for All

Rugged Access for All

The Complete Guide to Pushiking America's Diverse Trails

Christopher Kain

ROWMAN & LITTLEFIELD
Lanham • Boulder • New York • London

Published by Rowman & Littlefield
An imprint of The Rowman & Littlefield Publishing Group, Inc.
4501 Forbes Boulevard, Suite 200, Lanham, Maryland 20706
www.rowman.com

86-90 Paul Street, London EC2A 4NE, United Kingdom

British Library Cataloguing in Publication Information Available

Library of Congress Cataloging-in-Publication Data

Names: Kain, Christopher, 1971- author.
Title: Rugged access for all : the complete guide to pushiking America's diverse trails / Christopher Kain.
Description: Lanham, Maryland : Rowman & Littlefield, [2020] | Includes bibliographical references. | Summary: "This book showcases some of the greatest trails across the US that can be completed while pushiking-hiking with someone in a wheelchair, mobility chair, or stroller. Part narrative, part guidebook, this book validates that anyone can experience the natural landscapes our country has to offer, no matter what mobility challenges they may face"— Provided by publisher.
Identifiers: LCCN 2019057092 (print) | LCCN 2019057093 (ebook) | ISBN 9781538126608 (cloth) | ISBN 9781538126615 (epub) | ISBN 9781538168417 (paperback)
Subjects: LCSH: Hiking for people with disabilities—United States—Guidebooks | Wheelchair hiking—United States—Guidebooks | Hiking—United States—Guidebooks. | Trails—United States—Guidebooks. | People with disabilities—Travel—United States—Guidebooks.
Classification: LCC GV199.56 .K35 2020 (print) | LCC GV199.56 (ebook) | DDC 796.51087/3—dc23
LC record available at https://lccn.loc.gov/2019057092
LC ebook record available at https://lccn.loc.gov/2019057093

∞™ The paper used in this publication meets the minimum requirements of American National Standard for Information Sciences—Permanence of Paper for Printed Library Materials, ANSI/NISO Z39.48-1992.

Lisa, we're bonded forever!
Kellisa, we did it!
Egypt, the world is yours!
Everett and Kirsten, miss you guys!

Contents

Foreword

Patrick Gray and Justin Skeesuck

As fathers to some amazing boys and girls, we have sacrificed our wants and needs to make sure our sons and daughters are cared for, have a safe place to rest their heads, and know they are valued. The love we feel for our children is unique, there is an intensity to it that makes us want only the best for them, and we will do anything within our power to make it so. Fellow parents understand this. As mothers and fathers, we all embrace the desire to press in and learn from our children's perspectives, we share experiences with them, and we work to open their eyes to all the world has to offer. And if we pay close attention, we get to experience many of life's wonders through their eyes.

But does this love change when a child faces immense difficulty? Does the drive we have to provide for our kids shift when things don't go as planned? Imagine a son or daughter who can't walk, can't speak in a traditional sense, a child you have to care for every day of their life. What would you do for them—how far would you go to help them move beyond their perceived limitations? For some of you, this is your reality. For the rest of us, we can only wonder what we would do and marvel at the beauty the exists in such relationships.

Does this love change when a child faces immense difficulty? We don't believe so. A parent's love for a child seems to have unknown depths.

Does the drive we have to provide for our kids shift when things don't go as planned? For some, absolutely. For some, situations like this add fuel to the fire for parents who loves their child with reckless abandon. For some, the harder the situation, the more evident the resolve to do anything for a child.

In the pages that follow, you are invited into a number of adventures, a host of stories shared by a father and his daughter. *Rugged Access for All* is a guide for those looking to embrace all that nature has to offer—a guide for wheelchair users, stroller pushers, and anyone who desires to walk alongside or give a push to someone who needs it. But it is more than that—it is the result of a love between a father and daughter, a love that reminds us that life should be experienced with others at our side.

Introduction

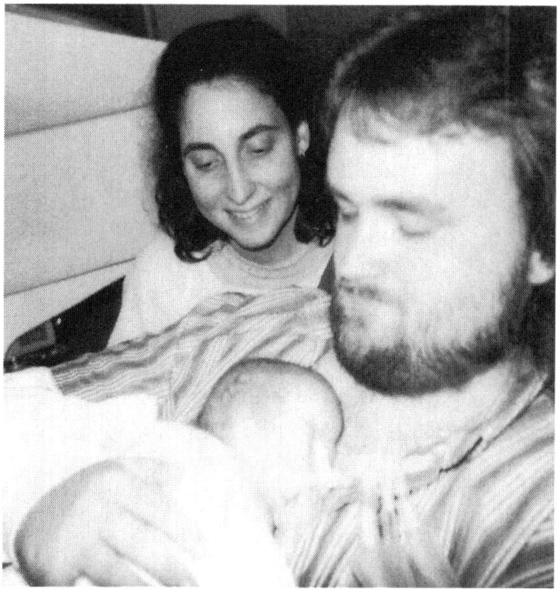

Family picture, 1999

Most fathers waiting in a cold hallway outside a delivery room expect to hear the words, "It's a boy" or "It's a girl." We already knew Lisa was pregnant with identical twin girls.

For us, the first words the doctor told me upon exiting the delivery room were, "Everyone's alive."

Even though Kellisa was only a few minutes old, she already exceeded her expected lifespan. At twelve-weeks gestation, we received the devastating news that Baby B had significant hydrocephalus. The doctor told us Baby B probably wouldn't survive the pregnancy, and if she was born, she couldn't survive more than a couple of minutes.

We traveled to see other doctors and even flew from Chicago to Florida to see a world-leading expert, and they all agreed with the initial prognosis. Kellisa's diagnosis was complicated because she was sharing the womb and placenta with her sister, Kirsten. They needed each other to live while inside Lisa. Kirsten was Baby A and didn't have any known complications.

The doctors told us Lisa's pregnancy was unlikely to go the full nine months. To give Kirsten a chance at surviving, we needed the pregnancy to last at least twenty-five weeks. Lisa was near death during the pregnancy due to the high-risk pregnancy struggling inside of her. There was nothing I could do but be there to help Lisa through the weeks.

Just three hours into Lisa's twenty-fifth week, her labor started. I rushed Lisa to the emergency room thirty-five miles away, where the doctors wanted to delay the girls' birth because every day significantly increased the odds of Kirsten surviving. The attending maternal-fetal medicine specialist was hopeful the delivery could be delayed another eight or nine weeks at a minimum, giving Kirsten better odds to survive.

Kirsten and Kellisa were in distress.

Less than six hours later, Lisa was rushed to the operating room for an emergency C-section. I wasn't allowed to follow Lisa. I remained in the hallway. Just before the doors closed, I heard a nurse say, "Anesthesia is on the way."

The doctor followed with, "We don't have time to wait," and the doors closed.

Twenty-four hours later, Kirsten would pass away in Lisa's arms from hemorrhaging. Her blood vessels weren't developed enough to survive outside the womb.

Lisa and I spent a few hours with Kirsten in a private room before a nurse came to take her. The hospital provided counselors, but we were in a daze where nothing seemed real anymore. Lisa was tired and in considerable pain. She was taken back to her room and given pain medicine, then drifted off into unconsciousness.

At this point, I had been up for thirty-six hours and felt like finding a dark corner to collapse in, but in a moment of clarity, I thought about Kellisa. She was fighting for her life in the neonatal intensive care unit (NICU) down the hall. She needed me. I needed her.

I went to be by Kellisa's side even though she was inside an incubator hooked up to a ventilator. Most of her two-pound, one-ounce body was covered with tape, tubes, and wires.

I stood gazing at Kellisa, trying to wake myself from what had to be a horrible dream. I couldn't begin to process the events of the past two days. I can only imagine how terrible I looked. We left our house at 3 a.m. the previous day, and I didn't get dressed since we were in a hurry. I was wearing an old T-shirt and a pair of shorts and was halfway through my second day at the hospital. A nurse was kind enough to bring a chair for me before I collapsed to the floor, creating an unnecessary emergency.

As I sat there, I couldn't take my eyes off Kellisa. I knew Lisa and I needed her to survive. Nine and a half years earlier, we lost our six-month-old son due to an incredibly rare heart defect. Despite two surgeries, doctors couldn't save him, and now we just lost a daughter after only twenty-seven hours.

In my fog, I leaned over as close as I could get to Kellisa and whispered, "I promise to provide you with the best life possible if you survive."

I needed to picture Kellisa as an adult, so I made a second promise, "I'll take you to all fifty states by your eighteenth birthday."

We moved from Chicago, Illinois, to Edgewater, Florida, when Kellisa was just six-months old. After the drive down, she had visited her first seven states. We were well on our way.

Kellisa kept her end of the promise and survived, but it wasn't an easy road for her. She's had twenty-two surgeries, hundreds of doctor's appointments, and thousands of hours of physical therapy so she could reach her full potential. Kellisa was very medically fragile for her first five years, and we rarely left the house because she was so sensitive. Life wasn't easy for anyone, but she was alive, and it was the only life we knew.

Kellisa would add developmental delays, cerebral palsy, and epilepsy to her diagnosis list in addition to the original hydrocephalus. She was on a heavy dose of medication to keep her seizures under control and slept with a C-Pap machine. Kellisa was in a wheelchair before her second birthday.

Lisa and I had enjoyed a reasonably active lifestyle before Kellisa was born. We loved to hike, camp, mountain bike, and kayak. I always pictured sharing the outdoors with our children, but those dreams seemed to fade away in May 1999.

Our outdoor activities were limited when Kellisa was a baby. We took Kellisa to the beach, a few local parks, and I carried her on a few short trails in her early years. We added a few more states to Kellisa's life list when we visited family members in Texas and Colorado. By her fifth birthday, Kellisa had visited fourteen states. But to be honest, taking Kellisa around the country wasn't high on the priority list. Like the doctors told us, keeping Kellisa breathing was the top priority, followed by a long list of other medical and therapeutic goals.

Kellisa's medical conditions started to stabilize around her fifth birthday. It was around this time she started coming out of her shell. Instead of a medically fragile child, Kellisa began to show the world her personality. I pushed Kellisa on a couple of trails in the summer of 2004 using her first wheelchairs. It was tough because we weren't on ADA trails. The wheels on her chair were hard and would sink into soft surfaces. But Kellisa loved those early adventures on the trails, and for the first time in years, I thought it might be possible to share an active life with Kellisa.

We purchased Kellisa's first jog stroller off the shelf of a warehouse club just before her sixth birthday. Kellisa was small for her age and was able to fit in without any problems. Once I had her in the jog stroller, a whole new world and life opened for us. I was able to take Kellisa on some of our local trails in and around Jacksonville, Florida. I found Florida trails perfect for pushing Kellisa because most were flat and free from rocks and other barriers. Even sand wasn't a huge obstacle because Kellisa was so light; we were able to glide over the sand without sinking too deep.

After a while, we started to venture a little farther beyond our comfort zones. We explored trails in neighboring states and began to travel with the jog stroller to experience trails in other parts of the country. It was during this time that I started to realize all trails weren't friendly toward jog strollers. I was stubborn to make the most demanding trails work for us. I would carry Kellisa through impossible sections or rely on brute force to propel her forward. I wanted Kellisa to go everywhere, even though I was learning the hard way that some trails just weren't meant to be for us. During these rougher trails, it was evident that Kellisa enjoyed bouncing around and had more fun on the challenging trails. We talked to her doctors, and everyone gave us the green light to hike at will. After I had to turn around a few times, I started researching trails in advance.

While we were becoming experienced hikers with a jog stroller, Kellisa started developing additional interests. She loved all forms of travel, with planes, trains, and boats at the top of her list. Kellisa's doctors placed few limits on her. She wasn't allowed to scuba dive, play football or hockey, and couldn't ride roller coasters with bars that come down over the head. Kellisa was free to experience everything else like any nondisabled kid.

We started exposing Kellisa to more experiences and learned that she preferred wild activities. She began riding horses with assistance, joined a T-ball little league, and took dance classes. The more Kellisa thrived, the more I was determined to provide her with opportunities.

Kellisa always struggled with her speech and communication, but I started to notice she was more talkative when we were out on a trail. She would try to say what she saw. It could take her six months of intense speech therapy to learn a few new words, but after a few days out on the trails, she could come back with five new words. I was motivated to get her out as often as possible. I was always interested in pushing our limits by finding longer and harder trails to attempt.

I was fulfilling my original promise of providing her the best life possible, but I wasn't working toward her visiting all fifty states. We still had years to reach that goal, and living in Florida, we were far from most states. While we were traveling quite a bit, we weren't planning trips to check off new states. By Kellisa's tenth birthday, she was just over halfway to our goal, with twenty-seven states visited.

It was around this time that I started calling what we do *pushiking*. Most people look at Kellisa in a wheelchair and don't see a hiker. If they did, I'm sure they assumed she took leisurely strolls down the sidewalks.

Kellisa deserves all the credit for our outdoor pursuits. Yes, I'm pushing her, but she wants to be out there enjoying the trails. Kellisa is my motivation to do everything in my power to get her places where wheelchairs weren't meant to go. The more Kellisa giggles, the more she learns. The more she talks, the more she thrives in the outdoors, the more I want to push our limits. I've always said, "Kellisa is a hiker; I'm just her arms and legs."

It was around this time we were becoming serious pushikers and would travel to specific trails as our destination so we could move the boundaries a little farther out. As Kellisa grew, we needed to purchase new jog strollers, and her last few were designed for larger children with disabilities. I would always buy jog strollers intended for trail use, but not all of them were made for our kind of trails. We broke a frame on one and snapped an axle on another. I learned the limits of jog strollers the hard way. I started traveling with essential tools to make trailside repairs. I know its cliché to say, but duct tape is the best tool to have in your pack while pushiking. I started to modify wheels by experimenting with tires made for wheelbarrows. I wanted to prevent flat tires, so I would proactively add products to the tubes to plug small leaks. The farther we went on challenging trails, the more prepared I needed to be. We'd been traveling with seizure-rescue medication for years. I would only administer the drugs if Kellisa had a seizure lasting more than five minutes. Having this medication allowed us to travel in areas far from medical centers. Kellisa's neurologist backed our adventures 100 percent, as did her pediatrician. We didn't do anything without their blessings. Thank you, Dr. David Hammond and Dr. Kim Dal Porto.

Kellisa was accustomed to being an only child when her sister, Egypt, joined our family. Kellisa was ten years older than Egypt. Kellisa and I continued to pushike across the country while Egypt stayed home with Lisa. We would go on a family vacation and incorporate trails where I could push Kellisa and carry Egypt in a carrier on my back. Eventually, Egypt was old enough to hike on shorter trails.

By the time Kellisa was fourteen, I had realized we had pushiked trails in thirty-eight states. I decided to add to my original promise. Instead of just visiting all fifty states, I promised Kellisa we would pushike at least one trail in all fifty states by her eighteenth birthday. With less than four years left to complete my promise, I needed to start planning strategic trips to reach our goal. We still had the two most difficult states to reach on our list to tick off, Hawaii and Alaska.

It was around this time that Egypt told an uncle, "Sometimes my dad forgets me when he takes Kellisa on a trip."

My heart broke when I heard how Egypt felt inside. I was devastated that she would think I forgot her. I was trying to keep things fair and was taking Egypt on father-daughter trips. We started earlier, and Egypt was far ahead of Kellisa at similar ages. I knew she didn't know or understand I was trying to be fair.

Egypt and I traveled to Memphis to see polar bears in a zoo because they were her favorite animal. I will always remember the disappointed look on her little three-year-old face when she realized she wouldn't be allowed to pet the polar bears. We traveled to see elk and bison in the wild. Egypt and I went to Mammoth Cave National Park so we could take a cave tour where wheelchairs and jog strollers wouldn't fit. But none of this mattered if she thought she was being left behind.

Even though Egypt was only four years old, I had a serious talk with her. I explained how Kellisa and I liked to travel to hiking trails, and we planned to visit all fifty states. I doubt she understood the fifty states component, but she said she wanted to join us on the trails. I decided to test her on a local trail before we traveled across the country. Egypt was able to hike by herself for about three miles. It was during one of these local hikes that something extraordinary happened. She asked if she could push Kellisa. I didn't see a reason to say no, and I moved out of the way. Egypt could barely see over Kellisa's chair but continued to push her for two-and-a-half miles without a single complaint. She was proud of herself when she was able to get Kellisa over a large tree root or around a large rock. I was convinced, and from then on Egypt would join us on our pushikes.

I went back and realized Egypt had already joined us on trails in twenty-one states. I decided Kellisa and I would pushike with Egypt in the seventeen states she needed to catch up to her sister. I was worried we wouldn't have time, but I didn't like the thought of Kellisa finishing her list before Egypt.

I was now on a mission to figure out how to get Egypt caught up while leaving enough time to finish Kellisa's remaining states. We started planning trips around states that we needed and tried to visit as many states as possible on each trip. It took a couple of years, but Egypt and Kellisa were now tied with forty-one states. After a big trip across the northern plains, a couple of Midwest states, and a quick stop in New England, we only had Hawaii and Alaska remaining. I purposely left Hawaii and Alaska for our last two, so we could have a big finish.

Kellisa was seventeen years old when we booked a trip to Hawaii and Alaska over Thanksgiving week. We flew to Hawaii first, where November rains did their best to prevent us from achieving our goal. On our last day, the rain finally stopped for a few hours. We took advantage of the brief window to pushike a trail in the mountains above Honolulu.

We flew a red-eye to Anchorage. Several hours after landing, I was completing my promise on a trail in Denali National Park.

Kellisa was seventeen-and-a-half years old to the day, and Egypt was sixteen days from being precisely seven-and-a-half when we were on that frozen trail in Denali.

After completing our goal, I didn't know how to answer people when they asked, "What's next?" I was so busy and stressed from the last few years, and I wasn't thinking beyond the fifty states. Some people would suggest pushiking across Canada or in as many countries as possible. While both were great ideas, I needed a break.

I created a blog for family and friends to follow our adventures, but it grew to the point where we had followers from around the world. We were featured in newspapers, online websites of major news organizations, and even made several TV news shows. People felt inspired by our story.

It was during this break I started to think about how we could reach more families with our story. Maybe we could provide the foundation for others to get out and enjoy a trail. In all our travels, we only crossed paths with one other child with disabilities on a real trail in a jog stroller. We saw a few wheelchairs in visitor centers and parking lots, but never out on a trail. I know we never saw any mobility chairs.

It had been a dream to write a book sharing Kellisa's story for years, but it never materialized. As I was resting, I started to think about a book focused on just pushiking. I was hoping to inspire families with young children and disabled members to get out on the trails. I knew from my years of experience how hard it is to plan and prepare for pushiking trips and thought I could share my knowledge with others. I also see the health benefits of recharging in the great outdoors while getting away, even for just a few hours, from the stress and demands of daily life.

Additionally, I saw the endless benefits pushiking provided to Kellisa and Egypt. Kellisa thrived in the outdoors while Egypt learned the independence and confidence that I know would give her an excellent foundation into her adulthood.

My goal isn't for families to do what we've done exactly. My goal is to provide inspiration and motivation to families who don't think hiking is possible because they have toddlers or disabled family members. I want those families to venture outside because wilderness experiences are beneficial for everyone, and everyone deserves the chance to get a little wild.

To create the core content for this book, Kellisa I traveled to all fifty states between October 13, 2018, and October 27, 2019, to find and pushike a wide range of trails to share with the world. I asked Egypt if she wanted to join us before I planned our first trip, and she asked if she could stay home with mom. Egypt is a little older now and has other activities and interests.

Egypt's average week is filled with music lessons, art classes, and rehearsals for plays at our church. Egypt told me she was proud and happy to hike in all fifty states, but she didn't need to do it again. I was confident she was making the decision for the right reasons and respected it. Egypt did ask if she could join us on one trail so she could be in the book. Egypt never wavered from her decision, and she joined us on a trail in Washington state.

Keep pushing!

Family picture, 2017

About This Book

The author and his daughter Kellisa

Kellisa and I traveled to all fifty United States to develop the content for our first book on pushiking. We've included 54 trails covering 142.1 miles with 7,219 feet of elevation gained.

The individual trails featured in this book range in length from four-tenths of a mile to more than seven miles. I've rated the trails from easy strolls along flat boardwalks to challenging climbs while navigating rocks and other obstacles.

Kellisa is fully disabled and dependent on a wheelchair, and she's outgrown jog strollers you can buy off the shelf. Her current mobility chair seen in the book was special ordered from France. Based on my fifteen years' experience pushing Kellisa, I believe any high-quality, all-terrain jog stroller will perform adequately on all the trails in this book. I would advise starting with easier trails before building up to moderate and eventually challenging trails. Only you know your child and your abilities. Be prepared. Check the weather. Carry everything you think you might need and know how to use your supplies before you need them. If I could offer only one tip it would be, don't be afraid to turn around.

Always discuss physical activities with your doctors before venturing too far in the wilderness. It's best to pushike with more than one responsible adult. And it's a good practice to leave your itinerary with someone who can initiate a search and rescue if you don't return by a designated time.

The majority of hikes and pushikes end without incident. However, be aware, every trail has dangers, and the fifty-four contained in this book all have their unique hazards. This book isn't intended to prepare you for these dangers. It's up to you to know what to expect on a specific trail and be as prepared as possible. Many trails go through bear and mountain lion habitats. Encounters with dangerous animals are infrequent, but you should still know what to do and how to respond if you encounter a bear, mountain lion, or other large predators. Snakes have the potential to be found on every trail in America. Most are nonvenomous, but if you are far away from help, a bite from a venomous snake can be deadly. Usually, snakes want nothing to do with humans and will avoid contact. Learn how to recognize where snakes like to hang out and what to do if you see one. My rule is to assume every snake is venomous and avoid them. Even tiny insects can be dangerous. Be aware of biting and stinging insects and take proper precautions when out in tick territory.

I mention dangerous wildlife not to scare you or prevent you from pushiking a trail, but to make you aware of what you might encounter. You might be surprised where you can find some of these dangerous animals. We live fifteen miles from downtown Sacramento, California, and I've seen rattlesnakes in my suburban backyard. Our town has posted occasional warning signs in my neighborhood when credible mountain lion sightings are reported in the immediate area. We also have bees who love attaching their hives to our house.

There are entire books written about the above subjects. I suggest reading as many as possible, so you are well prepared when out on the trail.

I do not offer commentary on cell-phone coverage. There are too many variables—phones, service quality, and plans—to report accurate cell coverage in any given area. I always carry my cell phone but assume it won't have service while I'm on a trail. If you want guaranteed coverage, you can purchase or rent satellite phones.

Both Kellisa and her sister, Egypt, thrive in the outdoors. They can sit quietly and watch animals for hours. Kellisa has always been developmentally delayed, and some of her most exceptional achievements have come while on a pushiking adventure. Egypt does not need her phone, tablet, computer, TV, or video games when she's immersed in the wild. She can go days without electronics when pushiking and camping. Egypt is eager to learn about local animals and history. She's been known to ask many questions while attending ranger-led activities. But when Egypt is home, she thinks she would wilt up and die without all her electronics.

This book is meant to be a resource to motivate and inspire. It's not a substitution for experience. Know your abilities and the abilities of those in your pushiking party. Start slow. Go for walks through your neighborhood or visit a local park with an easy walking trail. I recommend building your experience and confidence before venturing out on moderate and challenging trails.

Essential Gear for Pushiking

Essential gear

Below is a list of essential gear we take on every pushike. Some may argue it's too much, especially for a short trail. I would say no one ever plans to get lost or spend an unexpected night in the wild. I'm responsible for myself and another person, and I prefer to prepare for possible emergencies. The list below will keep you comfortable for a few hours and will get you through a night in reasonable comfort. I always consider where we plan to pushike. I add heavier clothes if pushiking in a cold environment. If we're pushiking in bear country, I'll pack a bell and bear spray.

- Baggy
- Buff
- Bug repellent
- Cell phone
- Compass
- Diaper
- Duct tape
- Emergency blanket
- Extra clothes
- First aid kit
- Food
  - Energy bar
  - Energy chews
  - Jerky
  - Meal bar
- Headlamp
- Jacket
- Map

- Matches
- Mirror
- Multitool
- Pack
- Prescriptions
- Rain gear
- Sunglasses
- Sunscreen
- Tether
- Towel
- Water bottle
- Wipes

Trails Overview

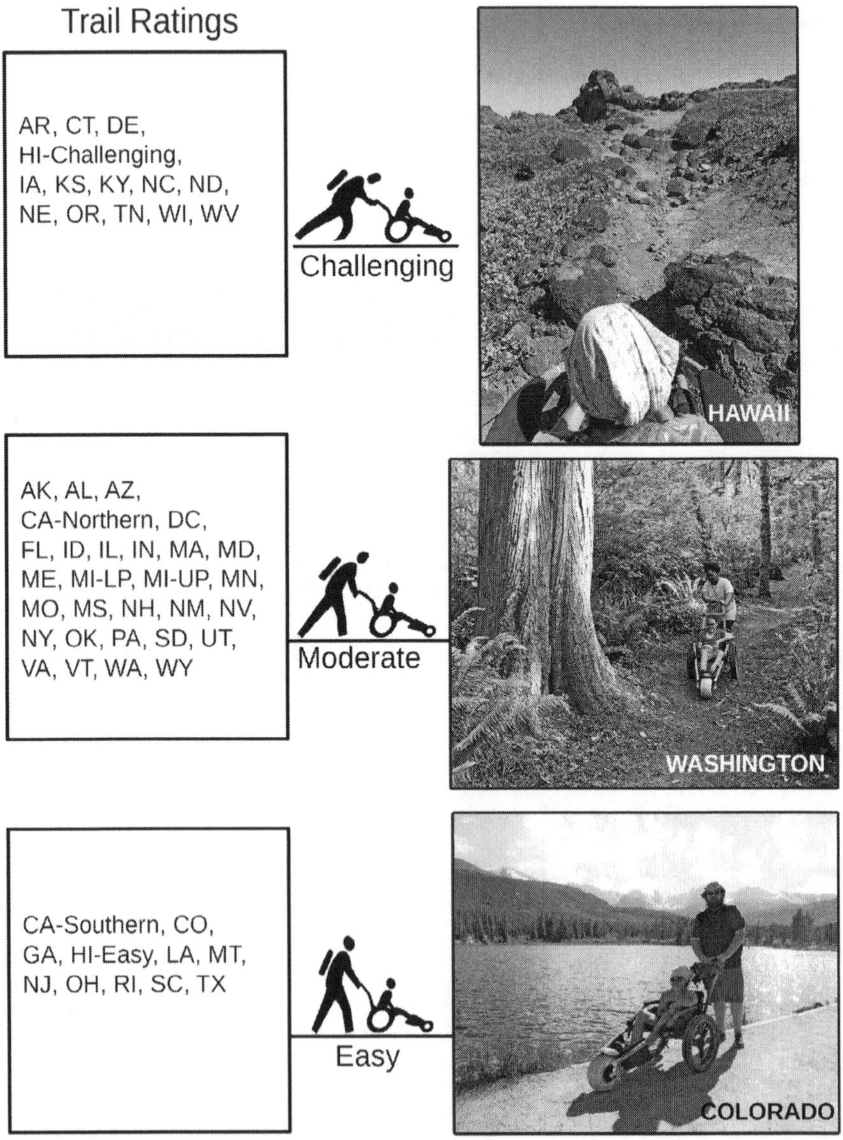

Graph by Cindy Bucher

Trail Distance

VA	7.0 - 7.9 miles
KS	6.0 - 6.9 miles
NM	5.0 - 5.9 miles
CA-Northern, TN	4.0 - 4.9 miles
AK, AR, IL, IN, MI-UP, VT	3.0 - 3.9 miles
AL, AZ, DE, FL, ID, MA, MD, ND, NY, OH, OK, SC, UT, WI, WV	2.0 - 2.9 miles
CA-Southern, CT, DC, KY, LA, MI-LP, MN, MO, NC, NH, PA, TX, WY	1.6 - 1.9 miles
GA, HI-Challenging, IA, ME, MS, NE, NJ, NV, OR, SD, WA	1.0 - 1.5 miles
CO, HI-Easy, MT, RI	0.0 - 0.9 miles

Graph by Cindy Bucher

Kansas

Trail Elevations

TN (712 feet)	Above 450 feet
AR, KS, WV	350- 450 feet
KY, NC, NM	300-349 feet
NE, WY	250-299 feet
DE, OR, WI	200-249 feet
AK, HI-Challenging, IN	150-199 feet
AZ, CO, IA, ID, IL, ND, PA, SD, UT, WA	100-149 feet
AL, CA-Northern, CT, FL, MA, MI-LP, MI-UP, NV, NY, OK	75-99 feet
CA-Southern, DC, MD, MN, NH, TX	50-74 feet
ME, MO, MS, MT, OH, RI, SC, VT	20-49 feet
GA, LA, NJ	7-19 feet
	6 feet
HI-Easy	3 feet
Virginia (Negative Elevation)	-230 feet

Graph by Cindy Bucher

South Dakota

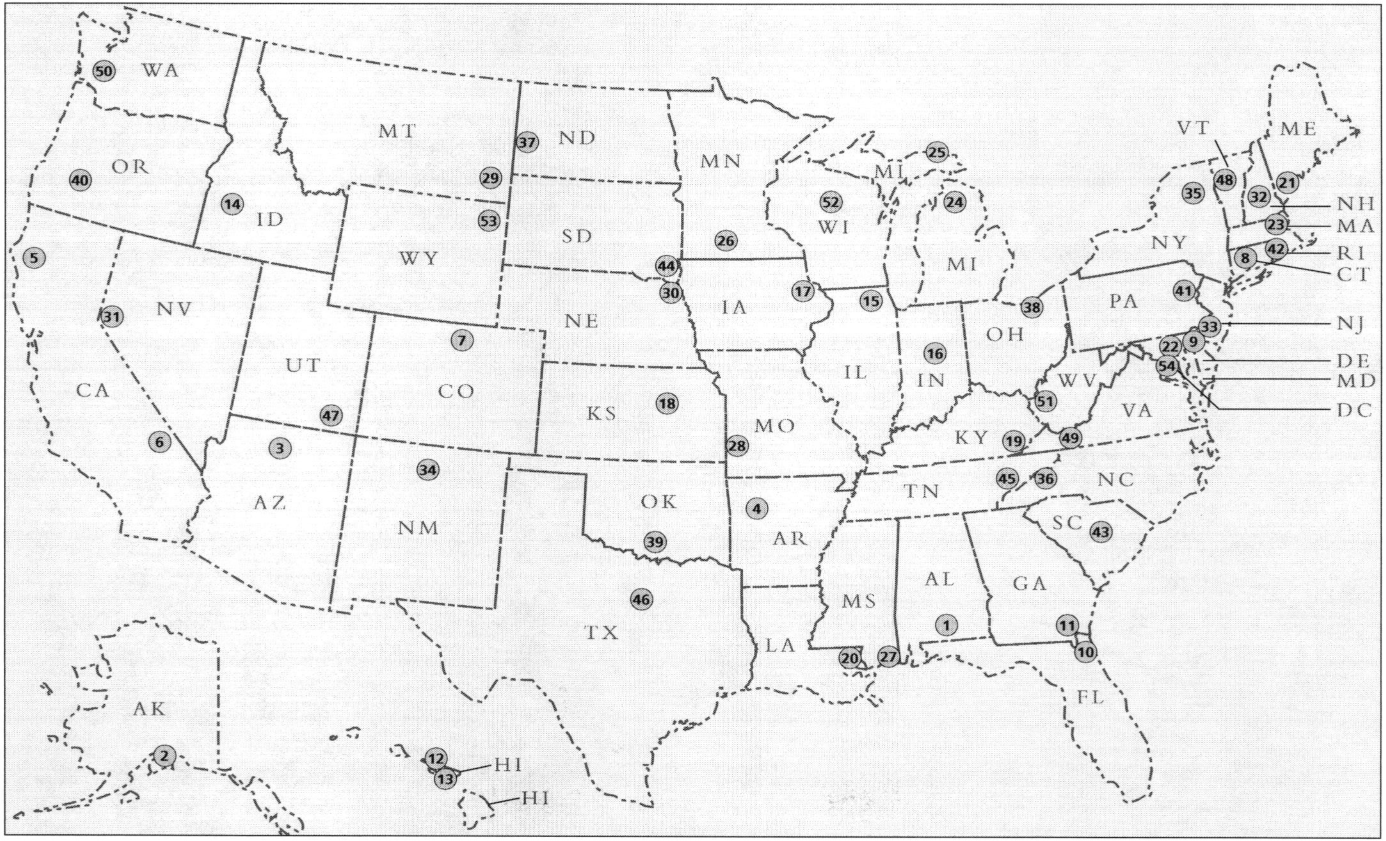

A map of all the trails covered in this book

1
Alabama

Trail name: Open Pond
Location: Open Pond Recreation Area
Distance: 2 mi
Duration (active): 55m
Average speed: 2.2 mi/h
Total ascent: 98 ft
Highest point: 280 ft
Difficulty: Moderate

I had the opportunity to explore Alabama trails on many occasions while living in Florida for sixteen years. I found most of the trails in central and northern Alabama to be too rocky for pushing Kellisa. We had more success on several trails in southern Alabama along the Gulf Coast, but those tended to be sandy, which makes pushing more difficult because the wheels sink into the sand. I was hoping to find a sweet spot in between the Gulf of Mexico and central Alabama for the perfect trail to pushike with Kellisa. I found several that looked like good prospects, and I selected the Open Pond Trail deep in the Conecuh National Forest. We were excited to be exploring a new area.

We started early from our hotel in Atmore, Alabama, to beat the midday heat on the first day of June. The drive through deep pine forests was beautiful. The occasional lakes off to the side of the road drew our attention to look for wildlife. The country roads were surprisingly twisty and hilly, which Kellisa always enjoys. She doesn't have the best trunk control, so her body shifts with the momentum of the SUV as if she were on a carnival ride. Since we fought severe traffic the previous day, it was a welcomed relief to have the roads all to ourselves.

As we drove through the Open Pond Recreation Area of the Conecuh National Forest, it was apparent that the forest service had recently conducted prescribed burns. Immediately, I was concerned that the Open Pond Trail would be closed for this maintenance. Since I didn't have a backup plan, this would be a significant setback for us. It would take at least an hour to return to an area with reliable cell service before we could even begin to research other trail possibilities.

When I approached the trailhead, my heart began to sink. The trail appeared to start in the middle of the worst part of the burned area. Kellisa and I were the only two in the parking lot, but I didn't see any trail closed signs. Before I went through the effort of setting up Kellisa's mobility chair and lifting her out of the rental SUV, I wanted to investigate the condition of the trail.

The trail seemed to be in good condition. The Open Pond Trail is a loop trail, and I looked in both directions and could see some greenery not too far away. The recent fire was out. I didn't even see any smoldering smoke remaining. The smell of burnt leaves was a bit strong, but I decided it was safe to proceed with our plan.

After taking a few pictures of Kellisa in her chair at the trailhead sign with the burned-out forest as the background, I started pushing her in a counterclockwise direction. I picked this direction because I could see the trail started going up a small hill. I preferred to get the more difficult part out of the way early since it was only going to get hotter.

The trail twisted through the blackened forest for several minutes before we emerged into an area that was spared from the burns. The trees, bushes, and ground were filled with many shades of green, orange, and brown. Compared to the beginning of the trail, this section seemed to be alive. We crossed a park road and immediately started going up another small incline on the narrow path. At the top, we were able to see Open Pond off to our left. The trail would circle the pond and eventually return us to our SUV.

We went through another burned area, but the trail remained wide enough that we could continue without any issues. It was peaceful always to have Open Pond below us a short distance away. The trail followed the natural contours of the small hillside, and we eventually worked our way down to the same level as the pond. We crossed another park road, and the trail entered a grassy area leading to the edge of the campground. The trail was impossible to follow through the grass, but it was easy to stay on course by following painted marks on the scattered pine trees indicating the correct direction. There were signs warning hikers that the pond had a resident alligator population and to keep a safe distance. Kellisa and I love observing alligators in their natural habitat, and I have a trained eye to spot them in the reeds or just below the surface of the water. No matter how much we wanted to see an alligator, they just weren't visible during our visit.

I pushed Kellisa out on a small fishing pier with seats to take in the view of Open Pond. I took a few pictures and scanned the water for alligators, but all we saw were a few birds fishing for their breakfast. We were back on the loop trail after a few minutes. Our path continued to be grassy as we worked our way between the campground and pond. At one point, the trail narrowed between a forested area and the water's edge. I proceeded with caution. It was difficult to see far ahead of us as the trail rounded a bend before heading back into the forest. Since it seemed like we were pushiking in prime alligator territory, I wanted to give them space to retreat.

It was not surprising that we didn't encounter any alligators. I've hiked hundreds of miles of trails in alligator territory and only seen them on, near, or crossing a trail a couple of times. Still, I always prefer to play it safe. If you are hiking with children who are not in a stroller, always keep them close and never let them venture anywhere near the water. Alligators usually don't attack adults because we are too big to be considered food, so they'd rather leave us alone. Small children, on the other hand, are the perfect size for an adult alligator's meal. Therefore, extra caution is necessary.

As we entered the forest again, the trail had a few more sections with small inclines before crossing a scenic wooden bridge over a dry creek bed. I left Kellisa in the middle of the bridge while I took her picture from many different angles. A trail branched off to our right, but it seemed like it was maybe a horse or mountain biking trail. We proceeded forward since that seemed to follow the general direction around Open Pond.

The trail dumped us out into a parking lot, but it wasn't the same one where we parked. No signs were pointing the way. I looked around a little confused before I saw the trail continue back into the woods a short distance away. Less than two minutes later, I was pushing Kellisa through another burned-out area, which eventually led us back to the trailhead. I was relieved that we were able to experience the entire trail so soon after a prescribed burn.

Shortly after leaving the Conecuh National Forest, I saw a road sign pointing to the exit for Lakewood Park, home of Britton Hill, the highest point in Florida at a modest 345 feet above sea level. I initially drove past the turn because we visited the state highpoint back in 2004. But then I thought, "I don't know if or when we'll ever be back in this area."

Afraid I would regret not stopping while we were so close, I turned the SUV around and drove a couple of minutes out of our way to Lakewood Park. Britton Hill is one of the few state highpoints where you can walk or wheel right up to the summit. I pushed Kellisa in the now brutal afternoon heat a short distance to the top of Florida. We had the park to ourselves, so we were higher than the millions of other people in the state.

I remember Lisa taking a picture of Kellisa sitting on the granite marker on the actual highpoint with me supporting her. Since I was alone with Kellisa, I did my best to snap a selfie of us in a similar position. After we got home, I created a two-picture collage of Kellisa's two visits to Britton Hill. I was a little melancholy while looking at how much Kellisa had grown over the fifteen years between her two visits. I was so glad we decided to make this little detour.

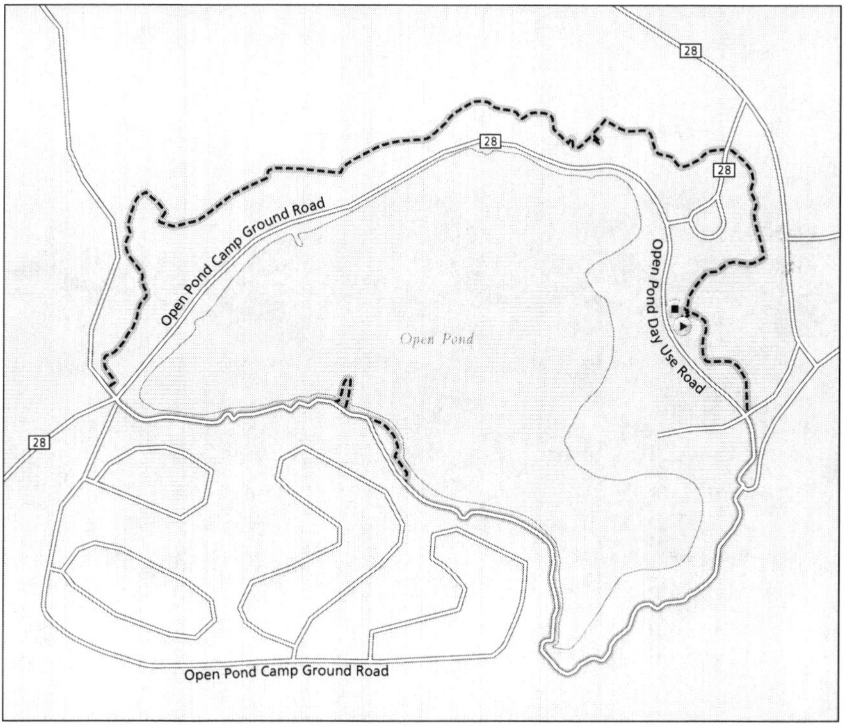

Open Pond Trail, Covington County, AL

2
Alaska

Trail name: Trail of Blue Ice
Location: Chugach National Forest
Distance: 3.9 mi
Duration (active): 1h 46m
Average speed: 2.2 mi/h
Total ascent: 171 ft
Highest point: 174 ft
Difficulty: Moderate

The temperature was −21°F on November 23, 2016, when we arrived at Denali National Park in Alaska for a pushike fulfilling my promise to Kellisa, and later to Egypt, to visit and hike a trail in all fifty United States by Kellisa's eighteenth birthday. We completed our epic adventure with precisely six months to spare. Egypt was only seven years old when she completed her goal of hiking in all fifty states with her sister.

With just over six hours of daylight, I had to plan our afternoon pushike perfectly. We had taken a red-eye flight from Honolulu to Anchorage earlier that morning after completing our forty-ninth state together. Both kids slept on the long flight, but I was too excited to sleep, and I was worried I would hit a wall while driving the four hours from the airport to the park. It was still dark outside when we left Anchorage on snow- and ice-covered roads. Just a little different from the 81°F weather we had enjoyed only twelve hours earlier while watching the sunset on Waikiki beach.

Driving north toward our destination, our first glimpse of Denali came when the rising sun lit the upper flanks of the majestic mountain. Brilliant oranges and yellows reflected off the high-altitude snowfields.

I was full of energy and ready to pushike when we arrived at Denali, but we decided to stop at the visitor center. We purchased souvenirs for the kids, collected the national park stamp, and talked to the ranger, who was excited to hear our story. We read the displays, and the kids posed for pictures. After quick bathroom breaks and sips of water from a fountain, I couldn't take it anymore, and I needed to pushike to end our long journey to fulfill my promises.

I didn't have a trail selected before our arrival; I was going on the hope that the path would find us. Since Denali was already frozen in a winter state, it was impossible to predict the weather and amount of snow we would face in advance. And to be honest, I didn't want to worry about Alaska while enjoying a few days in Hawaii. While driving the park road to the visitor center, we passed a snow-covered trail, and I knew it was perfect. I wasn't sure if it was a hiking trail, dog sled trail, or snow machine path. It could have been a narrow road. It was a path through the forest with a convenient place to park.

We didn't measure the distance we pushiked, but we spent just over an hour on our out-and-back trail adventure. We took pictures of the kids on the trail, the forest, and the sun, which was starting to set. Both kids were troopers with huge smiles from their accomplishment, and neither complained once about the frigid weather. I'm sure I would have cried out of my pride and utter relief, but I think my tears froze before rolling down my cheeks. You would think this was by far the coldest pushike of our careers, and you'd be correct that it was the coldest, but it was only a few degrees colder than our Minnesota pushike across frozen Lake Rainy in Voyageurs National Park.

When it came time to select a trail for this book, a path in Denali would have been a natural choice since I've been anxious to return when the park isn't in the depths of winter. However, while on a business trip in May 2019, I noticed a trail through the forest near Portage Lake Road, about eighty miles south of Anchorage. I had to pull over at the trailhead to investigate because from the brief sections I could see, it looked perfect. I discovered the trail was accessible, but mostly gravel with many boardwalks and bridges through deep forests under steep rising mountains covered with glaciers. It turned out to be the Trail of Blue Ice in Chugach National Forest, and I knew it would be an exceptional choice.

Online descriptions describe the Trail of Blue Ice as being five miles long with several side trail options. We planned to pushike the trail in two out-and-back sections over two days to keep the daily mileage and difficulty within the parameters of this book.

One huge concern to take into consideration before attempting any pushike in Alaska is bears. An encounter with a bear is highly unlikely, and most bears seen in the wild are seen from behind as they run away. But it would be irresponsible and dangerous not to have a plan. Since we would be pushiking in the homes of both black and brown bears, I decided to purchase bear spray in advance. This purchase was only the third time I bought bear spray, so I spent a considerable amount of time reading the directions and practicing holding the canister, getting familiar with where my fingers go and how to pull the trigger if needed. On rare occasions, when a bear does attack, hikers don't have a lot of time to make decisions, so you need to be ready.

Being prepared also includes knowing how to avoid a bear encounter in the first place. Most sources advise hikers to remain in groups and make noise, especially before turning a corner when you can't see around to know if there's a bear or not. You should also make noise when traveling through any known food sources for bears, like berry patches. Some people like to hike with a bear bell attached to their shoe or backpack to make a constant ringing noise. Many people don't like this artificial noise in the backcountry, while others will argue they don't work. I wasn't too interested in the debate on the merits of bear bells. It seemed like a reasonable way to enhance our safety, so I decided to purchase a loud bell from a local bike shop. I bought the loudest and easiest to use. Since they're designed to mount on a bicycle's handlebar, it was easy to adapt it to the handle of Kellisa's mobility chair.

I planned to ring our little bell every thirty to forty seconds and before any blind curves in the trail. Kellisa was sure to let out a giggle after each ring to further alert a bear of our presence. With the bear spray, bicycle bell, and Kellisa's giggles, I felt as prepared as possible before heading out on the Trail of Blue Ice.

The official trail guide mentioned the entire path was ADA compliant except for a 700-foot section at the beginning of the trail if you start at Portage Lake. It suggested a short road walk to avoid this area, which was too steep to be considered ADA compliant. I decided to start at Portage Lake and see if we could pushike this short nonaccessible section.

We arrived at the trailhead in the early afternoon. It wasn't hot, but the sun was intense. Knowing that heat and direct sunlight are seizure triggers for Kellisa, I decided to put a buff on her head for added protection since I wasn't sure how much of the trail would be under the canopy of the forest. With mountains rising straight up from the shores of Portage Lake reaching high into the clouds and the choppy waves, it was hard to pull ourselves away from such a beautiful view.

After a few minutes of standing in awe and taking pictures, I pointed Kellisa toward the inaccessible section of the trail. We found the path flat, a little narrow, and not too steep. It's probably beyond the specification to be considered ADA compliant, but not by much. I had Kellisa tethered to my body to be safe. We entered a small wildflower patch, and my bear senses went into high alert. I could imagine one just sitting to the side of the trail munching on the colorful berries growing in abundance. To our left, a fantastic view opened wide across Portage Lake to the glacier-covered mountains. The summits were still in the clouds, but we had nothing but sunshine above us.

The trail turned away from the lake and entered a dark forest. The high branches provided relief from the unrelenting sun, but the lack of light just heightened my awareness of our surroundings. We passed by some berry bushes before exiting out to a road crossing. It's at this point where you join the short road walk around the 700-foot section before continuing the fully accessible portion of the Trail of Blue Ice.

The forest continued on the other side of the road. Just before entering another open section with wildflowers and berries, we saw something in the middle of our path just beyond Kellisa's front tire. It was bear scat, and it was fresh enough to have still-visible steam rising from the pile. I quickly checked, looking in all directions for any signs of a bear. I asked Kellisa to be quiet for a second so I could listen as well. To my relief, we appeared to be alone. I could not tell if a black or brown bear left the scat, so I took a few pictures. I still had cell service and sent my wildlife biologist cousin, Matt, the photos to see if he could tell. He was not able to determine the bear type, and I had a decision to make; proceed or turn around.

We knew we were going to pushike in bear country, and we were prepared. Even if we turned around, we could still encounter a bear on the way back to the parking lot. Lastly, even if we found another trail, there is always a risk of seeing a bear in the Alaskan wilderness. There was only one option, and it was to continue our pushike deeper into the Alaskan wilderness.

I remained on full alert, spending most of my time scanning for bears. After a little while, I think it's only natural to let your guard down slightly and start to enjoy your surroundings. It was the case for me, although I was always ready with my bell and spray close at hand. The trail was mostly wooded, and we passed by several lakes. Every time the forest opened around us, we had terrific views of the surrounding mountains.

About a mile down the path, we were faced with a side trail. The Williwaw Nature Trail was to our right, and the condition of the path was like the Trail of Blue Ice, so I decided we should explore it. If we could complete the Williwaw Nature Trail, it would lead past several lakes, boardwalks to view salmon, and end at a campground near the Trail of Blue Ice. We would be able to make a little loop before heading back to where we started.

I was glad we chose the side trail. It offered some fantastic views up and down the valley. At one point, the trail followed a narrow strip of land between a lake and a river with a mountain rising straight up the other side. I was aware that bears probably ventured down from the nearby mountain to fish and feed on the local berries. I continued scanning the landscape, and a few birds flying around were the only wildlife we would see on our pushike.

Eventually, we circled several lakes and entered an area with boardwalks and wooden bridges. We were able to see giant salmon swimming in place in the crystal-clear water. It looked like you could reach down and pick them up. We didn't try, but it was tempting.

After our break to view salmon, we pushed our way through the campground on a quest to rejoin the Trail of Blue Ice. We just headed toward the back of the campground following the path of least resistance and naturally ended up where we needed to be. To divide the trail into two even parts, we would have had to continue a little farther, but since we were at the end of a natural loop, it seemed like the perfect spot to start back toward our rental SUV.

Since the Williwaw Nature Trail wasn't a perfect loop, we joined the Trail of Blue Ice farther along than where we turned off. Several long lengths of boardwalk over the wet areas greeted us. The amount of birdlife increased, but despite our best efforts, we didn't see any other creatures. It wasn't long before we were back to the intersection where we turned off for the nature trail.

Even though we were on the same trail, it seemed very different when viewed in the opposite direction. When an out-and-back trail stays in the woods, everything can look the same, but on this trail with mountains and glaciers in every direction, everything looked like we were on a new path.

I returned to being on high alert for possible bears in the area as we neared the bear scat still on the trail. When pushiking in bear country, I always wonder if there were bears that saw us without us seeing them. I have the same thoughts about mountain lions. When we reached the road crossing, I decided to follow the road back to the parking lot to finish the ADA compliant section.

I'm not a fan of road walks because being hit by a distracted driver scares me more than surprising a bear. I was relieved when we made it back to our SUV without any cars passing us. I loaded Kellisa in the SUV, and we headed back to Anchorage.

My plan for the following day was to pushike the remaining section of the Trail of Blue Ice before flying home. While at the hotel that night, I realized we wouldn't be too far from Kenai Fjords National Park, and it looked like there was a trail we could navigate to get close to a glacier. I looked up the mileage and determined we would have time to visit a new national park and still have time to complete the Trail of Blue Ice.

We woke up to a perfect weather forecast and started our ambitious day with an early morning departure. About ninety minutes into our drive, we passed the turnoff for the Trail of Blue Ice. I started having doubts we would have time despite being on schedule with time to spare built in. I started running the mileage and times in my head to be sure. A speed trap by a state trooper returned my attention to the road. I was thankful I had the cruise control set to the speed limit even though it angered many drivers as they came up from behind us and sped past at their first opportunity. I wanted to enjoy the scenery and didn't want a ticket to ruin our trip.

Just past the trooper, Kellisa started having a seizure. I checked the time but continued to drive while keeping an eye on her. Once a seizure hits five minutes, or Kellisa stops breathing, I need to start administering rescue medications while calling 911. Kellisa's epilepsy is mostly under control with drugs, and the few that break through rarely last more than forty-five seconds. A few reach two to three minutes, and one or two a year go beyond five minutes.

Around the two-minute mark, Kellisa started to struggle with her breathing, and her body began to jerk in her seat violently. At this point, I knew we were in for a significant seizure, and I was almost positive it would reach five minutes. Right when we needed it, there was a rest area with an emergency phone. I pulled off the road and parked near the emergency call box. I jumped out of the car and ran to Kellisa's side, where I could drop her seat back and turn her on her side, promoting more comfortable breathing. Despite the difficult breathing, her lips were keeping their color and not turning blue.

With one eye on Kellisa, I scanned the parking lot. Although there were many parked cars, I didn't see anyone. I'm guessing this was also a trailhead and a place to park for a popular fishing hole. I was able to grab my phone but didn't have any bars. I reached for the bag with the rescue medication to get it out and prepared so I would be ready to administer it once the seizure reached five minutes. I knew we were far from any medical center, and I started to do calculations to determine the closest town that might have a clinic of any size. I was formulating a plan in my head. Since I didn't have service and was so far from help, I decided that I would race back to the parked state trooper once I gave the rescue medication. My thought was that he would be able to call for help or drive us at a high rate of speed to the nearest medical center.

The seizure hit five minutes while Kellisa was still gasping for air and violently shaking in the front seat. Her rescue medication is ten milligrams of Diastat administered rectally. It may sound awful, but at this point, I'm just going through the necessary procedures without thinking. I always wish Lisa was with me at these moments. While I feel I perform solidly, I appreciate another set of eyes and someone to share in the decision making. I also draw great strength from the fact that Lisa trusts me enough to manage Kellisa in faraway places.

It doesn't take long to administer the medicine for Kellisa, and she usually emerges from the seizure within twenty to thirty seconds. For some reason, the drug didn't have its usual effect on Kellisa. It didn't even slow the seizure down, much less stop it. Another minute passed and still nothing. I wasn't sure what to do since this had never happened before. Therefore, I never discussed what to do in this situation with her neurologist. I started reading all the information on the prescription packaging, and it didn't advise one way or another if it was safe to give a second dose if the first one didn't work.

I knew Diastat knocks Kellisa out shortly after breaking the seizure. It doesn't matter what time of day it is, where we are, or what we're doing, Kellisa falls into a deep sleep. This known response to the medication made me afraid to give a second dose. Seconds seemed like minutes, and after another full minute, Kellisa still had her coloring but showed no signs of emerging from the seizure. At this point, it was now the second-worst seizure that I've witnessed.

Kellisa's first known seizure when she was just a baby started on my lap. Knowing nothing about seizures, we called 911 once we realized what was happening. Paramedics arrived in minutes and rushed her to a nearby hospital. The worst seizure she has ever had lasted forty-five minutes and left Kellisa paralyzed for a week. She was hospitalized for that week to have numerous medical tests. The intensity of that seizure seemed to stump the medical staff. Thankfully, she has not had another seizure like that one.

It took a while for Kellisa's neurologist to find the right combination of seizure medications since all people and their seizures are different. Once our trail adventures and travels started taking us far from cities and major hospitals, I started asking Kellisa's neurologist for advice. He loved hearing about Kellisa's experiences and thought they were good for her. He encouraged us and provided us with the following restrictions: no scuba diving, playing hockey, or riding roller coasters with the bar that comes down and around the head. Other than that, he gave us the green light to proceed with a life of adventures. He did train us in the use of rescue medications and advised us that it is the same prescription medication a paramedic or ER doctor would use to stop a seizure. This information gave us the confidence to start pushing the limits. Fortunately, we rarely need to use rescue medication at home or while traveling.

Since I decided not to give the second unit, this was quickly getting to a point where I needed professional help. I put Kellisa's seat belt back on but left her in a reclined position to help her breathing while I raced back to the state trooper. I was hoping he was still there. Even if he was in the middle of writing a ticket, I planned to interrupt him and maybe make the day for the unfortunate driver he pulled over.

I thought he was only a few miles back, but it was farther than I remembered. I was confident we didn't pass his little turnoff, and even if he were gone, we would likely run into him pulled over somewhere. At least that was what I was telling myself. Kellisa's seizure was approaching nine minutes when I saw the turnoff just ahead. I was going well above the speed limit but turned off while breaking in a cloud of gravel dust. To my horror, the trooper was gone. I was confident this is where he was just fifteen minutes prior. The direction I was driving was the same for the closest medical center, but we were still a long way away.

Just as I was about the speed off, I heard the familiar sound of a great gasp for air. I looked over at Kellisa and saw her half-paralyzed face and knew for sure she was finally out of her terrifying seizure. A few minutes after she emerges from a severe seizure, Kellisa usually has a half-smile and tries to giggle a little to let us know she is OK. Despite feeling a great sense of relief, my heart was still beating out of my chest.

I started talking to Kellisa, "What happened? Are you OK? You almost gave dad a heart attack!"

She continued to look at me with her eyes still glossed over while continuing to smile and faintly giggle. I wanted to cry but didn't have the energy. I knew our day was over because Kellisa would be in a deep sleep soon. I calmed myself with a few deep breaths and butterfly taps before I started the drive back to Anchorage for our evening flight home.

I was thankful for our pushike the previous day. I knew the trail would be there for another attempt on a future trip. I couldn't help myself from feeling a little disappointed we didn't accomplish our plans since we traveled so far. Kellisa was sleeping a few minutes later. We had an entire afternoon to kill, and I wasn't sure how to pass the time. When we reached the turnoff for the medical center, I decided to pull off to see if there was a local park where I could park, and maybe I could join Kellisa with a nap of my own.

I found a secluded little park covered in the shade from towering pine trees. I backed into an open spot and reclined my seat. This situation left me emotionally drained, and I fell into a deep sleep. Kellisa woke up first several hours later, and she had regained the full use of her body. She was asking to eat something. I checked the time, and we had just enough time for a nice sit-down dinner before our flight home. While we waited for our dinner, I told Kellisa we would return someday to finish our pushike on the alluring Trail of Blue Ice.

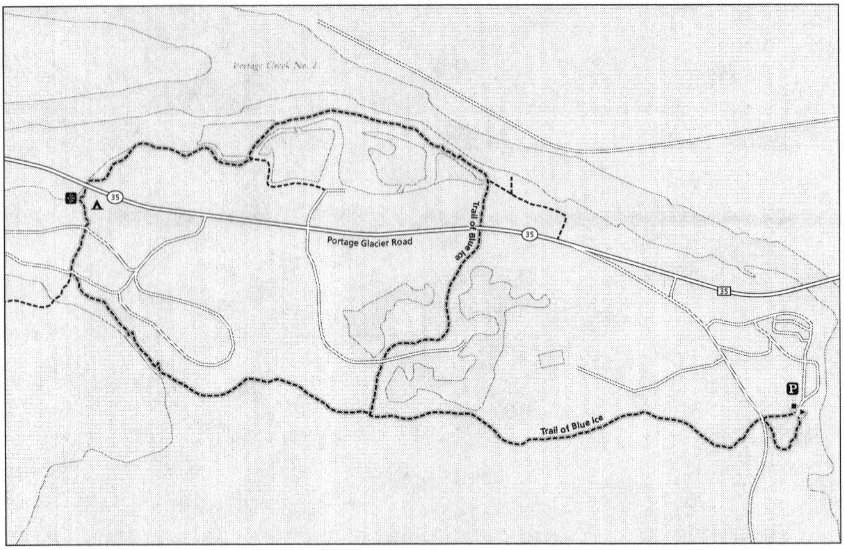

Trail of Blue Ice, Portage, AK

3
Arizona

Trail name: Shoshone Point
Location: Grand Canyon National Park
Distance: 2.1 mi
Duration (active): 57m
Average speed: 2.2 mi/h
Total ascent: 144 ft
Highest point: 7,314 ft
Difficulty: Moderate

Deciding to pushike in Grand Canyon National Park was one of the easier decisions I had to make for this book. We traveled to visit family on all our family vacations when Kellisa was a baby and toddler. Since we lived in Florida and most of our family was split between eastern Texas and the Midwest, we didn't have an opportunity to explore the West until Kellisa was seven years old. We went to Grand Canyon National Park on that trip in March 2006. I remember not checking the weather before we left because we just assumed all of Arizona was hot and dry, so you can imagine our surprise when we arrived to find temperatures in the teens and snow on the ground along the South Rim. We had fleece jackets but had to scramble to purchase gloves and a blanket to cover Kellisa in her jog stroller.

I had pushed Kellisa on a few trails in the southeast and had high hopes for testing our limits on the trails in Grand Canyon National Park, but the snow and ice relegated us to the sidewalk trails along the South Rim. Despite the winter conditions, the Grand Canyon was majestic. We saw it colored with hues of gray and blue from the overcast days instead of oranges, reds, and browns. The canyon was no less spectacular. While it was fun pushing Kellisa through the snow on the sidewalks, I left wanting to explore natural surface trails with her in the park.

We returned to Grand Canyon National Park in June 2009 for our first overnight backpacking trip with Kellisa. I had secured a permit for a trail on the North Rim months before our trip. Kellisa was still in a jog stroller, and I had it loaded up with our water and some camping gear. I thought it would be easier to push extra weight instead of adding it to my already fully laden backpack. I underestimated the difficulty, especially when you consider we traveled from sea level to an altitude of more than 8,200 feet.

The guidebook I purchased for the trip described the trail I selected as an old road. I didn't research beyond the book or look for any trip reports with pictures. I figured, how hard could it be to push Kellisa up an old roadbed? The Cape Royal Trail is a four mile out-and-back trail that gains almost 500 feet. The trail turns around at the rim and has a campsite near the edge where permit holders can pitch their tents. I learned right away that I severely underestimated the difficulty, and we weren't ready for such an adventure. The trail was steep and filled with large rocks and boulders. It was too hard pushing Kellisa in her jog stroller with probably thirty extra pounds of gear while wearing a forty-pound backpack.

Instead of leaving defeated, we pushiked as far as we could. We ended up going less than a half-mile up the trail before we found an area where we could go off-trail to find a campsite for the night. Lisa joined us on this excursion into the wilderness, and I promised I would do all the work around camp. I set up our tent under tall pine trees away from the trail, inflated our air mattress, fluffed the sleeping bags, and cooked a fantastic backcountry dinner. The three of us fell asleep immediately and didn't wake up until the following morning completely refreshed after being drained from our pushike to our camping spot.

My permit was for one night only, so I packed our gear, and we returned to our rental SUV. We spent the rest of the day like most of the other tourists in the park, driving from viewpoint to viewpoint and taking pictures. All the stops had paved sidewalks making it easy to take Kellisa to see what everyone else was seeing. We would not revisit the park until October 2019.

After carefully reviewing our trail options, I selected the Shoshone Point Trail along the South Rim. It was another trail following an old roadbed, but more than ten years of pushiking experience would make me better prepared than I was during our last visit. We arrived at the park and bypassed the visitor center and all the viewpoints as I drove straight toward the trailhead. I was concerned the trail would be popular on a beautiful fall weekend morning, and I had read the parking area was small. I wanted to avoid parking a mile away on the side of the road.

I had taken a screenshot with the directions to the trailhead because I read the trail was unmarked, and you just parked near a gate blocking the trail. One of the reports told readers the entrance to the trail was located between Mile Markers 245 and 246 on Highway 64, the East Rim Drive. I drove the entire mile several times without seeing any gate or cars parked. I even drove a couple of miles past without finding the trailhead. I wasn't sure what to do, so I decided to turn around and drive to the visitor center, where I could ask a ranger for directions.

After passing the mile stretch where the trailhead was reported to be, I continued toward the visitor center. I passed a parking lot. It was unmarked, and I didn't see a gate, but I was between Mile Markers 244 and 245. I decided to turn around to investigate. As soon as I pulled in, I knew we were in the right place because I saw a gate blocking a rough-looking road hidden in a back corner of the lot. Cars filled the parking lot, but the spot closest to the trailhead was open.

I was anxious to hit the trail and immediately started getting the mobility chair and our gear ready. Before I had Kellisa out of the rental SUV, I saw a young couple coming off the trail. I said, "Excuse me, do you know if this is the Shoshone Point Trail?"

The man replied, "I don't know" and continued walking to their car.

His companion was a little friendlier and added, "I think so, but I'm not sure. You can reach the viewpoint with that thing," as she looked at Kellisa's empty mobility chair.

I thanked her, and after double-checking our gear, I lifted Kellisa into her trail chair, and we set off on what I was hoping was the Shoshone Point Trail. There was enough room to push Kellisa around the gate without having to go under or over the barrier. What a difference ten years makes. The road seemed very similar to the one that I found so difficult at the North Rim. It wasn't as steep, and we were at a slightly lower elevation, but I was able to push Kellisa around or over all the rocks in the broad road.

The trail started through a pine forest without any hint that we were near the Grand Canyon. I knew we were in mountain lion country, so I kept scanning our surroundings for any movement or wildlife sightings even though it was doubtful we would encounter the elusive predator. Even with a dozen other cars in the parking lot, we didn't see any hikers on the trail. After close to a mile down the path, I could start to see the view through the pine trees spreading out. I knew we were getting close to the rim.

It was surprising how developed the area around the rim was with picnic tables and a bathroom. We saw a few families enjoying a picnic, but we pushed past them to go right to the rim, where the Grand Canyon spread far and wide in front of us. We noticed others posing for pictures at various points along the edge, and it didn't take long before I started taking photographs of Kellisa.

The road was gone, but pushing Kellisa along the rim remained relatively easy on the well-worn paths. Even though we were at the edge, I could see Shoshone Point sticking out into the canyon a little farther down the rim. I started making our way toward Shoshone Point when the trail got narrow and rocky. It was also close to the edge. There was room to fall without going over, so I continued. We were almost there when people started passing us from both directions. A lot of the visitors were young and running around from rock to rock to try to take the best and most daring pictures. A few even passed us on the side with the drop-off.

While we were safe, it felt like we were pushing ourselves into a dangerous situation, and I wasn't comfortable proceeding to the tip of Shoshone Point. I decided to carefully retreat with Kellisa until we were back on safer ground. We continued to soak in the views while taking additional photos. I was now ready to relax and was envious of some of the picnickers as they enjoyed elaborate spreads. One family even lugged a cooler to the viewpoint. Kellisa and I had to settle for the water and energy bars I had in our pack.

We spent about an hour at the viewpoint before heading back down the out-and-back trail. The entire trail was never steep, but most of it was at a subtle incline between the trailhead and viewpoint, meaning most of the pushike back would be a descent. I allowed gravity to be my friend and use its force to guide Kellisa down the trail. I still held on to the handle as I steered around the rock obstacles but did less of the pushing. I knew we were descending at a good clip but was still surprised at how fast we reached the trailhead.

Back at the parking lot, a few hikers talked to us about the trail, and they were also wondering if this was the Shoshone Point Trail. Kellisa received several compliments on her super cool chair. Kellisa always loves receiving compliments and thanked the hikers by blowing them kisses. As we were leaving the parking lot, I couldn't help but think about returning to the Cape Royal Trail on the North Rim for another attempt at backpacking to a campsite along the rim.

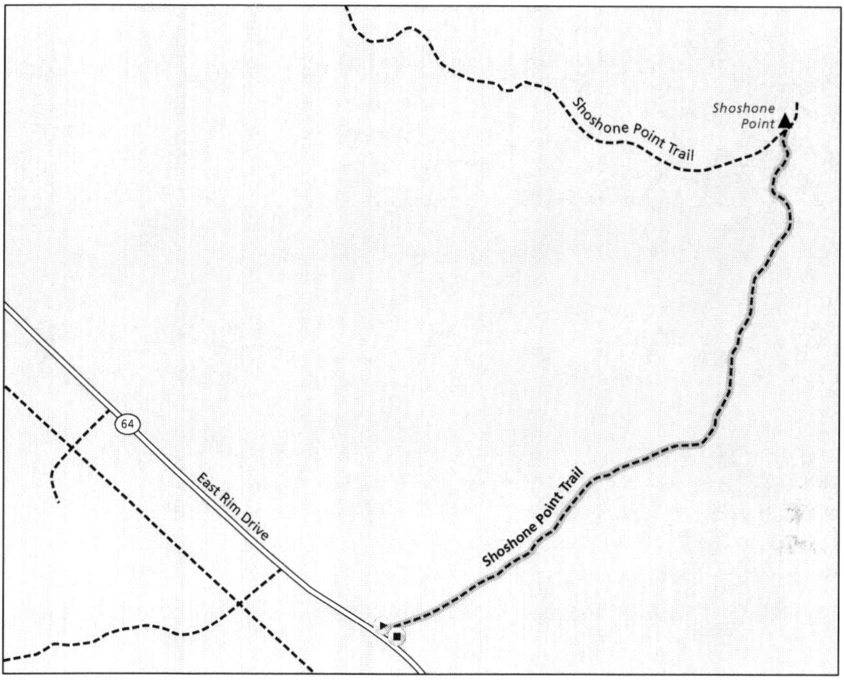

Shoshone Point Trail, Grand Canyon Village, AZ

4

Arkansas

Trail name: Bench	**Average speed:** 2.0 mi/h
Location: Mount Nebo State Park	**Total ascent:** 440 ft
Distance: 3.9 mi	**Highest point:** 1,575 ft
Duration (active): 1h 58m	**Difficulty:** Challenging

We approached 1,350-foot Mount Nebo late in the afternoon just ahead of the thunderstorms. The drive to the trailhead is worth the trip to Mount Nebo State Park if you enjoy switchbacks with grades up to 18 percent. The timing and forecast were far from ideal, but we arrived at the trailhead prepared and ready to pushike the Bench Trail. Our chosen path circles the mountain just below the summit on a wide natural bench that was used as a rough road in the 1880s when the area was developed as a resort complete with a hotel, log cabins, and a store. Most remnants of this development are long gone. We were drawn to the park because the trail followed what promised to be a high-quality remnant of an old roadbed.

We decided to pushike the loop trail clockwise. This route meant a short, but steep road walk to our trailhead. When pushing Kellisa on steep sections of road or trail, I always tether her chair to my arm for safety reasons. If I slip, trip, or worse, Kellisa will stay attached to my body instead of flying uncontrollably down an incline. You need to worry about drop-offs when hiking with kids, but even a slight incline can send a jog stroller or off-road mobility chair out of control toward trees, rocks, cars, or cliffs. Inclines may not look dangerous to an average hiker who might skin a knee with a slip, but they could be life-threatening or even fatal to someone inside a wheeled device. It only takes a few seconds to tether up, and we always make it a priority to be safe.

The trail was wet with standing puddles from recent rainwater sitting on top of the impervious rock of the bench. Everything was so green and lush; the path almost had a tropical or rainforest quality to it. To our right, the mountain rose toward its lofty summit in the low-lying clouds. The forest to our left was dense with an occasional view through the trees, which made it clear there was a steep drop-off to the valleys far below.

One of the unique features of this trail is that it has several backpacking campsites along its route. We want to return someday when we have more time to spend a night or two perched high above Arkansas. On this afternoon in October, all the campsites were vacant. The falling darkness was exaggerated under the thick forest canopy as the sunlight was fading fast.

To our surprise, several small waterfalls were adjacent to the path. I knew we didn't have time to linger, so we were off after a few quick photographs at each minor cascade. Kellisa enjoyed being pushed through the small streams of water flowing across our trail. Around the halfway point, we passed Fern Lake just as the local mosquito population was readying for their nightly assault. Since we were the only people on the trail, Kellisa and I were the dinner menu. We both suffered from many bites before I could lather us up with strong insect repellant.

With insects chasing us, night falling, and the threat of rain, I increased our pace to Kellisa's delight. She is always happier when going fast or cruising over roots and rocks. The trail started to have some severe inclines, which slowed our progress. I noticed a few declines to this point, but not enough to justify our new rise in elevation. Most hikers might barely see the change in elevation, but when pushing more than 100 pounds, it's not only noticeable but challenging.

It seemed like every time we reached a new height, I could see the next rise after a drop in between. I wanted to stop to get my headlamp out of my backpack but didn't want to make it easy for the mosquitoes. I was considering looking at the trail map to see if there was any shortcut back toward our rental SUV, but in the end, we just kept moving forward.

I enjoy hiking in the dark, especially when I'm familiar with the trail. The forest is beautiful under the setting sun or the light of the moon. Since this was my first time on the trail, I was worried about a barrier preventing further progress and sending us back down the path to where we started at the trailhead. As we rounded new corners and conquered new inclines, I was always hoping to see the end.

I was disappointed at least a dozen times when we emerged out of the darkness to a small clearing where the Bench Trail was a little wider and didn't have the same canopy cover. It wasn't nearly as dark as I thought. We were able to slow the pace a little so that we could enjoy the trail at a less frantic speed. The mosquitoes stopped attacking us, but I think it had more to do with being in a drier area with less standing water and trees. After a short distance, we entered the forest again and immediately heard the mosquitoes dive-bombing from all directions. The repellent was holding them off, but the constant buzzing was annoying.

After a few more curves in the trail, I could see an opening a short distance in front of us. A gate blocked the path. I was confident the trailhead parking would be just beyond the gate. We could go over, under, or around the gate if needed to complete our pushike. As we approached the gate, I could see our SUV waiting for us still illuminated by the fading sun. The gate was locked and completely blocked the trail, but we were able to navigate around it between several large boulders. Kellisa enjoyed this off-trail ramble as it took us up a steep embankment and back on top of pavement for the last several feet back to our ride.

Just as we finished our pushike, I realized that directly in front of our SUV was the best view of the entire trail. In my hurry to start the pushike, I completely missed this vista when I parked. The trees parted in a way that we could see forested valleys below dotted with many small lakes. Since we were in the open again, the mosquitoes left us alone to enjoy the breathtaking views. I was already planning to return someday to this fantastic trail so we could camp in the backcountry.

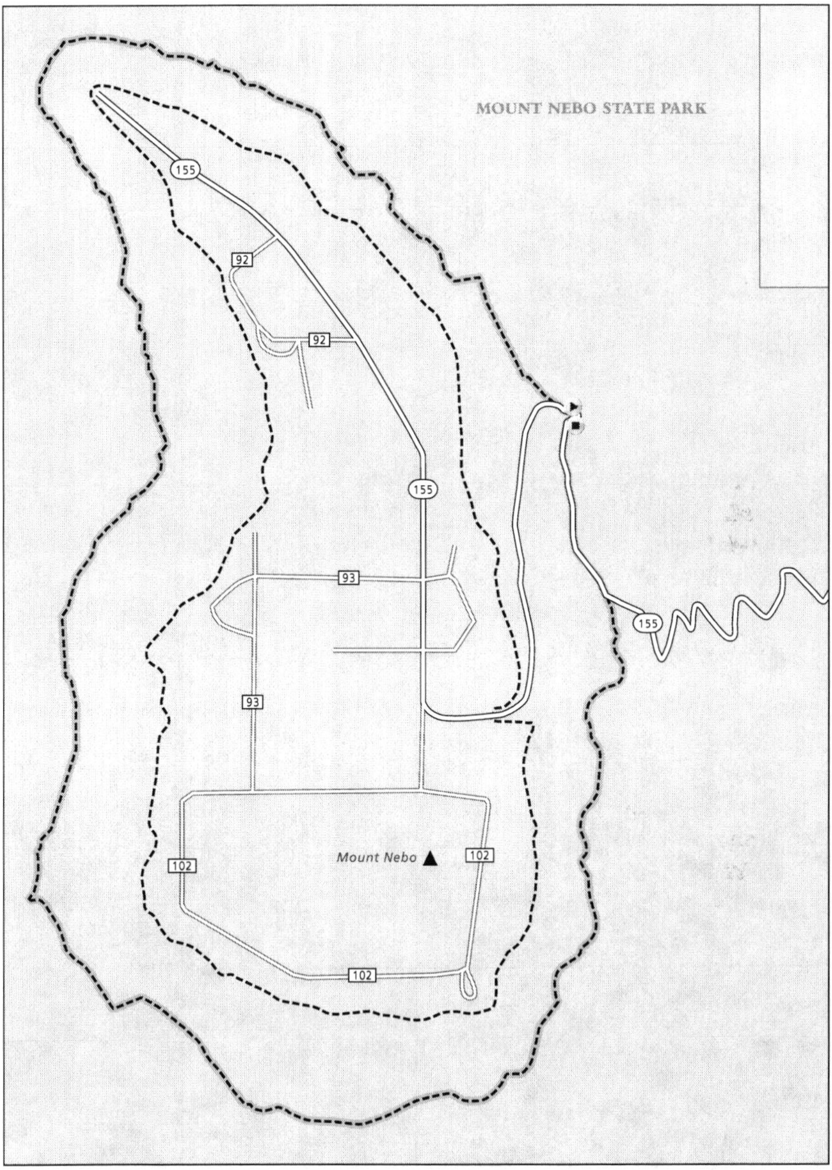

Bench Trail, Dardanelle, AR

5
Northern California

Trail name: Drury-Chaney Loop
Location: Humboldt Redwoods State Park
Distance: 4.5 mi
Duration (active): 1h 45m
Average speed: 2.6 mi/h
Total ascent: 82 ft
Highest point: 139 ft
Difficulty: Moderate

Once I decided to split California into two chapters, I didn't have an exact trail in mind. I knew the path would be somewhere in the redwood forests along the northern California coast. Redwoods can be found in a few small groves in southern Oregon and along the northern coast of California. We've visited the redwoods multiple times, and many of the trails are perfect for pushiking. The trails are wide and mostly free from obstacles. I believe there is less ground cover and brush under towering redwoods because so little sunlight penetrates the canopy. Nothing can prepare a person for their first visit to a redwood forest with trees reaching as high as 300 feet. In some spots, dozens or even hundreds of these legendary trees surround hikers. Kellisa and I have pushiked many miles through the redwoods. Egypt joined us on each adventure, but this time she wanted to stay home with mom.

Since we've pushiked many great trails in the redwoods, my thought was to select one of our favorites. But I was faced with a problem since we loved them all; it was impossible to pick a favorite. Some of the remaining redwood groves are quite small in acreage, and the trails are usually short. While these trails are no less spectacular and worth a visit, I wanted to feature one of the longer trails. I thought about Muir Woods National Monument just north of San Francisco because the park has an excellent trail system with several miles suitable for pushiking, but there are a few drawbacks that prevented me from selecting Muir Woods. Since it's so close to San Francisco, it's often very crowded. Parking can be a problem, and once in the woods, the trails can be packed and difficult to navigate when pushing someone in a jog stroller or mobility chair.

One of our favorite areas of the redwood forests is found in Humboldt Redwoods State Park with the thirty-one-mile drive through the Avenue of Giants, a highlight of each visit. The challenge was finding a trail that would be new to us. My research led us to the Drury-Chaney Loop. We found the parking area adjacent to the Avenue of Giants. Within a few minutes of our arrival, I was pushing Kellisa from a small open picnic area into a dense, jungle-like forest. The redwoods were reaching for the sky far above our heads.

The Drury-Chaney Loop is a lollipop trail and is rated as wheelchair accessible because gravel was spread over the full trail. The path is also free from obstacles and only has minimal elevation changes. Kellisa can propel herself in her manual wheelchair with ease at home, school, stores, and so forth, and for reasonable distances. I'm not sure she could move along the Drury-Chaney Loop trail. That's not to say others in wheelchairs couldn't push down this trail. I do want to be clear; it's more of a challenge than wheeling down a paved surface in the forest.

Some redwood trails can be hard to follow due to the lack of ground cover, but we found the gravel trail easy to follow. The forest floor surrounded the path in a lush green carpet-like covering. The trail felt exotic as we continued our pushike through this majestic example of the old-growth forest.

Tucked between the famous Avenue of Giants and the primary 101 highway, this grove was surprisingly free of road noise. We heard an occasional motorcycle or truck braking. In between those sounds, it was eerily quiet, adding to the ambiance of our pushike.

Once at the beginning of the loop section, we decided to pushike in a counterclockwise direction. There was a scenic log bridge to our left, and I wanted to save it for the end of our loop because I knew I would want to take Kellisa's picture on the bridge. The trail went between some of the most towering trees in the grove. I took a few steps away from Kellisa to take her picture and was surprised by how small she looked in her mobility chair next to the giant trees. We passed through a redwood that had fallen over, and its trunk was taller than me, making me feel tiny in comparison. As the loop circled, it was at its closest point to the 101 highway, and we could hear a constant buzz from the roadway. It was easy to forget about this intrusion because I was preoccupied with looking at my surroundings in complete awe.

It doesn't matter how many times we visit the redwoods or how many miles we've pushiked, we are always blown away when under their presence. I notice Kellisa looking up and around more than usual when on a trail surrounded by redwoods. She often points to the most massive trees and up to the canopy, which can be 300 feet above our heads. It can feel like you're in a dark canyon set in another world.

We completed our loop at the bridge over a small creek where I snapped many pictures of Kellisa with the trees forming a dramatic background. I was feeling good, the weather was perfect, and Kellisa was having a great time, so I decided we would pushike the loop a second time. For our repeat loop, I reversed directions. It was like pushiking a new trail since we saw everything from new angles and different lighting. It never felt like we were passing the same redwood twice.

The Drury-Chaney Loop is listed as a 2.4-mile-long trail. Since we pushiked the loop twice, our mileage total reached 4.5 miles. I usually feel a little melancholy when we complete majestic trails because I'm sad the experience shared with Kellisa is over. I was ready to find another path in the redwoods to pushike, but we had a long drive home, and Kellisa had school the following morning.

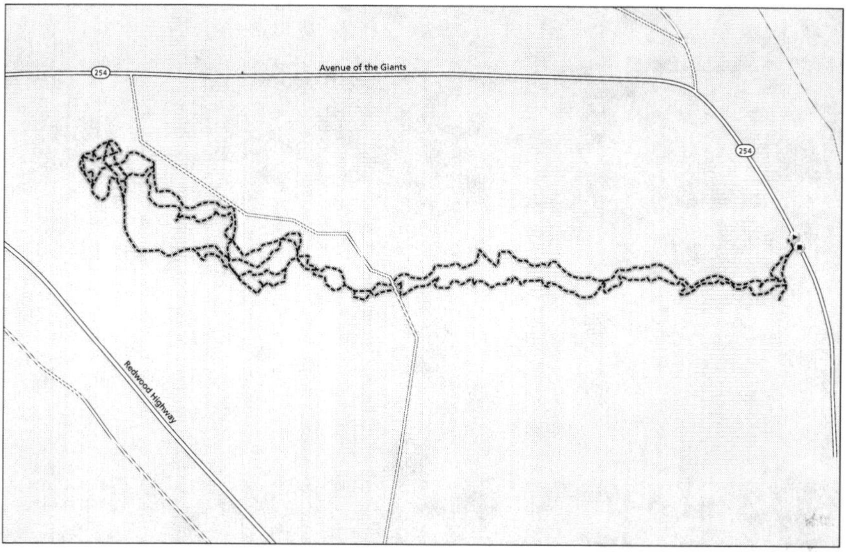

Drury-Chaney Trail, Pepperwood, CA

6

Southern California

Trail name: Badwater Basin	**Average speed:** 2.0 mi/h
Location: Death Valley National Park	**Total ascent:** 62 ft
Distance: 1.8 mi	**Highest point:** -217 ft
Duration (active): 56m	**Difficulty:** Easy

Kellisa's first pushikes in California happened back in November 2010 when we stayed in Death Valley National Park for the week of Thanksgiving. It was an unusually cold week in the desert, which limited our time spent outside. Our trip was the first vacation we took with Egypt. Since Egypt was a baby, I had her on my back in a carrier while I pushed Kellisa on several of the park's more accessible trails.

We moved to Roseville in northern California in early 2016 when my job relocated me from Florida. We've taken many day trips and a few long weekends as we get to know the outdoors of our new and diverse home state. California has a little bit of everything from lofty mountain ranges to enormous deserts to sunny beaches and everything in between. It was a challenge deciding where to go for our California trail. Since I couldn't pick just one, I decided to split the state in half and select one trail in the south and one in the north.

To narrow my selection, I wanted to consider some of the landscapes unique to California. While other states have deserts, Death Valley stands out for a few reasons. It has the lowest spot in the United States at 282 feet below sea level. Death Valley is also one of the hottest places on earth. The 134°F day in the summer of 1913 was the hottest temperature ever reported on earth, and the 201°F surface temperature reported in 1972 is also a world record. Death Valley is also extremely dry, averaging less than three inches of precipitation annually.

I decided we would return to Death Valley for our southern California pushiking trail. I picked a weekend in March to make the long drive hoping to find reasonable temperatures when we arrived. I asked Egypt if she wanted to join us, but she opted to spend a fun weekend at home with mom.

Badwater Basin is the lowest point in the park and for that reason, a popular stop for tourists. There's a short boardwalk leading from the parking area to the sign marking the low spot and a small spring-fed pool. While most visitors congregate around the sign for picture taking and then leave, it's possible to walk (or push) beyond the boardwalk to venture out on the vast salt-crusted basin. You could walk for miles with minimal elevation changes. Fifteen miles away from the low point is a towering mountain range with the highest peak reaching more than 11,000 feet above the valley.

Once off the boardwalk, there isn't a designated trail. The idea of wandering around without limits appealed to me. I was hoping to pushike at least five or six miles, but the weather dictated otherwise. It was brutally hot, even in March. Without any shade to protect us from the sun, Kellisa was at risk to suffer from heat-triggered seizures, so I needed to limit our time out pushiking. Death Valley received a rare rainstorm a few days before our visit. Rainwater soaked Badwater Basin, creating a weird mixture of sloppy and crusty salt to push through. Kellisa's mobility chair's wheels became caked with this substance, making pushing difficult.

Like many trails we've experienced in national parks, once you move away from the parking area, we usually have the path to ourselves for the most part. While we could see dozens of tourists waiting for their turn at the low point, Kellisa and I were all alone once we pushiked about a half-mile beyond the boardwalk. The basin was relatively flat, and I wasn't able to detect elevation changes.

Even though the salty ground wasn't bumpy, it did make loud crunching sounds as I wheeled Kellisa over the surface, which she found funny. The views seemed endless as we looked to the north and south. It was odd seeing snow-covered mountains to our west, directly in front of us while we were suffering under the blazing sun. I wondered if any hikers in the mountains were looking down at us tiny specks wishing they were in the warm valley far below.

After spending about thirty minutes wandering around on our own, I decided it was time to turn around. We headed back toward the crowds because I wanted to limit Kellisa's exposure to the direct sunlight. I had skipped taking Kellisa's picture at the low point when we first arrived due to so many people. I was hoping Kellisa could pose for a photo on the way back. When we made it back to the boardwalk, there were still many people, but Kellisa was doing good, and I pushed her to the line waiting to stand next to the sign. It didn't take long for our turn, but Kellisa was done at this point and refused to smile for her picture, which is extremely rare as she almost always flashes her beautiful smile for the camera. I took this as a sign she was ready to cool off in our air-conditioned SUV. I pushed Kellisa the remaining short distance to end her second visit to Death Valley.

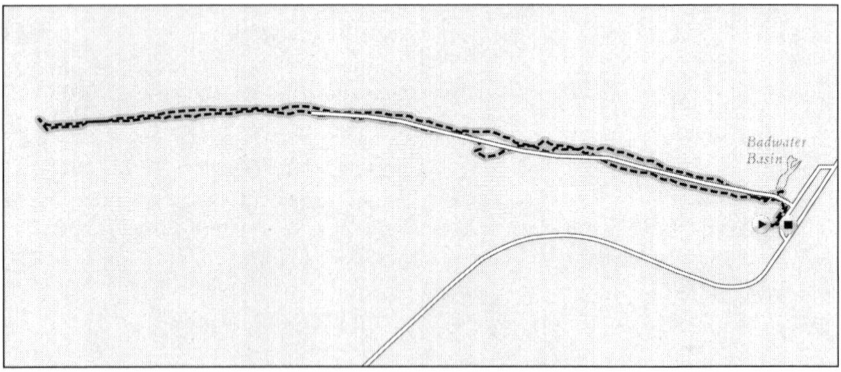

Badwater Basin, Furnace Creek, CA

7
Colorado

Trail name: Sprague Lake Loop
Location: Rocky Mountain National Park
Distance: 0.9 mi
Duration (active): 28m
Average speed: 1.9 mi/h
Total ascent: 148 ft
Highest point: 8,731 ft
Difficulty: Easy

The Sprague Lake Loop Trail in Rocky Mountain National Park is short and fully accessible, two of the attributes I usually avoid when selecting a trail. But to overlook this trail would be a severe mistake. What the path lacks in distance and ruggedness, it more than makes up for with its location deep within a national park surrounded by towering mountains on all sides. This path is also proof that a trail can be developed in the middle of a wilderness, and with a few accommodations, it can be available for all to enjoy. The Sprague Lake Loop Trail is the definition of total inclusion.

Kellisa's first visit to the park was in June 2014 for a pushiking and backpacking adventure. Egypt joined us on this trip. As we were approaching the park, Egypt had her first view of 14,259-foot Longs Peak and asked if we would be hiking to the top. I summited Longs Peak in 1996 and knew there was no way we could attempt the mountain dominating our view with Kellisa. Egypt wanted to understand why, and I explained that the trail was too steep and full of rocks and boulders. Quite simply, there was no way to push Kellisa to the top.

Egypt was outraged and demanded change. She wanted to know what she could do to right this wrong. Egypt didn't think it was fair that others could hike to the top of a significant mountain but her sister had zero chance of getting there. After discussing our options, Egypt decided to write a letter to then-President Obama. She wanted to demand he instruct his friends to build a trail to the summit of Longs Peak so Kellisa could enjoy it like everyone else.

When we returned home a few days later, the first thing Egypt did was ask for a sheet of paper and pen. She started writing her letter before I had our bags through the front door. We had to mail it right away. Sadly, we never received a response, so the accessible trail to the top of Longs Peak is still just a dream.

Colorado has many promising trails for pushiking. My dream list is long, but when it came time to select a trail for this book, we thought the inclusion of the Sprague Lake Loop Trail made the most sense. Kellisa and I arrived at the park late on a June afternoon. We were hoping for more time in the park, but Denver traffic was a nightmare, and we had a late-night flight to catch out of town. Since we had to be focused, we drove right to the trailhead. The parking lot was full, but we were able to find an open disabled spot which saved us a considerable road walk from an overflow parking area.

The trail is wide, flat, and not level. A trail can be flat, free from roots, rocks, and other barriers while ascending and descending along the way and, therefore, not level. The path starts with a picturesque little bridge over running water. The beginning is gorgeous, but there were too many people around for us to enjoy the views. I wheeled Kellisa around the visitors like we were in a video game. It didn't take long to get through the obstacles and start our loop around the lake.

We decided to go clockwise because I remembered going the other direction five years earlier with Egypt and wanted to mix it up a little. The trail is compacted gravel, which makes the experience feel a little more like a hike than a walk in a neighborhood park. Plus, I love the sound of Kellisa's wheels crunching over the small rocks as we pushike.

The trail was moderately crowded, with many young families enjoying their visit. Kellisa usually says "Hey" to everyone she encounters on a path and has an almost perfect record of hikers and backpackers saying "Hey" or "Hi" back. Many even give her a high five.

Sadly, not many returned her cheerful hello, and I could see Kellisa sinking back into her shell. Too many people in everyday life act like Kellisa doesn't exist. Based on years of past experiences, Kellisa rarely says "Hey" when out in public at a store, the movies, and so forth. I would conclude due to its easy access and short length that this was more of a tourist trail than a hiker's trail. Sad.

Instead, Kellisa turned her attention to nature. She enjoyed pointing at the brilliant blue lake just a few feet away and up toward the mighty mountains with their remnant snowfields high above. I engaged Kellisa, and we communicated the best we could. She was having a great time. At one of the most scenic spots along the trail, I posed Kellisa for a few photographs with Sprague Lake and Hallett Peak at 12,713 feet in the background. After taking several shots, a middle-aged woman approached us and asked if she could take a picture of us together. I gladly accepted her photography offer and stood behind Kellisa with a smile.

I thanked her and was appreciative since it's rare for Kellisa and me to be in pictures together. I've almost given up trying to use a timer. Kellisa thinks it's hilarious when I run behind her chair after setting the self-timer. Most pictures taken this way show Kellisa looking up and away toward me while laughing.

Continuing down the trail, we were just past the halfway point when we witnessed something we don't often see. A woman was being pushed in a wheelchair by a man. In all our trail adventures, but not counting an organized wheelchair hike we attended in 2017 in Rainier National Park, I believe this was only the second time we've ever seen someone else in a wheelchair out on a trail. We stopped so that Kellisa could say "Hey."

The lady smiled, and she seemed labored while the man continued to push her in the opposite direction. Not sure what to make of the brief encounter, I went back to pushing Kellisa while admiring the alpine views. Maybe two-thirds around the lake, we came to a side trail leading to a backcountry campsite only reservable by those with disabilities.

When we first pushiked this trail with Egypt, we camped two nights at that campsite. We had to state that Kellisa was disabled when we made the reservation by phone, and then the park rangers had to see Kellisa in person before issuing our permit. It was Kellisa's third or fourth time backpacking, but our first with Egypt. The site was perfect with a bear box to store all our food and scented items along with a picnic table and privy. We spent a beautiful three days enjoying the backcountry like a nondisabled family.

Since only campsite permit holders are allowed on this side trail, we continued down the loop trail with our memories and thought that we need to return someday to camp again. As we were nearing the end of the path, we noticed a large gathering of people blocking the trail in front of us. We were surprised to see an elk a short distance ahead in the water minding its own business while several dozen tourists snapped pictures like crazy. I'll admit we took a few photos before weaving our way through the onlookers.

With so many people watching the elk, I was hoping to find the bridge near the trailhead empty. I wanted to take a few photos of Kellisa on the scenic bridge. Many other people shared my same idea, dashing my hopes. I took what I could in between others jockeying for position. It's hard to imagine a better trail in Colorado for those with wheels than the Sprague Lake Loop Trail.

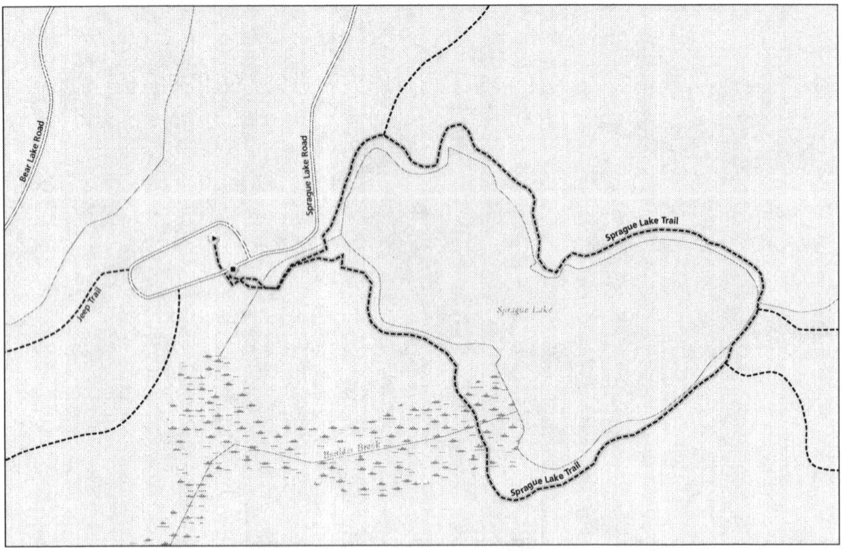

Sprague Lake Loop Trail, Estes Park, CO

8
Connecticut

Trail name: Bull Hill
Location: Bull Hill Preserve
Distance: 1.7 mi
Duration (active): 46m
Average speed: 2.2 mi/h
Total ascent: 85 ft
Highest point: 619 ft
Difficulty: Challenging

I initially selected the Little Pond Boardwalk Trail in western Connecticut for inclusion in this book, and we gave it our best attempt to pushike the trail but fell short of our goal. We drove to the trailhead through three hours of heavy rain. It was still raining too hard to venture out when we arrived at the trailhead, so we decided to drive around to explore the surrounding forested area. The trail was in the White Memorial Conservation Center, along with more than fifty miles of other trails throughout the heavily wooded area. While driving through the pine forests, we only saw a few other visitors and a few boggy areas before the rain slowed down a little. It was hard to tell while driving exactly how hard the rain was falling, so I pulled over to roll down my window. Kellisa thought it was hilarious when I stuck my arm out my window to check the weather. Once I was satisfied, I rolled down Kellisa's window so she could feel a little rain on her arm. Kellisa found her wet arm even more hilarious than mine.

It wasn't ideal conditions, but I thought we could attempt our hike with our ponchos protecting us from the elements. I opened the back of our rental SUV to act as a roof to keep Kellisa's mobility chair as dry as possible while loading her and covering her with her poncho. I need to be careful to arrange the poncho in a way so that all of the water runs off her body and mobility chair. If not done just right, the rain tends to puddle where the seat meets the back, and I didn't want Kellisa sitting in water for our pushike. Once satisfied, I put on my poncho and grabbed our gear before heading into the pine forest.

The trail was wide and free from all obstacles. The fresh smell of pine during a rainstorm was soothing to my senses. There were a few puddles to push through, but the ground was compacted enough that we didn't encounter any mud. I knew the trail would cross the Bantam River on a bridge before reaching the boardwalk circling Little Pond. Just before the bridge, we had to decide which way to follow the loop. I could see the bridge to our right, so I decided to circumnavigate Little Pond in a counterclockwise direction. The trail was muddy and full of rocks as we approached the bridge. It was tough going, but it was a short section. We made it through and crossed the bridge, only pausing briefly to take in the far-reaching views of the river area.

The boardwalk started shortly after the bridge. It was just wide enough for Kellisa's back tires, but there was no room for error. The wood was also very slippery. I had to take my time watching every step to keep Kellisa on the boardwalk while making sure I didn't slip off. It wasn't a huge drop-off, but enough to where we could potentially get hurt. The boardwalk continued through some marshy and wooded areas. We reached a set of stairs leading to a second bridge. While stairs aren't a guaranteed obstacle, I needed to check them out to formulate a plan. The stairs were steep and narrow. The only way to make it work would be to back up the stairs while pulling Kellisa up one step at a time. We would need to cross the bridge by walking backward to be in the correct position to climb the stairs because there wasn't enough room to turn around. While not ideal, this would be doable for us with minimal risk.

However, I was worried about the potential for another set of stairs on the other side of the bridge. I've never attempted to go down a set of stairs backward, and I wasn't going to entertain the idea of starting the practice in the rain. I could have left Kellisa for a minute to verify if the second set of stairs existed, but the stairs I could see looked slippery. I knew it was time to turn around for safety reasons.

As we were retreating, the rain was still a constant drizzle. I checked Kellisa to make sure she was staying dry and the poncho was doing its job. I decided to try the loop trail in the opposite direction once we made it back to the intersection with the path leading back to our SUV. I hoped to reach the other side of the second bridge before turning around again. If possible, we would complete 99.8 percent of the trail, and I would consider it a successful pushike.

A short distance past the intersection, the trail took a considerable turn for the worse. Deep mud and large rocks blocked the path. I was hoping this would be a short section of difficult trail and struggled to push Kellisa forward. After a few minutes, the conditions weren't improving. I decided to throw in the towel and make our way back to the SUV. The rain continued to hold off, and we ended up going 1.6 miles on our wet adventure. I had to decide if this was enough for the book. I wanted it to be our Connecticut trail but just wasn't satisfied with the quality of the pushike.

It was too late in the day to find another trail, and it would be a couple of days before we had time in our schedule to attempt another trail in Connecticut. I was scrambling to select a new trail when I found a rough trail up Bull Hill. From the pictures and trip reports, it looked like a real climb to a summit with outstanding views.

The Bull Hill Preserve was created in 2017. The trail to the viewpoint is a rough 4x4 road with large rocks and boulders along most of the route. Since the road is wide, I could push Kellisa around most of the more substantial obstacles. The trail passes large rock outcroppings scattered throughout the forested hillsides while being surrounded by lush ferns. The trees were mostly green, with some reds and oranges on an autumn afternoon during our visit. The ferns varied from vibrant greens to a few with rustic brown colors.

Even though the trail only gained 85 feet from the trailhead to the top, every step was up unless we were going sideways around a large boulder. The trail wasn't steep, just unrelenting in its constant incline. Besides passing a man and woman on their descent, we had the remote trail to ourselves. I knew it was a short out-and-back trail at only 1.7 miles long round-trip, so I was expecting to see the top around every turn. Progress was slow, and I could only hope the view would be worth the effort.

We finally rounded a bend, and I could see the end a short distance ahead. However, we still needed to conquer the steepest section of the trail before we would finally reach the top. I was hoping I wasn't looking at a false summit. I could see the forest give way to shorter brush before becoming an exposed rock at the summit. There were a few scattered trees nearby and a bench at the highest point. I took a few deep breaths and started our final assault on Bull Hill.

I was carefully watching the rocks in front of us, but they were easy to roll over at this point, and a few minutes later, we ran out of trail. The view spread out before us in three directions. We could see lesser hills covered in fall colors. The skies were gray, but there was no sign of rain. We earned every one of the 85 feet gained in elevation on this pushike, and we decided to savor our time on top. Kellisa enjoyed looking out and feeling the breeze on her face and through her hair while I took pictures of her from every possible angle. I was tempted to sit on the bench to take a break, but I was worried I would fall asleep or wouldn't be able to get up again. I opted to start our descent without sitting down to play it safe.

I thought the descent would be challenging, but it was quite easy since it was all downhill. The rocks and boulders were easy to navigate as I let gravity do most of my work. I just steered Kellisa around the boulders that her mobility chair wouldn't fit over. Our momentum carried us back to our SUV in a quarter of the time it took us to reach the top of Bull Hill.

It's not often we find a trail suitable for safe pushiking with such a rewarding view from a summit area. This trail was a challenge, but we were rewarded for our effort. We enjoyed the time we spent together, not only at the top but on the journey to and from the highest point on Bull Hill.

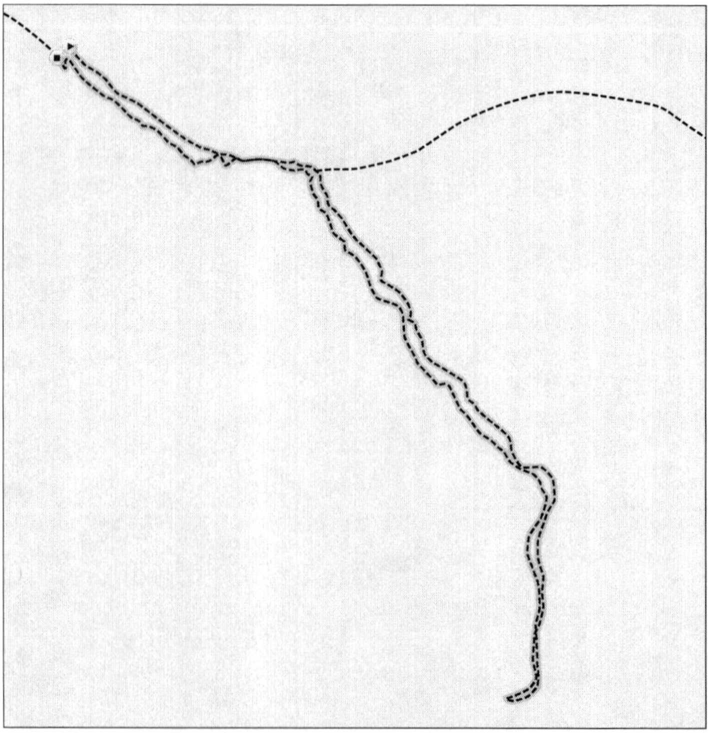

Bull Hill Trail, Woodstock, CT

9
Delaware

Trail name: Tulip Tree & Hidden Pond
Location: Brandywine Creek State Park
Distance: 2.6 mi
Duration (active): 1h 15m
Average speed: 2.1 mi/h
Total ascent: 213 ft
Highest point: 331 ft
Difficulty: Challenging

I left Delaware surprisingly tired after one of the most challenging pushikes covered in this book. I was expecting an easy trail in a state not known for mountains or even hills, and what we experienced broke all the stereotypes of trails in Delaware that were in my head.

We were planning on pushiking the First State National Monument Trail in Brandywine Creek State Park, but we never reached the trailhead. I was confused while driving around the park, looking for the right parking lot, and decided to stop at the visitor center for directions. I parked in a disabled spot and noticed a kiosk not too far in front of our rental SUV. I decided to check it out before going inside the visitor center. As I got closer, I could see a promising trail starting just past the kiosk. There was a star marking "You are here."

For the first time since driving inside the park, I knew where I was, but where was the trail we wanted to hike? I quickly found it, and we were close. But I was drawn to the trail in front of us. The kiosk didn't have any description or rating, so I had no idea what to expect. The trail was less than a mile long and had a passive name, Tulip Tree. The kiosk did warn the trail wasn't accessible, but that alone never stops us. I was hoping for a long trail and saw it connected to the Hidden Pond loop trail. I would be satisfied with the mileage if we combined both trails but was worried that I didn't know anything about these trails except the first thirty feet of the Tulip Tree trail looked easy enough. We rarely pushike a trail with such little advanced knowledge, but I figured we could always turn around and drive to our intended trail. We decided to take a chance on the Tulip Tree and Hidden Pond trails.

I pushed Kellisa through an opening in a medieval-looking stone wall. In hindsight, the wall should have been a warning because those large rocks weren't moved a great distance to be stacked up. The forest was deep and dark, with little sunlight reaching the ground. The natural surface path was damp, but not muddy. Pushing was easy, but after maybe 100 yards, the trail became rocky. Kellisa enjoyed the bouncing as we proceeded down the Tulip Tree trail following the path of least resistance since the rocks were covering the entire trail.

The pushing was a challenge, but we were having fun, and I wanted to see where the trail would lead us. Since there wasn't any solid footing, I did take my time to watch most of my steps because I was worried about twisting or even breaking an ankle. I would only take a step if I knew where I'd safely plant that foot upon landing. It didn't take long to find a steady rhythm down the path. Suddenly, the trail started to descend gradually. I began to have second thoughts. Pushing Kellisa down a rocky trail is challenging, but pushing her up when we would also be fighting gravity is usually more complicated. I considered turning around, but I didn't want to push her through the rocks we just navigated. I was hoping the backside of the loop would be smoother.

The trail gave us a short break as it transitioned from the Tulip Tree to the Hidden Pond trail. I hoped we were past the most challenging section when the trail became steeper as it descended toward Brandywine Creek. The trail was less rocky but a little muddier for this section. At this point, turning around would be a real challenge, and I kept hoping the right decision was to keep going forward. We were working our way through the forest when Brandywine Creek appeared in front of us.

We noticed a lot of debris along the edge of the river scattered around in the forest, everything from a rusty old kid's bicycle to a sizeable beat-up cooler. I could only figure the area flooded at some point, depositing strange trash in this remote area. Off to our right, we could join the Freshwater Marsh Preserve Nature Trail. I thought a path called a nature trail would be tame and straightforward enough to follow, but it didn't lead us back to where we were parked, plus the trail looked overgrown after a little exploring. I decided to continue the Hidden Pond loop trail, still hoping it would be an easier path back. The Hidden Pond loop followed Brandywine Creek. The creek was flowing fast and looked more like a river to me, but it was in no danger of breaching its banks. I kept looking for Hidden Pond, but the only water we saw on the trail was the creek.

The trail turned away from the creek to start its path back toward the Tulip Tree trail and, ultimately, the parking lot with our SUV. The trail began to ascend a forested hill with several large rock outcroppings. The trail was wide, free of mud, and only had minor roots to push over. So far, I was feeling good about all the decisions I made out on the trails. It wasn't long when we reached a junction with a connector trail leading to a road that leads back to the visitor center. I thought about bailing on the trail and taking the road back. I knew we still had significant elevation to gain but thought it would be easier pushing Kellisa on pavement compared to a rocky trail. I wasn't familiar with the road, and it seemed like the cars were going between 45 and 55 miles per hour. I couldn't see if there'd be a sidewalk or shoulder for us.

I decided to stay on the Hidden Pond loop trail, knowing I could turn around and take the road if it became too difficult to proceed. The path remained wide with a constant incline, but never approached being too steep or rocky. We were enjoying the rock outcroppings and significant hills in all directions. We had no idea Delaware contained this type of terrain. If you dropped me in the forest blindfolded with no sense of knowing where I was and asked me what state I thought I was in, I would have probably answered Virginia or West Virginia. I doubt Delaware would have even made my top thirty guesses.

The trail eventually reunited with the Tulip Tree trail, and I was fearful as we passed through another rock wall that we would find the trail rocky again. We were now close enough that I decided to force myself to dig deep to push Kellisa and finish these trails without turning around, but the trail remained pleasantly moderate. The grade remained gradual, and the rocks were smaller and more spread out than they were at the beginning of our pushike. We were making significant progress when I could see another rock wall ahead of us, and a clearing beyond, which I guessed was the grassy area around the visitor center and its parking lot.

We passed through the rock wall and could see the visitor center, and I knew I parked our SUV on the other side. The decision to continue turned out to be correct. I think I found the trail harder than it was because I wasn't mentally prepared for the challenge, but at the same time, it was fun exploring with a certain number of unknowns. A simple pushike in Delaware turned into one of our favorite adventures. I'd recommend the trails only if you pushike the Tulip Tree and Hidden Pond trails in a counterclockwise loop, so the most challenging sections are on the descent.

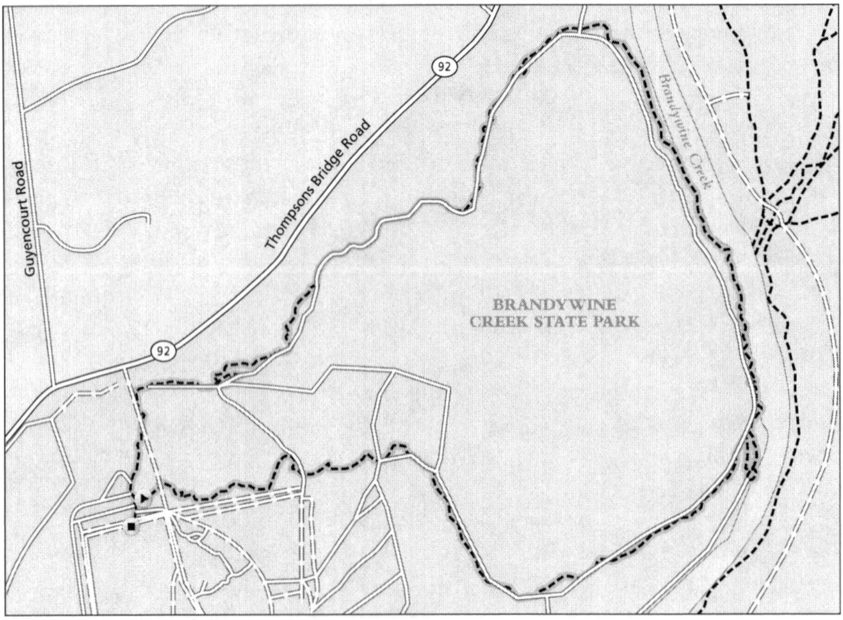

Tulip Tree Trail, Winterthur, DE

10
Florida

Trail name: Spanish Pond
Location: Fort Caroline National Memorial
Distance: 2.6 mi
Duration (active): 1h 10m
Average speed: 2.2 mi/h
Total ascent: 85 ft
Highest point: 59 ft
Difficulty: Moderate

We moved to Florida from Illinois when Kellisa was a medically fragile six-month-old baby still fighting to survive. Her doctors advised that getting away from Chicago's cold winters would be suitable for Kellisa's health. When my job wanted to relocate us, we took advantage of the opportunity and never looked back.

In Kellisa's early years, all our energy went to keeping her alive. She had multiple doctor appointments every week and endless therapy sessions so she could reach her full potential. Since she had an original life expectancy of no more than a few hours, it was impossible to know how her life would develop. Kellisa also had multiple surgeries each year, half of them were on her brain. I couldn't imagine finding the time to go hiking. I never had the thought of taking Kellisa out on a trail, especially once we realized she probably would never walk. Even if she did learn how to walk, it would be with a great deal of help and only for short distances.

Slowly, as Kellisa's health began to stabilize, we started to venture outside a little. Kellisa was extremely sensitive to sound, so we had trouble taking her out to restaurants, stores, or other populated places. We found comfort spending time outdoors and lived near the ocean. Kellisa enjoyed our visits to the ocean, which included short walks along the beach and laying out on a blanket, feeling the ocean breeze on our faces. Baby Kellisa would stick her tongue out with a smile whenever the breeze would hit her straight in the face.

Everything changed when I accidentally stumbled upon an article that described an ADA trail in Georgia. I didn't even know there was such a thing since we were still getting used to Kellisa using a wheelchair. She was two when she received her first wheelchair.

Kellisa had just turned five when we "hiked" the short ADA trail in Georgia, and I immediately wanted more. I struggled to push Kellisa's bulky and heavy wheelchair on paths not made for wheels, but I was determined. I knew there had to be a better way and found it when I purchased a jog stroller off the shelf at a local warehouse club. Pushing Kellisa on trails was now very possible, so I thought we could hike anywhere. It didn't take long before I came crashing back to earth. Many trails had obstacles we couldn't wheel over or around, like steps, stairs, and rocks, while other trails were too sandy or narrow.

Most of our early hikes were close to our home in Jacksonville, Florida. Eventually, I found trails well suited for pushing Kellisa. In our sixteen years in Florida, we hiked many trails in every part of the state. As our experience grew, we would venture to other parts of the country while continuing to push our boundaries.

With so much experience to draw from, it was difficult at first to select a trail for this book. My first thought was to visit one of our favorite national parks, the Everglades. There we were sure to see alligators and had options ranging from short trails to trails more than ten miles long. My second thought was the rugged and remote trails in the Ocala National Forest in central Florida. But I kept going back to our favorite trails in and around Jacksonville since we had hiked those the most and missed them dearly.

I would write about one of our favorite trails, but which one? After going back and forth, I selected the trail system at Fort Caroline National Monument. I narrowed it down to the Spanish Pond Trail plus short sections of the Willie Browne and Timucuan trails. We would start at the Spanish Pond parking lot and continue to the shell mounds overlooking Round Marsh. As an extraordinary treat, we had Kellisa's best friend since eighth grade, Jenny, join us on this out-and-back trail adventure.

I wanted an early start since the high temperature was going to be near 100°F, so I asked Jenny to meet us at the trailhead at 8 a.m. At 8:15 a.m., I was awakened by a text message from Jenny, "Hey, I'm at the trailhead."

Somehow, I overslept. I wasn't sure if I forgot to set the alarm or in a tired fog, I turned it off instead of hitting snooze. Either way, I felt horrible and quickly texted Jenny back, "Just woke up, very sorry. Be there at 9:15 a.m.!"

We pulled into the parking lot and immediately saw Jenny patiently waiting for us. She ran up to our rental SUV, where she shared hugs and kisses with Kellisa. It had been a year since they saw each other, and they were so happy to be together again. Seeing Kellisa and Jenny reunited brought tears to my eyes.

It was already getting hot, so we wasted little time before heading out on the trail. Jenny started pushing, which Kellisa thoroughly enjoyed because she knew it was something extra special. I gave them some space and lingered behind them a short distance. My heart filled with joy as I heard them giggling along the path together.

They stopped after a short boardwalk to observe a gopher tortoise just off the side of the trail. Kellisa enjoyed being so close to the wildlife while Jenny and I took turns snapping pictures. After a few minutes under the scorching sun, Jenny took off jogging while pushing Kellisa. It was getting hot, and I remembered the trail was about to embark on a steep little incline with more sand than solid ground. I was comfortable hiking at a leisurely pace as they disappeared around a turn.

It didn't surprise me to find Jenny taking a short break when I caught up with them. Kellisa was still giggling away. I took a turn pushing Kellisa through the jungle-like forest. One of the things I love about this trail is its location in the middle of Jacksonville. There are more than 1.5 million people in the metro area, and yet on this trail, you feel like you're in the middle of nowhere lost in another time. Few hikers and the lack of road noise contribute to this feeling.

When you think of hiking in Florida, hills probably aren't at the top of the list of thoughts, but the trail system at Fort Caroline has several short ascents and descents. There is also a significant amount of bone-rattling roots across the trail. Fortunately, most of the trails are under a thick canopy protecting users from the harsh Florida sun. After a downhill section at the edge of the forest and marsh, we began pushiking over mounds made from shells. The mounds are left from the native inhabitants who used the nearby St. Johns River and Atlantic Ocean as food sources. There is a viewing tower at the end of the trail.

When Kellisa was smaller, I would carry her up the stairs whenever we had the opportunity for a bird's-eye view. However, when Kellisa was nine or ten, this practice became too complicated and often dangerous. I could leave Kellisa for a couple of minutes so that I could take in the far-reaching views, but I decided long ago that I will never go somewhere without Kellisa when she is out on the trail with me. In my opinion, it is just not fair.

While standing at the bottom of the tower, we could see the ships docked across the marsh at the Naval Station Mayport. Some might feel this takes away from the wilderness experience, but I always found it interesting to see such massive ships. Due to the oppressive heat, we didn't linger long and retraced our steps back to the shade of the forest for a little relief.

Jenny and I traded turns pushing Kellisa. After one of the times Jenny took off running behind Kellisa, they waited under an enormous oak tree for me to catch up. As I snapped a few pictures of Kellisa, Jenny started to climb around in the tree's massive limbs. Kellisa couldn't stop giggling while watching Jenny bounce around above her. I took a few pictures and then retreated to watch them play from afar. I enjoyed watching Kellisa in her element with a true friend. It's not often we get a glimpse of a "normal" life with Kellisa. I couldn't help but wonder if Kellisa could feel jealousy because she couldn't climb around like a healthy twenty-year-old. As I continued to observe them, I realized Kellisa was more than happy with her level of participation in the game they were playing.

The only animal we encountered on our return hike was a well-controlled little dog who took an instant liking to Kellisa and Jenny. I made small talk with the dog's owner while the girls had a great time showering the dog with attention that the dog repaid with wet kisses.

Our return to the trailhead turned into an impromptu photo session as the girls posed while I took pictures. Some were serious, but most of them were silly, which was alright with me. Since I don't get a lot of pictures of myself with Kellisa out on a trail, I asked Jenny to take a few. No one wanted this reunion to end, but Jenny had commitments, and I was hopeful to pushike two more trails that afternoon.

A part of us will always consider Jacksonville home, and some of our favorite trails will always be in and around the "First Coast."

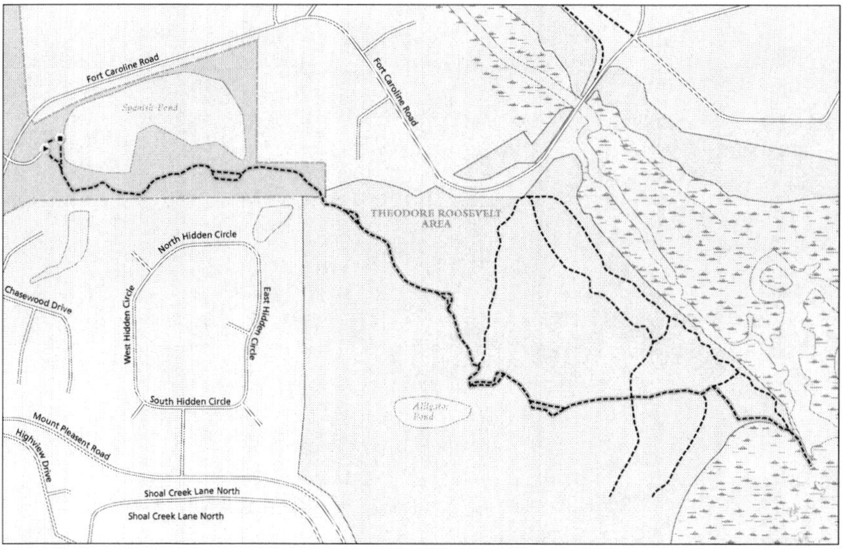

Spanish Pond Trail, Jacksonville, FL

11
Georgia

Trail name: Chesser Island Boardwalk
Location: Okefenokee National Wildlife Refuge
Distance: 1.5 mi
Duration (active): 37m
Average speed: 2.4 mi/h
Total ascent: 7 ft
Highest point: 144 ft
Difficulty: Easy

Since Jacksonville, Florida, is close to the Georgia state line, we often found ourselves heading north into Georgia to explore new trails. Some of our favorites were Driftwood Beach on Jekyll Island and Amicalola Falls State Park in the mountains of North Georgia near the southern terminus of the world-famous Appalachian Trail. But there is no doubt on our absolute favorite, the Chesser Island Boardwalk Trail in the Okefenokee National Wildlife Refuge. It may be a surprise to learn an "easy" boardwalk rates so high with us. But it was just over an hour from our house, and we were always guaranteed wildlife sightings. We've been taking Kellisa there since she was a baby. I carried Kellisa during our early visits because she was small for her age. At four years old, she only weighed twenty-two pounds. On our many visits, we saw everything from alligators to snakes to bobcats to birds. The wildlife refuge never disappointed us, and the Okefenokee holds a special place in our hearts.

Without being long or difficult, the Chesser Island Boardwalk Trail takes its visitors deep into the largest blackwater swamp in North America. The boardwalk is the only way to "hike" out into the swamp. The alternatives include seeing the swamp by boat and slogging through the swamp. We've enjoyed several guided boat tours into the Okefenokee Swamp. These tours are a relaxing way to learn more about the resident wildlife, early settlers, and local flora of the swamp. *Slogging* is the term for hiking in and through the swamp. Since slogging is impossible with a wheeled device, our favorite way to experience the swamp is the Chesser Island Boardwalk.

The trailhead is at the end of a seven-mile swamp drive after you pass several other trails and many roadside ditches that often fill up with water. If you look closely as you drive by slowly, you can usually spot alligators hanging out in the ditches. On a few visits, we've even seen large snakes sunning themselves on the asphalt. One time, we waited patiently for a water moccasin to finish crossing the road. It was in the middle of the road, where it coiled up and displayed its famous cottonmouth with exposed fangs. The kids enjoyed observing this natural moment from the safety of our SUV. It became apparent after fifteen minutes that the snake had claimed this section of the drive, so we slowly and carefully navigated around the snake. Egypt was convinced we would drive over the snake and kill it. I shared the same concern. I knew I would avoid running it over but was fearful it would try to slither away and get caught under the rear tires. Fortunately, it held its ground and remained unharmed.

The Chesser family homestead is near the trailhead. The family settled on the island in the late 1800s and remained there until the late 1950s. It's worth the time to walk around the homestead to learn about living in the swamp. If you time your visit just right, you will find interpreters in period clothing playing the role of the Chessers describing life in the swamp in great detail. As much as I love the Okefenokee, I can't imagine living in the middle of the swamp without modern conveniences.

There are a bathroom and a small picnic area near the trailhead. After a short sidewalk, you reach the boardwalk, and it quickly disappears into a forest. The surrounding ground is usually muddy or even filled with standing water, making it a prime area to look for snakes, frogs, and other small creatures taking refuge in the relative safety of the wooded environment. A few minutes into the walk, the boardwalk emerges into the swamp with views so far and wide that first-time visitors will be left speechless.

The look of the swamp has changed drastically over the years since we started visiting. In 2011, a lightning strike during a period of a drought sparked a massive wildfire that burned approximately 75 percent of the Okefenokee. We visited not long after the fire was extinguished entirely, and most of the trees were gone, leaving only blackened stumps. The boardwalk was also a casualty of this fire. After the complete devastation, it was hard to imagine the swamp ever recovering. We were afraid that the boardwalk would not be replaced.

We returned a few times a year and were amazed at how fast some of the green and brown colors started returning to the Okefenokee. You could still see charred trees and limbs, but new growth was slowly overtaking the dead areas. It took a few years, but the boardwalk was rebuilt.

When we arrived on an early June afternoon to pushike the boardwalk and document it for this book, the temperature was 100°F. I don't remember a single day in our sixteen years of living in the area that reached triple digits. Since it was so hot, I was thankful I selected a short, easy, and familiar trail to feature. The fact that it was one of our favorite trails in Georgia was a bonus.

The boardwalk is an out and back that ends at a large wooden lookout tower. On the way to the tower, the boardwalk makes a few slight turns, so you're not just walking in a straight line. Several benches are spaced along the walk with a roof to provide some relief from the blazing sun. Usually, we wouldn't stop, but on this day, we were grateful to use them as a resource to cool down a little while sipping water and pouring some over our heads.

It was on our second break that we witnessed a good-sized adult bobcat emerge from the swamp coming to a sudden stop after it jumped on the boardwalk. The bobcat was maybe twenty yards away and was staring right at us. I tried to get my camera in a position to take a picture, but the bobcat turned and ran away down the boardwalk. I was able to get a blurry image of its backside. Before we could take more than a couple of steps, it jumped from the boardwalk and disappeared in the swamp brush.

I pushed Kellisa to the spot where it jumped off, and we stopped quietly, hoping to see him again. After a few minutes, we concluded the bobcat was long gone. We continued on our way to the end of the boardwalk when we heard an unusual sound coming from the water on our left side. I looked over and saw a large mother gator resting her head on a rock that was jutting up from the swamp water. At the very top of the rock were a couple of baby alligators. We were excited to observe the mother and her babies at such a close yet safe distance. The protective mother allowed us the opportunity to take several pictures. The mother must not have felt threatened because she was hanging out while watching us off to the side as her babies wrestled a little for the top position. Happy with our encounter, we continued toward the end of the trail, leaving the new family in peace.

The end of the trail features a high wooden tower surrounded on three sides by a densely forested part of the swamp. The fourth side has open views out across the vast swamp. When we reached this tower, we noticed numerous giant spiders resting on their webs, which were suspended from the many trees around the tower. Keeping with my own rule, I did not climb the tower for a better view since I couldn't safely take Kellisa with me.

Even though we were now in the shade, we didn't stay long. We began the short backtracking to the trailhead. We were hoping to see the mama gator with her babies again, but in the few minutes since we left them, they had disappeared entirely.

I've lost track of how many times we've enjoyed the Chesser Boardwalk Trail, and the record remains perfect; we've never been disappointed. After the fire, we visited several times before the refuge rebuilt the boardwalk. I would use Swamp Drive as a trail to push Kellisa through the swamp and pine forests. It was amazing to see how quickly nature could devastate an area, then watch the recovery process as the Okefenokee transformed back to lush green swampland. Even though we now live on the other side of the country, we still hope to return many times.

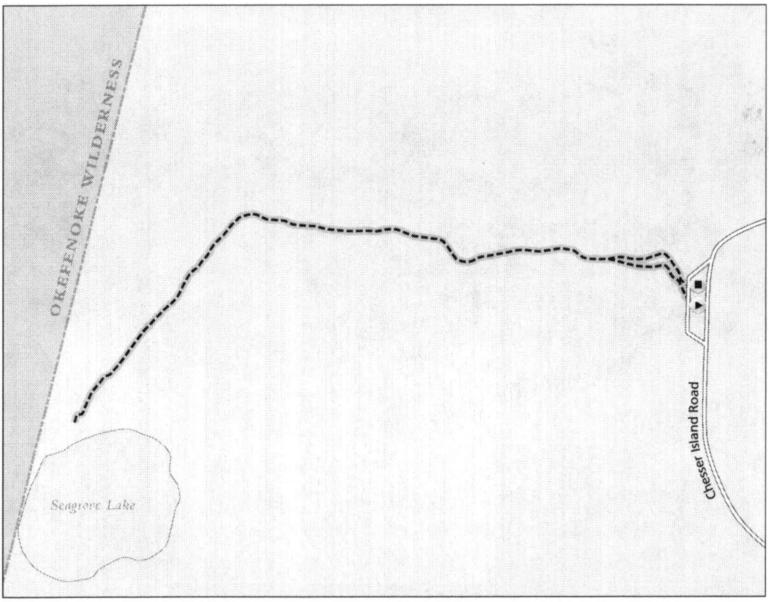

Chesser Island Boardwalk, Folkston, GA

12

Hawaii, Difficult

Trail name: Ohai Loop
Location: West Maui Coast
Distance: 1.3 mi
Duration (active): 59m
Average speed: 1.3 mi/h
Total ascent: 174 ft
Highest point: 355 ft
Difficulty: Challenging

Kellisa and I flew to Kahului, Hawaii, for our second visit to the island state. Once we landed, it meant we both visited each of the fifty states at least twice. I like to keep lists and track our travels, but I was surprised also to learn that Kellisa had visited forty-one states at least three times.

Our objective for the weekend was to pushike at least one trail while exploring the island a little for a possible return vacation with Lisa and Egypt. The airport was open to the weather just beyond the gate area, and as soon as I pushed Kellisa outside, a wall of humidity hit us. It was warm, but that didn't bother me as much as the humidity. It's funny because I grew to love the humidity when we lived in Florida, but after three and a half years in the dry climate of northern California, I lost my affinity for humid conditions.

We arrived late and had to take a short train to get our rental SUV, which Kellisa loved. I made reservations in advance for a campsite near a beach about a half-hour drive away. Since it was dark, I couldn't see the mountains rising around us or the ocean that I knew was just to the side of the road. I was a little concerned about setting up camp after dark. The turnoff for the campground was confusing because it was so dark, and GPS wanted me to turn down the wrong driveway. It took a few minutes, but I eventually found the correct driveway. When we arrived, the park office was closed, and I used the flashlight on my cell phone to read the after-hours arrival procedures. We were assigned a specific site number, but there wasn't a map of the campground.

I could see a large parking lot filled with cars, vans, and SUVs just beyond the small office. I decided to drive over there, hoping the site would be easy to find, but I ended up even more confused. I circled the parking lot and didn't see a single site number or tent set up anywhere. It looked like everyone was sleeping in their vehicles. I circled a second time and still didn't see any tents.

I found a parking spot and was considering sleeping in our front seats when I noticed a young woman walking by our SUV, and I decided to ask her for information. I didn't want to scare her. I turned on the interior lights, and it caught her attention. I hoped she noticed Kellisa in the front seat, so she didn't feel threatened when I opened my door and said, "Excuse me, do you know where I can find the campsites?"

The woman stopped and replied, "You just park anywhere and sleep."

I thought this was odd because someone at the campground assigned us to a site, so I said, "I have a reservation for site #22."

Her response was simple and not very helpful, "We're camping over there," as she pointed to an older cargo van where I could see a man working on the inside.

Even more confused, I thanked her before sitting back inside the air-conditioned SUV. I was telling Kellisa our predicament with the hope of figuring out our next move. It was too late to try to find a hotel room. I started to think about how best to make sleeping in the SUV work when the same woman startled me by knocking on my window. It was so dark outside I didn't see her approach our SUV. I rolled down my window, and she asked if we had a tent. I responded that we did, and she pointed to an area and said she saw tents set up in that direction. I thanked her and decided to go check it out since I couldn't see anything from our parking spot.

I grabbed the flashlight and decided to check it out before grabbing all our gear. I found a path and could see some torches and campfires in the distance, along with a few glowing tents from headlamps moving around inside. I wanted to find our site before returning to the SUV. The numbers were hard to find on the scattered campsites, but after five minutes of stumbling around, I found #22. Now I had to find my way back to the parking lot.

I was a sweaty mess before I hoisted my heavy backpack over my shoulders and started pushing Kellisa to our site. I was hoping it would cool off, but since it was already after 9 p.m. and pitch-black outside, I didn't like our odds for a comfortable night of sleep. I set the tent up by flashlight and left the rainfly off, hoping it would allow an ocean breeze to cool us a little once we settled down for the evening. I opened our sleeping bags and threw them inside. After dropping our stuff on the floor, I lifted Kellisa from her chair and placed her in the tent. I crawled in behind her and rearranged her on top of her sleeping bag. I still had to give Kellisa her tube feeding, which is always a challenge without a solid surface to set down the open containers containing liquids. I'm always worried that I will spill water or formula all over the inside of the tent, but tonight's feeding was uneventful.

It was still uncomfortably hot when it was time to help Kellisa get in position for bed. I decided to let her fall asleep on top of her sleeping bag. I also settled in on top of my bag when I immediately regretted my decision to leave our air mattresses at home. I was hoping, since the campsite was near the ocean, that we would be sleeping on the sand (and we were), but it also had many rounded rocks, which made laying directly on top of them uncomfortable. I apologized to Kellisa for my mistake, but her twenty-year-old body didn't seem to mind as much as mine. I wanted to save the weight and space since it was only two nights, and I would already have my hands full with Kellisa. It was a hard lesson, and I won't make the same mistake again.

Despite feeling like I was lying in a warm puddle, sleep seemed to happen fast but didn't last long. One of our neighbors was camping with an infant who woke up five times during the night screaming. I'm guessing the child was hungry, and it would take a few minutes each time before quiet returned. Thankfully, Kellisa slept through these outbursts, but I had a difficult time falling asleep each time.

The sun rudely woke me up before 7 a.m. local time. I was not a happy camper as it was already 87°F, and the humidity was just as high. I knew I would never fall back asleep, but I laid in the tent for another hour before my aching body forced me to get up and out. I moved slowly and quietly so Kellisa could sleep in a little longer.

Now that it was light outside, I could see a towering mountain rise in front of our tent and the ocean through a few trees behind our site. If I listened carefully, I could hear the waves hitting the beach. Our site had a picnic table where I sat while enjoying a granola bar and some warm water. While sitting there, I saw a lady emerge from the only tent between ours and the ocean, and she was holding a small baby. It wasn't long before the baby was screaming again, and this time the cries woke Kellisa.

Typically, I get upset when someone wakes Kellisa before she must get up, but I understood the baby couldn't help it. Honestly, I was ready to start our day after such a miserable night. It didn't take long to give Kellisa her morning medicine and liquids before packing up what we needed for the day and heading off to find our trail.

I selected the Kanahena Trail in the Āhihi-Kina'u Natural Area Reserve because it ran along the Pacific Ocean over a lava bed. I carefully researched the trail, and by all the photos and reports I could find, it seemed possible to pushike with Kellisa. As the road to the reserve ended, I became concerned about the number of cars parked along the side. I continued driving to find the parking inside the reserve packed with vehicles. People were leaving their cars anywhere there was enough room, which added to the chaos in the small lot. It was challenging to turn around once I reached the end without finding a spot. I didn't want to start and end this pushike with an unnecessary road walk, especially since it was now in the nineties outside. Just as I completed my slow turnaround, I noticed a car's reverse lights come on, and I held my ground until they backed out. It was a tight fit, but I found a spot near the trailhead.

I drank a quart of water to hydrate my body before I even got out of the SUV. I left the air running for Kellisa while I got her chair and our gear ready so that she could enjoy a few last minutes of comfort. The constant breeze off the ocean was appreciated, but it was not enough to make the conditions pleasant. With Kellisa in her mobility chair, I started pushing her toward the trailhead, where we met with our first obstacle. We had to navigate up, over, and around several large chunks of lava. I looked ahead, and the trail seemed better after this beginning section.

We were on top of a black lava field stretching from high above directly into the Pacific Ocean below our right side. The views were mind-blowing, with waves crashing over the lava rocks sending spray high into the air. We could see a couple of islands just off the coast.

The condition of the trail deteriorated after only twenty yards. I found myself lifting Kellisa's mobility chair over large lava rocks with jagged edges. I was worried about getting a flat tire or worse, multiple flat tires. I checked the tire pressure, and so far, they were holding up. I started having doubts about continuing.

I saw a large blowhole a short distance down the trail with people gathered around watching and taking pictures. I set the goal to make it to that area and decide if we wanted to go farther. By the time we reached the blowhole, we had the area to ourselves, which made taking photos easier. I tried to time the pictures perfectly to capture Kellisa with the ocean water spraying into the air behind her. I never got a perfect picture with Kellisa looking and smiling at the exact second the water was rising behind her from the lava.

With the sun beating down on us, I decided to continue because it looked like we were halfway to where the trail turned inland just enough to be in the shade of a forest. But I still had to navigate through many lava rocks.

The going was slow and painful since I was continually lifting Kellisa and her mobility chair to maneuver past the lava rocks. I couldn't see it from a distance, but we reached a small beach. I thought it would lessen the difficulty of this trail, but I knew I was wrong as soon as Kellisa's tires sunk in the sand. Now I was struggling to push Kellisa through deep sand, which was possibly more challenging than the lava field. I only proceeded forward because we were getting close to the forest. I was hoping for some relief from the sun, and I knew the trail had to get more comfortable.

I was wrong again as the shade provided by the trees offered a minimal reprieve from the brutal sun, and the trail found a way to get harder. The path turned into a jagged rock scramble. I dug deep and forced our way another fifty yards deeper into the forest. I stopped to look ahead and decided it looked even worse. I didn't want to admit what I knew almost from the beginning, that this trail was not at all suitable for pushiking.

In defeat, I turned Kellisa around to start making our way back when we saw several goats wandering around on top of some of the more massive rock formations. Kellisa and I both enjoyed watching them navigate their way around the lava rocks with ease.

I was dreading the entire pushike back to our SUV. I knew we were in paradise, but the battle of every step forward was draining me. As I was pushing Kellisa back through the sandy beach area, I noticed a rough-looking 4x4 road. I could see a fence with no trespassing signs, but the road was on our side of the fence. I didn't know where it led, but it was heading in the general direction toward the parking lot. Even though I had been wrong many times so far on this trail, I decided to push Kellisa down the road. It was filled with large rocks and ruts but was wide enough that I could make our way around most of the biggest obstacles. My only real concern was if this road would somehow connect to where we needed to go. Even though it was more comfortable than the lava rocks near the ocean, it was still tough, and the last thing I wanted to do was backtrack down this road only to retrace our path over the lava field. I didn't know what to do, but I decided to follow the road.

Eventually, my hopes and fears collided. I could see the road we were pushing down ended at the parking lot where we left our SUV, but there was a closed gate blocking the entire route. I knew I couldn't get Kellisa up and over the gate. A fence was extending out on both sides, making our options appear dire. I knew we had to find a way because backtracking was no longer an option. As we got closer, I could see a small opening between the gate and fence on one side. It didn't look like I could push Kellisa through it, but I was confident we would get off this road soon. I tried squeezing Kellisa's mobility chair through the opening even though it was apparent there was no way it would fit. After backing her up, I went through alone to figure out what to do next.

My best option was to carry Kellisa through the opening between the fence and gate before setting her down. I would then lift her mobility chair up and over. The only problem with this plan was the area was filled with jagged lava rocks. I didn't see a comfortable place to set her down. Even though Kellisa can sit up pretty well for someone with cerebral palsy, if she starts to fall over, she will continue until she lands on her side, or worse, her face. With all the sharp rocks, I was afraid she could get hurt if that happened. I was standing there mentally and physically defeated when I saw a relatively flat rock just off the trail. It looked just big enough for Kellisa to fit. I knew Kellisa was likely to giggle and curl up when I carried her to the rock, so I had a serious talk with her before I lifted her up and over my shoulder. I told her in a stern voice, not to laugh or giggle. She looked at me with a face like she didn't understand why she was getting in trouble, which was precisely the reaction I was hoping to get. I proceeded to lift her and quickly carry her to the rock where I set her down. I told her, "Don't move. I'll be right back."

I made sure she was as stable as can be, and she sat there like she was in trouble. I grabbed her mobility chair and lifted it up and over the gate before setting it down directly in front of Kellisa. I was still worried she would fall over, so I didn't waste any time getting her back in her mobility chair before pushing her back to our SUV, where I blasted the air conditioning on high to cool us off.

In the end, our little lava field adventure lasted just forty-five minutes and covered only 0.44 of a mile. While the views were unbelievable, and it will be fun to remember the blowhole experience, I felt like we were leaving the trail unsuccessfully in our ultimate goal of writing a chapter that readers can use as a reference.

We had a second day on Maui, and I had planned to pushike another trail, even if I didn't need it for the book. I had a new sense of urgency to complete a trail since this was our only opportunity to visit Hawaii. My second trail was on the other side of the island. I decided to drive there to make our attempt even though my body was suffering. I didn't want to wait until our last day on the island.

The drive to the Ohai Loop Trail took longer than expected due to the twisting road that rounded the northern end of Maui. It would be hard to find a more beautiful drive, but we had a trailhead to reach, although my sore muscles appreciated the extra time, giving them a chance to recover a little.

As soon as we reached the trailhead, I was concerned. I could see a significant portion of the trail winding along the coast far below my vantage point. Even though everything I read in advance rated the trail as "easy," it looked far from easy, and I had severe doubts before starting. It was now late in the afternoon, and we didn't have any other trail options, so I decided to at least give it a try.

The trail started descending to the intersection where it met the loop portion of the lollipop trail, and I needed to make a decision. We could have gone straight or to our left. Looking straight ahead down the path, it didn't look too tricky from the parts I could see. The way to the left seemed daunting. The trail continued its descent toward the cliffs rising from the ocean, and I could see several large rocks posing an immediate problem. I decided to go left because I wanted to descend the difficult part of the trail, and I hoped the ascent going in this direction would be easier. This decision also meant I didn't want to turn back once I made it past this area.

The trail would lose most of its 174 feet early when pushiking the Ohai Loop Trail in a clockwise direction. It was challenging to navigate over and around the large rocks in the middle of our path, but I didn't have to lift Kellisa's mobility chair. It was hard to let gravity assist because the trail was narrow with dense foliage on both sides. The views were unobstructed; even Kellisa, sitting in her mobility chair, could look out and see the rugged coastline and waves crashing far below. All the surrounding greenery was under three feet in height.

As we made our way down the path, I was worried about gaining all the elevation we just lost. It was equivalent to a seventeen-story building, and I was solely responsible for getting Kellisa safely back up the trail. The trail remained mostly flat with a few elevation changes as it followed the curves of the island high above the ocean. The pushing was more straightforward, but many rocks still littered our path, slowing our progress.

The trail reached a section where it got narrow as it followed the slope along a wall heading out in the ocean a short distance. We only had a few inches to spare with Kellisa's back wheels, but this section was mostly free of rocks allowing me to concentrate on following the path. The landscape rose directly to my right and dropped away to the ocean on my left. A slip or fall along this section would be bad. I would not recommend this trail to anyone with a fear of heights or anyone who doesn't have a tether for the jog stroller or mobility chair.

It didn't take long to reach the top and round the bend to start heading back away from the edge. The trail remained rocky, but still not too difficult. I only had to lift Kellisa and her mobility chair once over a large rock. The trail continued to hug the coastline. I knew the trail was only a little over a mile in length, and it seemed like we already covered twice that distance.

The hot afternoon sun was starting to wear me out, and I kept drinking water. I forced myself to take a few sips every few minutes, even if I didn't feel thirsty. I knew Kellisa was hydrated because I gave her sixteen ounces of water in the car at the trailhead before we started.

There was a second section where the trail got steep with significant drop-offs on one side before again rounding a bend to head away from the edge. This incline had a few large rocks which required special care to push around. Once on safer ground, I noticed a couple hiking the loop in the opposite direction. In a few minutes, our paths would meet. When they did, I asked them about the condition of the trail coming down from where they started.

The lady looked at Kellisa in her mobility chair and said, "I think you'll be OK with that thing going up."

With great relief, I smiled and thanked her. The feeling only lasted a few seconds because the man followed with, "There are a few rocks, and you might have to turn back."

He then pointed in the direction we were coming from, and that was the last thing I wanted to hear, so I thanked him as well before proceeding to follow the trail in a clockwise direction. I was hoping the lady was correct. The path remained rocky but was a little wider in the middle section of the Ohai Loop Trail.

It seemed like hours had passed before the trail finally turned back in the direction of the trailhead. It also meant we would start gaining the 174 feet we lost earlier on our loop. A large boulder was blocking the entire trail just a few steps into the first significant incline. I couldn't push Kellisa around because the hill rose almost straight up on our left and to our right was the low-lying dense foliage typical along this trail. My only option was to lift Kellisa and her mobility chair up and over.

I was worried about my footing since I didn't want to fall or drop Kellisa. I also wanted to be careful not to hurt my back or any other body part. We were still far from the trailhead, and the unrelenting sun remained high in the sky above us. We couldn't afford an injury. Once I was confident in my position, I went through my plan several times in my head as a way of checking it for success. After a minute, I lifted Kellisa and set her down on the other side in one fluid motion. My back was a little sore from going through an awkward movement, but I was familiar with the feeling and knew it wasn't anything to worry about too much.

I knew we still had probably a half-mile to cover, and most of the remaining trail would be a climb. I was hoping the path would be free of rock obstructions. As the trail closely followed the contours of the hillside, we found ourselves in the shade several times, and it made a huge difference. The temperature seemed to drop fifteen degrees each time the shade sheltered us from the sun. I used each opportunity to cool off a little and check Kellisa for any signs of the sun getting to her. She was doing great and having a wonderful time between our rock hopping and the ocean breeze in her face.

I noticed Kellisa's tongue out during most of our pushikes on Maui, and it brought back many memories from when we visited the ocean during our years living in Florida and Kellisa would always stick her tongue out. It looked like she was licking the salty ocean air. While enjoying one of our rests in the shade, I realized we had been gaining considerable altitude without any major rock obstacles. When we reached the end of the loop, I was surprised how quickly we completed the back half of the trail. Before ending our pushike, we followed a short paved path leading to a small lookout above the parking lot. The view was beautiful but paled in comparison to some of the sights along the Ohai Loop Trail.

I was relieved to complete a quality pushiking trail in Hawaii. The Ohai Loop can challenge every other trail in this book for the titles of most significant challenge and most beautiful. While we were able to complete this trail, we've been pushiking for many years and have a mobility chair specifically built for demanding trails. I would not recommend this trail for anyone new to pushiking or anyone who didn't have a jog stroller or mobility chair rated for tough terrain.

After two demanding trails, the last thing I wanted to do was spend another hot and humid night sleeping on rocky ground. I decided to look for an affordable hotel for our last night. I was hoping to find a decent rate since it was a Sunday night. Not many places had vacancies, but I booked the cheapest room on the website and hoped for the best. If our room had air conditioning and a shower, I knew we'd be alright. But first, we had to return to our campsite to pack up our gear. I already knew I made the right decision to book a hotel when I saw our neighbors with the baby still in the spot next to ours. It didn't take long to throw all our gear in my backpack, and forty-five minutes later, we were relaxing in the comfort of a hotel room on the ocean. It was a pleasant surprise since I didn't pay for an ocean view room because we were looking at it all day from beautiful, but demanding, trails.

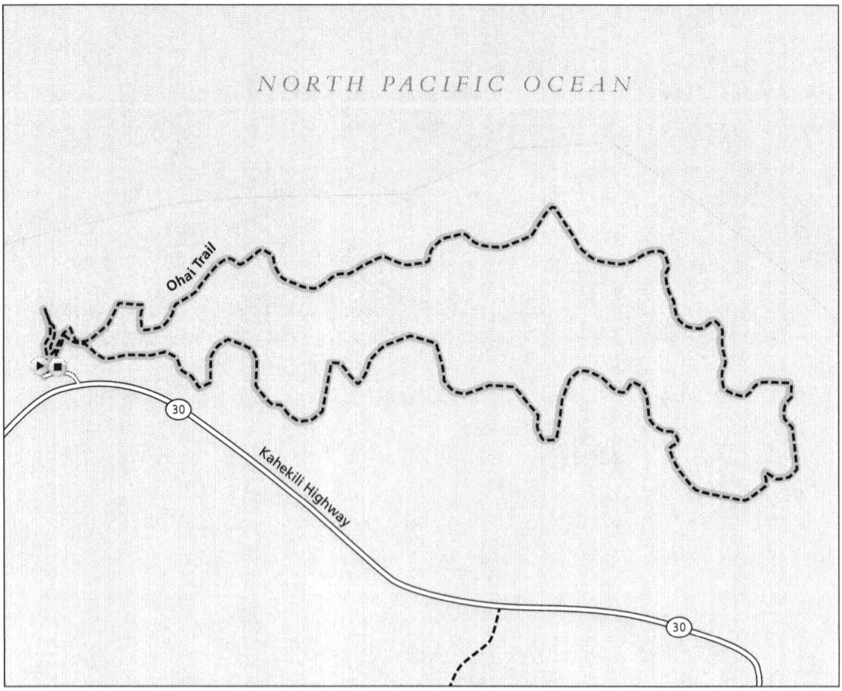

Ohai Loop Trail, West Maui Coast, HI

13
Hawaii, Easy

Trail name: Kealia Boardwalk
Location: Kealia Pond National Wildlife Refuge
Distance: 0.8 mi
Duration (active): 27m
Average speed: 1.8 mi/h
Total ascent: 3 ft
Highest point: 58 ft
Difficulty: Easy

Kellisa and I had most of a day to explore Maui before catching our evening flight to Oakland. I originally planned to pushike the Ohai Loop Trail. Since we completed it the previous day, I thought we could drive up a volcano to visit Haleakala National Park. The entrance was just over an hour from our hotel, allowing enough time to spend a few hours exploring the park. I thought we completed the most beautiful drive along the northern coast of Maui earlier in our trip. But then we drove from sea level to near the summit of a volcano at more than 10,000 feet above the Pacific Ocean. As we ascended, we drove through several layers of clouds. The volcano road rivals any of the high routes that we've driven on the mainland over the Rockies or Sierra ranges. The road had many switchbacks as it passed through several different environments.

Kellisa and I learned from a ranger that the road we were driving climbs 10,000 feet in the shortest distance of any road in the world. Near the summit crater, we passed through lava fields on both sides. It was windy and quite cold at the summit despite 90°-plus temperatures at the base of the giant mountain. Instead of getting out to explore, we just enjoyed the views from our rental SUV. Since we were mostly looking out over a sea of clouds, I'm sure it reminded Kellisa of looking out the window on an airplane.

Our time on top was short, and we began the long descent back to sea level. It was fun passing through the clouds. We had views of the ocean beyond agriculture on both sides of the road. As we were descending, I realized we would have a couple of hours before we needed to be back at the airport. I started thinking about pushiking a more accessible trail on Maui to balance out the challenging trails of the previous day in case someone wanted an easy pushike while on a relaxing vacation.

On our way to the Kanahena Trail the previous day, we passed the Kealia Pond National Wildlife Refuge, and I could see a boardwalk trail following the shoreline. I decided to spend our remaining time on the island visiting the refuge. The boardwalk is an excellent location to view migratory birds making brief stops as well as local birds making their homes in the sanctuary. I'm not good at bird identification, so I don't even try. All I can say is we would see several types of unusual birds that I'm confident we had never observed before this visit.

The boardwalk followed the shoreline for approximately four-tenths of a mile. In between the beach area and boardwalk was a narrow strip of trees offering a buffer for the ocean winds. Several access points were connecting the boardwalk to the beach. I didn't want to deal with pushing Kellisa through sand shortly before boarding our long flight home, so we just followed the boardwalk. There was a shallow water pond on the other side of the path with a two-lane highway just beyond. Tall mountains rose to lofty heights in the distance.

I pushed Kellisa to the end of the boardwalk, where we enjoyed the best ocean views for several minutes before turning around. Since we still had time, we made several stops to watch the birds drinking, feeding, and just hanging out on the ponds. We only saw three other people on the boardwalk.

The boardwalk wasn't long, but I could imagine spending several hours at the refuge, especially if you spent time on the beach. The boardwalk provided a clean surface for pushing and wheeling. If I kept a lifetime birding checklist, I'm sure I would have been able to check at least a dozen new birds off my list. Even though the path was close to a major highway, the ocean breeze seemed to cancel out most of the road noise, making this a tranquil place to escape for a peaceful pushike.

Kellisa and I arrived at the Kahului Airport with plenty of time to return our SUV, ride the train, and print our boarding passes before moving through security, and we enjoyed personal pizzas while waiting for our flight to board. We left Maui only forty-five hours after we arrived, but we left with experiences and memories that will last a lifetime.

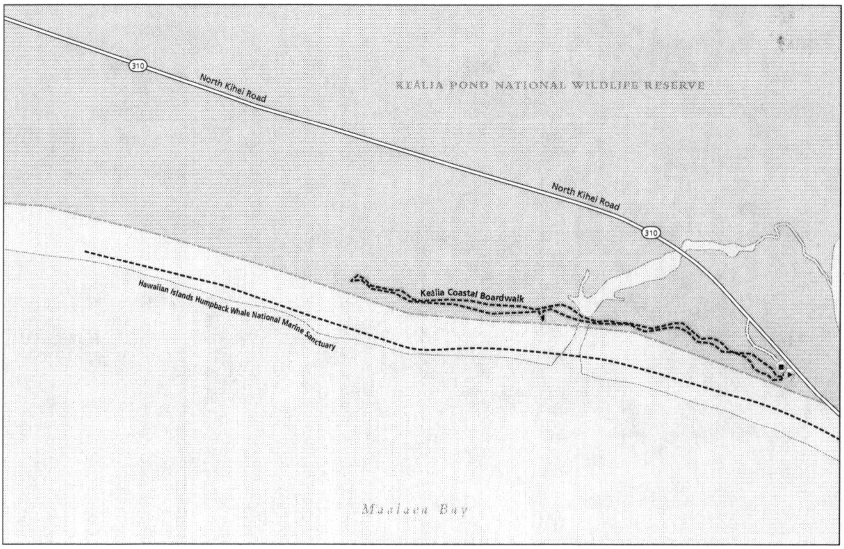

Kealia Boardwalk, Kīhei, HI

14
Idaho

Trail name: Oregon #103 and Rim #102
Location: Oregon Trail Preserve
Distance: 2.1 mi
Duration (active): 1h 6m
Average speed: 1.9 mi/h
Total ascent: 102 ft
Highest point: 3,026 ft
Difficulty: Moderate

Kellisa and I planned a day trip to Boise to pushike a trail in Idaho for inclusion in this book. I was initially looking for an urban trail since Boise is both the state capital and largest population center in Idaho. I found a few typical walking and biking paths along with many challenging trails in the mountains rising near the city. Nothing was jumping out at me until I discovered the Oregon Trail Preserve. Since Kellisa and I would fly up in the morning and return later that evening, the fact the trail was just a few minutes from the Boise Airport was an added convenience.

Once we landed, I pushed Kellisa to find our rental SUV, and within a few minutes, we were looking for a place to grab a quick lunch before our pushike. After eating cheeseburgers, we drove down the expressway for a couple of miles before exiting and driving through a suburban residential area. The trailhead parking area is on East Forest Drive near the intersection with South Kelton Place. Before I even got out of the car, I could see some of the trails, and it looked perfect for pushiking. I also had views out across a valley to higher mountains in the distance. The preserve had a water fountain and bathrooms for visitors.

It wasn't hot, but we would be pushiking under the midday sun. I decided to apply some sunscreen before we started down the trail. The preserve has several trails making loops of varying distances. I didn't have a set plan for which trails we would explore, and I figured we could make it up as we went. We started off going counterclockwise on the Oregon Trail #103. There were beautiful houses and backyards to our right and considerable views on our left with low-growth scrub surrounding the trail. Its surface was flat and wide enough for Kellisa's wheels, and the well-compacted gravel and sand reminded me of a desert hike.

The trail system had well-marked intersections making it easy to see where you are and aided in planning where we wanted to go next. We decided to start looping back on the Rim Trail #102, which ran close, but never at the edge of a significant drop-off. A fall from this edge would be fatal. From several different viewpoints, we could see that the rim went straight down to the valley below, which was filled with several subdivisions. Many deep-red trees jumped out in a sea of green trees and roofs far below. In the distance, to the northwest, we could see the higher buildings in downtown Boise. It was hard to believe an urban area could harbor a natural resource as grandiose as the Oregon Trail Preserve. The only noise along the rim was an occasional breeze.

Each viewing area along the Rim Trail had informative signs. We stopped at each one to enjoy the views and learn a little more about the history of the region. The Boise River was meandering through the valley under towering mountains rising on the far side. Unfortunately, most of the Rim Trail is directly under power lines. Besides being unsightly, every time the wind would die down, we could hear the buzzing sounds coming from the power lines.

The trail system was popular with joggers. We saw several young women out for a run along with a couple of men who looked to be in their seventies running down the trail. Most were friendly and gave us a polite "Hi" or smile as they passed us. Kellisa thought it was funny they were moving so fast. I think she wanted me to start running, so I reminded her that we were pushikers and not joggers.

The trails were free from rocks, and without trees we didn't have to worry about roots to roll over. I might have been able to push Kellisa along the trails in her manual travel wheelchair. My only worry would be about possibly sinking in the sand with the hard and narrow wheels, which would make pushing her difficult. But if the ground was compact enough to support her weight and keep the wheels on top, these trails might be accessible to some wheelchair hikers. Even if it was possible, I was glad to have Kellisa's mobility chair, which made pushiking the trail system a breeze for me.

We stopped at a couple more overlooks before reaching an intersection. We could continue forward on a trail leading to the bottom of the rim. I couldn't see enough of the path to assess if we could make it down and back up safely. It looked wide and clear, but I just wasn't sure. With some doubt, I decided to circle back up to the Oregon Trail, where we could complete our loop back to our trailhead.

I was excited to find such a wild trail system in the middle of a suburban environment. The trails were popular, but they didn't feel crowded. Dogs are allowed on all the trails in the Oregon Trail Preserve provided they're on a leash, but we didn't see any during our visit. Kellisa and I returned our SUV and had just enough time to enjoy a nice dinner at the Boise Airport. We flew back to Sacramento with another stunning trail to add to our pushiking resume.

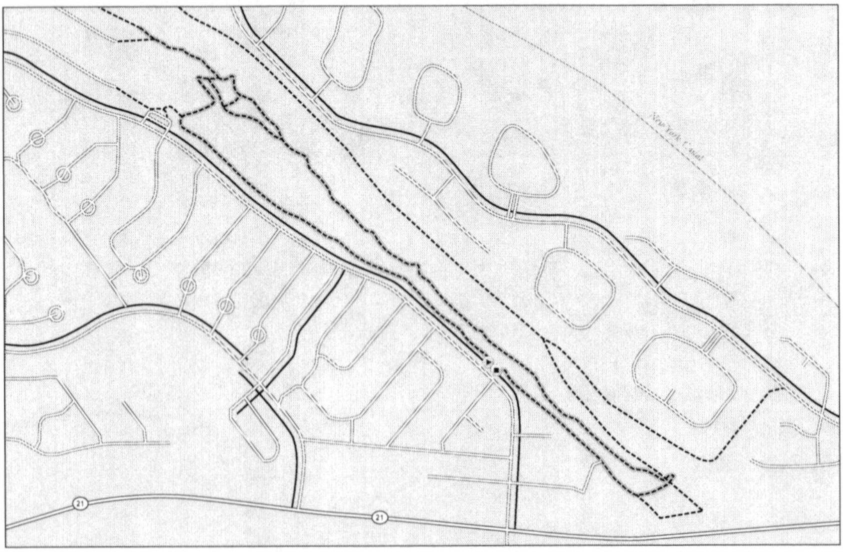

Rim #102 Trail, Boise, ID

15
Illinois

Trail name: Interpretive and Tamarack View
Location: Volo Bog State Natural Area
Distance: 3.4 mi
Duration (active): 1h 33 m
Average speed: 2.2 mi/h
Total ascent: 125 ft
Highest point: 796 ft
Difficulty: Moderate

Illinois was my home state for the first twenty-eight years of my life. Lisa and I hiked many miles of amazing trails from the Shawnee National Forest in southern Illinois to some of the great trails near Chicago to Apple River Canyon in the far northwestern part of the state and countless trails in between, including trails to the spectacular canyons and waterfalls of Starved Rock and Matthiessen State Parks.

Kellisa was born in Chicago and spent the first six months of her life in the state before moving to Florida for the next sixteen years. Most of Kellisa's Illinois residency was spent in the hospital fighting to survive, so it's not surprising that we didn't hike any trails during this difficult time. Over the years, we would return to visit family often, but Kellisa was seventeen years old before we shared a trail in Illinois. Illinois was the forty-eighth state where Kellisa and I shared a path when we pushiked a trail at White Pines State Park in November 2016. Kellisa's younger sister, Egypt, also joined us on our original quest to pushike at least one trail in all fifty states. The three of us completed our goal at Denali National Park later in November 2016.

For this book, we selected the Volo Bog State Natural Area. The area was designated to protect the 47.5-acre bog and the surrounding woods, prairies, savanna, marshes, and shrubland. Created from melting ice at the end of the Wisconsonian Glaciation, Volo Bog is the last surviving open-water quaking bog in Illinois. Chicago's far northwestern suburbs have now encircled Volo Bog. Thankfully, the early preservation efforts, which led to a National Natural Landmark Designation in 1973, saved it from being developed.

When I was growing up, I had an aunt and uncle who lived near Volo Bog, and I remember visiting the natural area a couple of times. A cherished highlight of those visits was walking on floating planks over the vast bog. These fond memories made me want to return to this trail to experience it as an adult. After careful research, I was confident I could push Kellisa on the half-mile Interpretive Trail over the bog. I was slightly less sure we could navigate the 2.75-mile Tamarack View Trail. My main concern was mud from melting snow. We were also visiting late in the day. So if we weren't finished pushiking the trails before the park closed for the day, our rental SUV would get locked in for the evening.

Wanting to complete at least one trail, we started with the Interpretive Trail. This short loop takes visitors over and through Volo Bog. The trail consists of wooden dock sections, boardwalks, and a path of wood chips. Kellisa enjoyed the bouncing effect as we crossed the floating dock. The views were unobstructed, and only the distant sound of traffic reminded us that we were in the suburban outskirts of Chicago.

The open-water section of the bog had a layer of ice from the unusually cold Midwest fall. Small patches of snow were also visible on the sides of the trail. The dock transitioned to a narrow boardwalk. With careful navigation, it was possible to continue pushing Kellisa deeper into the bog. We were now in a forested section of the bog that was still surrounded by water on both sides. Snow and ice on the boardwalk from the lack of sun penetration slowed our progression. With the sun fading, the temperature was plunging, and the gray gloom of the sky added a particular eerie element to our hike.

After completing the Interpretive Trail, we had a difficult decision to make. We could play it safe and retreat to our SUV, or we could continue our adventure. Under ideal circumstances, we would have time to complete the longer Tamarack View Trail. Kellisa wanted more. I wasn't going to argue, but with night falling fast, we had to be serious.

The trail started with a quick hill climb through a prairie that left me gasping for air. Breathing in the cold air wasn't helping. Thankfully, the trail was mostly free from mud since it was partially frozen. Despite its cold condition, the path was not icy or slippery. I was pushing Kellisa over a hard surface that crunched as we moved forward. The hills were relentless, and we were falling behind our tight schedule to complete the loop.

The trail entered a forest with all its leaves on the ground. The path was wide and easy to follow. The hills were constant. It felt like we were a million miles from Chicago.

With the environment on this unique trail completely changing every few minutes, the trail exited the forest. A floating walkway with a warning sign stating the uneven surface could be slippery was our next challenge. A little snow covered the walkway, which only added to our excitement as we bounced up and down and from side to side. Kellisa loved every second. I was glad we made the decision to pushike this trail but still worried about getting locked in for the night.

The floating walkway dumped us back out on a frozen path cut through a savanna grassland. I was eager to continue forward since I could see we had hills to conquer in our immediate future. Despite the cold air and developing brutal wind, I was working up a sweat which necessitated removing my fleece. It didn't take me long to cool off. Since Kellisa was sitting for this adventure, I left all her winter gear on her.

We entered another forest with several viewpoints of the setting sun disappearing over the bog. I was concerned we would be cutting it a little too close with the park closing. But it was too beautiful not to stop to capture the moment with pictures. The path led us deeper into the forest, where it was starting to get dark. I picked up our pace and started thinking about what we would do if our SUV got locked in for the night. I could hope to find a ranger and plead for our release. I could play the foolish father card, begging that my daughter not be punished for my mistakes. If necessary, I could call a cab to take us back to our hotel tonight and return in the morning to retrieve the SUV. I knew our lives weren't in danger but was fully aware that it could be a costly mistake to attempt this trail. I wasn't happy with the available options, but sharing this extraordinary trail with Kellisa was well worth the possible price.

I was hoping to see the parking lot in the distance around every bend in the path. Finally, I was able to see the signs at the trailhead. A minute later, I could see our waiting SUV. A quick look at the clock on my phone, and I knew we would make it out in time. We were the only car in the lot and left the park with less than five minutes until closing time.

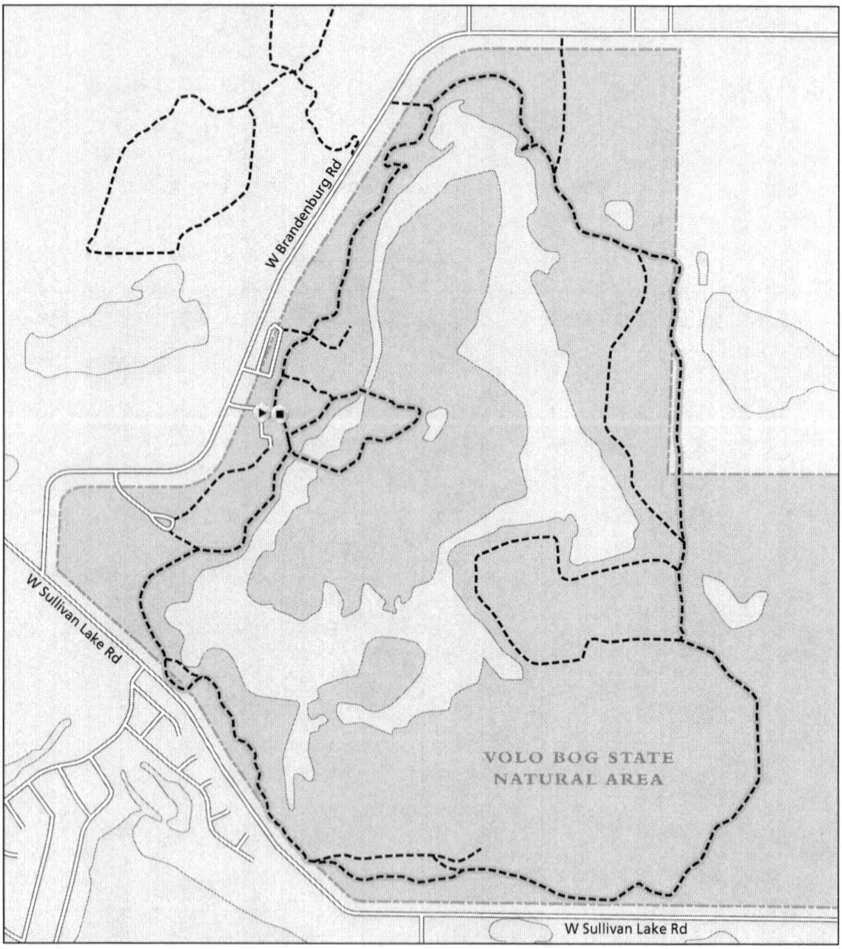

Tamarack View Trail, Ingleside, IL

16
Indiana

Trail name: Blue Trail Loop
Location: Eagle Creek Park
Distance: 3.1 mi
Duration (active): 1h 30m
Average speed: 2.1 mi/h
Total ascent: 157 ft
Highest point: 886 ft
Difficulty: Moderate

Eagle Creek Park in Indianapolis is a place where you can find true wilderness inside the largest city in Indiana. Eagle Creek is one of the ten largest municipal parks in the United States. We were pleasantly surprised to find a large lake, rolling wooded hills, and many others enjoying an early winter morning when we visited Eagle Creek Park in late November.

With many trail options in the park, we chose the Blue Trail Loop because it circled a bird sanctuary on a narrow spit of land in the middle of a lake before finishing with a gentle path through densely forested hills. The beginning of the trail was perfect for chairs because it was wide, paved, and straight. The surface was covered in damp leaves, making it a little slippery. We didn't travel to Indianapolis to pushike on a paved trail, so we were thankful when the path changed to a natural surface as we approached a creek. Despite the dreary overcast morning, we had prolonged views over the chilly water. The forests were mostly devoid of leaves with a small scattering of trees holding on to their golden-hued foliage, making the views even more dramatic.

Unlike so many trails, we explored the path with many other hikers and runners. Despite the cold, many families were out enjoying the great outdoors. Unfortunately, and like most pushikes, we didn't encounter anyone else using a jog stroller or mobility chair. The trail never felt crowded, even with the constant presence of people. We stopped many times for pictures and to observe birds flying or diving for a meal.

Once we completed the semicircle following Eagle Creek, we had a choice to make. We could follow the shoreline back toward the trailhead or continue on a longer loop through the forest, which would also return us to our trailhead. It was cold, but we were feeling good and decided on the longer loop.

The trail immediately went up a rocky hillside. Kellisa loves when the trail gets steep. I never know which she enjoys more, the bumps or the sounds of me struggling behind her. If I had to guess, I think it's a little of both. The trail became more difficult than I expected. I briefly considered turning around, but Kellisa's giggles and cheering motivated me to keep pushing forward.

The trail was wet but not muddy due to the presence of leaf debris. I might not have been able to push Kellisa up the inclines if it had been muddy. The wet leaves made it slippery, so I tethered myself to Kellisa for safety. Once we topped out on the first hill, the trail circled above the water before dropping down across a narrow ravine. After Kellisa stopped giggling and we found our rhythm, I noticed that the forest was silent. Now that we were away from the water's edge and bird sanctuary, we were the only hikers around. We would finish the second part of the trail without seeing another person.

The trail continued its surprising climbs and drops through the woods. For those who think central Indiana is flat, Eagle Creek Park is there to prove the Hoosier state isn't all flat farmland! We crossed a paved road, which could have led back to the trailhead, but we continued our loop. Shortly after crossing the road, the trail skirted around Lilly Lake. We paused for a short break with the hope of observing wildlife, and a couple of deer rewarded us for our efforts. Leaving the lake, we felt recharged for the final push through the forest. The hills on the backside of the loop were less intense before the trail turned mostly flat.

This section of the forest came alive as the golden leaves surrounded us. The path narrowed, and it felt like we were walking through the halls of a grand palace. We paused many times to take pictures hoping to capture the colorful beauty all around us. I even pushed Kellisa off-trail to immerse ourselves in nature fully. After taking over a hundred photos, I was hoping we would have one or two keepers.

The trail ended much as it started with a long, straight path through the forest leading us back to the trailhead. If we lived near Indianapolis, there is no doubt that Eagle Creek Park would be our home trail system.

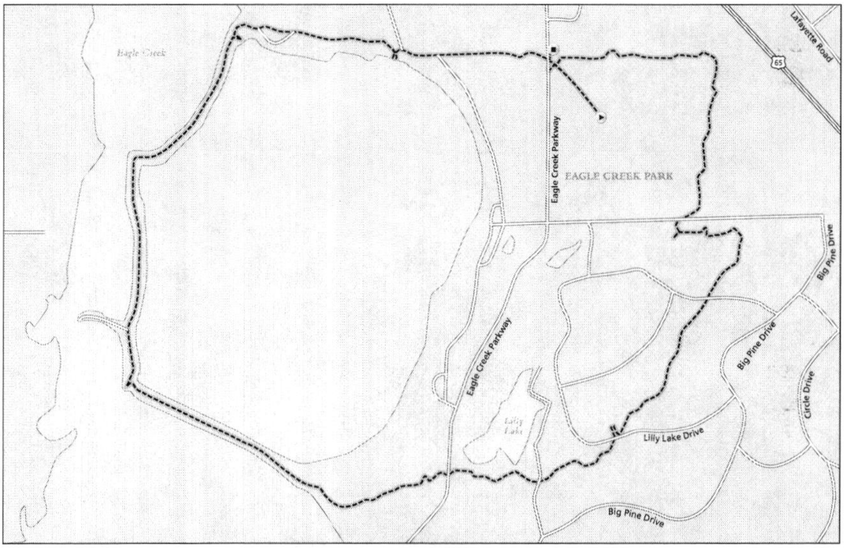

Blue Trail Loop, Indianapolis, IN

17

Iowa

Trail name: Overlook
Location: Whitewater Canyon Wildlife Area
Distance: 1.3 mi
Duration (active): 48m
Average speed: 1.6 mi/h
Total ascent: 131 ft
Highest point: 1,035 ft
Difficulty: Challenging

Anyone who's driven across Iowa on I-80 for 306 miles would think the entire state is made up of farms, and they'd be mostly correct. Iowa is the largest grower of corn in the United States and a leader in soybeans, hogs, and egg production. Kellisa and I visited Iowa in September to pushike a trail for this book. My first thought was to try to find a giant corn maze instead of a real trail. I knew from previous trips to Iowa that the state has high bluffs overlooking the Mississippi River in the east and even a canyon in the far western part of the state. Wanting to bust the myth that Iowa was all flat farmland, I decided to find the perfect trail to prove it.

In my research, I learned Iowa has three real canyons. While none are world famous or considered one of the world's natural wonders, they are unique finds deep in the Heartland. After reviewing trip reports and pictures, I selected the trail system at Whitewater Canyon Wildlife Area in the northeastern part of Iowa.

As we drove through the slightly rolling hills of rural Iowa, I couldn't help but be concerned about the dark clouds dominating the western horizon. I knew the area saw strong thunderstorms the previous day. I was worried about the condition of the trail. I was worried we might be turned away by the mud. Now, I was concerned we'd be stopped by a thunderstorm before even starting. It was warm, and we had our rain gear. I wasn't too concerned with a downpour, but I could see lightning in the distance, which is enough to prevent a pushike. You don't want to be outside on a trail with lightning striking in your general area.

We were the only vehicle in the parking lot, and I had a decision to make: to pushike, wait out the storm, postpone our hike, or find another trail. The skies to the west remained dark, but about ten minutes had passed since I witnessed the last flash of lightning. We were hoping to do a several mile loop pushike but decided we only had time to safely attempt the Overlook Trail to a scenic overlook.

The trail started through a field of wildflowers filled with hundreds, if not thousands, of butterflies fluttering all around. I knew we were on a tight time frame to complete this trail, but we couldn't help stopping every few minutes to observe the butterflies. Kellisa was drawn to the largest butterflies as they spread their colorful wings. Many flew across the trail within several feet of us. A few even landed on Kellisa and her mobility chair, which made her smile. It felt like we were walking through a large butterfly enclosure in a botanical garden.

The ground was wet but not muddy since mowed flowers and grasses were covering it. I was surprised that the terrain was rolling just enough to make our pushike challenging. I always have bug spray packed, but I'm hesitant to apply it to our bodies unless it's needed. Despite the recent rains, there wasn't any sign of biting marauders.

We continued to follow the Overlook Trail through several junctions. I was tempted to alter our new plans of a simple out-and-back trek to the overlook since the rain looked like it would hold off. I hadn't heard any thunder since we started the pushike, but we maintained our course. The hilly terrain was constant as we approached a forest of dense trees. I could tell from the map we were close to the scenic overlook.

As soon as we entered the forest, it was like a switch was flicked. The mosquitoes came out in a swarm as they started to dive-bomb us from all directions. I quickly grabbed the bug spray and liberally applied it to all of Kellisa's exposed skin before taking care of my own body. Thankfully, the thirsty bloodsuckers made a hasty retreat into the forest. I was relieved to see Kellisa only had three or four bites from her short exposure, and I had maybe eight between my arms and legs.

Satisfied that we had repelled the lethal army, I started pushing Kellisa deeper into the forest. After taking a few steps, I could see the trail suddenly drop through a series of many steps cut into the hillside anchored by railroad ties. The trail immediately ascended the other side of the ravine. I wasn't expecting this drastic change in elevation. From my vantage point, I could see both sides were muddy now that we were under a canopy of tree cover. I couldn't help but think this was a perfect location for a bridge to span the ravine.

I had another decision to make: continue to the overlook or retreat and maybe take another trail through the hilly wildflowers? I knew if we continued, it would be difficult due to the mud. The return pushike would be more challenging since there would be mud covering the wheels and my boots. I also had to consider that I couldn't keep an eye on the weather under so many trees. I decided we were hiking a canyon in Iowa and would try a step or two. If I felt comfortable, we would proceed to the overlook at the edge of the canyon.

I double-checked everything, including our tether before taking the first slippery step down the stairs. Fortunately, each step down was long enough for Kellisa's mobility chair to rest without having a wheel hanging over the next level down. Also, due to significant erosion, the railroad ties were higher than the ground, making them act like an additional break. I took my time lowering Kellisa one step at a time with short breaks on each landing. Once we were at the bottom, the trail in front of us looked a lot higher and steeper. Again, the steps going up were sufficiently long enough to rest with each lift and push up a level. The mud wasn't as much of an issue as going down, but I was slipping back with each time I lifted and pushed the mobility chair up a step.

As we neared the top, I was worried about what we would see. I've been on many trails where there's a series of ups and downs through ravines before leveling out. Afraid this might be the beginning of that type of trail, I was relieved when we reached the top to see the overlook. I was excited as we neared the end and wanted to take in the views. I continued to push Kellisa to the vantage point atop a rock outcropping. Far below, we could see Whitewater Creek snaking through the canyon with forested dolomite cliffs rising on both sides. The setting seemed more dramatic due to the effort it took to reach this majestic spot and the fact that we didn't see the canyon until we were at the edge.

I wasn't looking forward to retracing my steps through the muddy ravine, but I also knew we couldn't linger at the overlook because I could see the dark clouds were still just to the west of the canyon. As I started to push Kellisa back toward the muddy steps, I noticed more resistance than expected. The mud was caked around the wheels to the point of reaching the frame, which made pushing Kellisa difficult. I didn't notice it in my excitement to reach the overlook, but now it needed to be addressed. I knew I had to attempt to clean her tires even though the displaced mud would almost immediately be replaced with new mud. I looked around for a strong enough stick to scrap as much of the mud off as possible. Once the wheels were mostly clear, I decided to clean off my hiking boots, allowing for a fresh start down the ravine.

It didn't take long before I was up to ankles in sloppy mud, and the mud again slowed Kellisa's tires. I just wanted to be done and reach the top of the other side. I decided to forgo stopping at each step and just pushed Kellisa down and back up as fast as possible without taking any additional risks. I was careful to keep her mobility chair safely tethered to my body and watched my every step. Kellisa was giggling due to the bumps in the steps and she finds my struggles extra funny. I was breathing hard by the time we completed our second descent and ascent of the ravine.

I needed to catch my breath and take a few sips of water, but knew we were near the exit of the forest and still in the mosquito danger zone. I pushed on before we could get attacked for a second time. I didn't take a break until we were clear of the forest and surrounded by the butterflies again. For the first time during our pushike, I heard thunder in the distance as I was taking sips from my water bottle. I felt like we still had some time before the rain finally caught up to us but didn't want to push our luck. I wish the weather would have held out just a little longer so we could have explored some of the other trails in this beautiful wilderness area.

The first drops of rain started to fall as we approached our rental SUV, still the only vehicle in the parking lot. The mosquitoes were waiting for us as they seemed to appear out of nowhere as I lifted Kellisa into the front seat. I quickly closed her door and hastily tossed her mobility chair in the back before running to the driver's seat. Kellisa curled forward with giggles as I spent several minutes swatting the dozen or so mosquitoes that made their way inside the SUV. As we drove away, I made a promise to return to Iowa someday to pushike the other two canyons in this surprisingly beautiful Midwestern state.

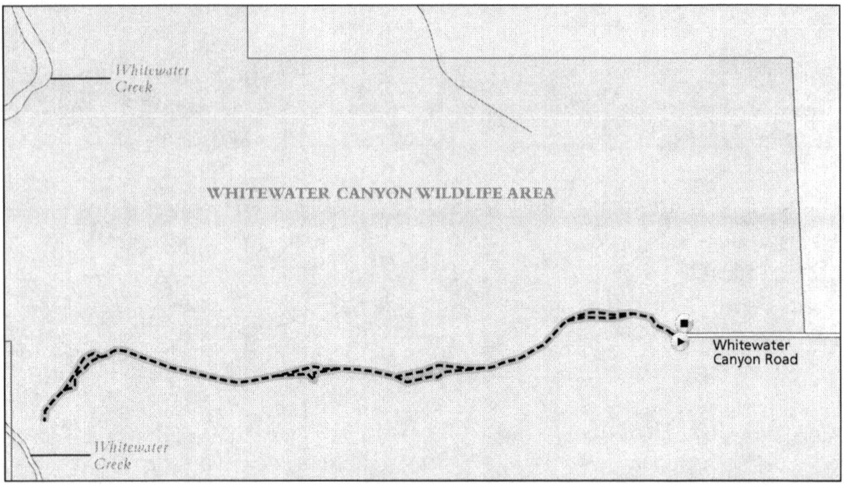

Overlook Trail, Dubuque County, IA

18
Kansas

Trail name: Scenic Overlook
Location: Tallgrass Prairie National Preserve
Distance: 6.2 mi
Duration (active): 3h 9m
Average speed: 2.0 mi/h
Total ascent: 351 ft
Highest point: 1,483 ft
Difficulty: Challenging

I've wanted to pushike with Kellisa through the Tallgrass Prairie National Preserve for years. I read an article written to attract tourists to Kansas, featuring the natural wonders in the state. The main picture showcased an old farm road twisting its way through the hilly Tallgrass Prairie. I knew right away the trail would be perfect for us.

I pushed Kellisa inside the visitor center at Tallgrass Prairie National Preserve in Kansas. We were welcomed with an unusual greeting: "With those wheels, you can hike any trail out on the prairie."

Instead of making a quick judgment about Kellisa's disability and what we can't do, the park ranger behind the desk saw the possibilities with our mobility chair. He asked if this was our first visit and inquired about the trails we planned to hike. I confirmed this was our first visit and shared our plans to reach the Scenic Overlook, 3.2 miles beyond the visitor center. The ranger explained that the entire Scenic Overlook Trail followed an old ranch road the park uses during the summer for bus tours. Since it was October, dodging buses wouldn't be on our list of concerns. The kind ranger only had one warning. He wanted us to be aware and cautious of the bison who occupy the Windmill Pasture, which is surrounded by a fence with gates and cattle guards across the road.

Since 75 percent of our pushike would be through Windmill Pasture, we were told not to approach the bison. We needed to remain at least 125 yards away from the 2,000-pound animals that can charge with little warning. The ranger explained the bison could run faster than us and have horns made for gorging. I was surprised at the stern warning about the gentle-looking giants of the prairie. Who knew bison could run thirty-five miles per hour and have a six-foot vertical jump? The ranger explained that visitors to Yellowstone National Park were more likely to be attacked by a bison than a bear.

Lastly, we were advised of three options if we found the bison herd blocking the road. First, we could turn around; second, we could wait for them to move; and third, we could venture off-trail and go around. Later in the afternoon, I would be thankful for this brief yet informative conversation. It's always a good practice to discuss your plans with a ranger or someone else familiar with the local hazards when traveling to a new environment.

Tallgrass prairies once covered 140 million North American acres from Manitoba, Canada, down to Texas and Louisiana. The prairies covering the midsection of the continent were a mostly pass-through country for early pioneers heading west. The Native Americans used the prairies for hunting bison, which provided large amounts of food and materials used for clothing and shelters. Once Europeans traded guns with the Native Americans, sustenance hunting was easier. Also, many bison were slaughtered by new settlers in an attempt to control the native population. At the beginning of the 1800s, bison approached as many as 60 million across North America. Tragically, their numbers fell to less than 1,000 by 1900. Today, roughly 30,000 live on protected lands while an additional 500,000 exist on private lands.

The tallgrass prairie landscape would change forever in 1837 when John Deere developed a plow strong enough to till most of the prairies to prepare the land for agriculture. Less than 4 percent of tallgrass prairies survived this agricultural revolution. Most of the remaining tallgrass prairies are in the Flint Hills of eastern Kansas and the Osage Hills of the north central region of Oklahoma. The low-lying hills survived plowing due to the rocky soil, and cattle ranches eventually sprung up to exploit the remaining prairies.

Tallgrass Prairie National Preserve is one of the newer additions to the national park system, created in November 1996. The land consists of the historic Spring Hill/Z Bar Ranch, which raised cattle from 1878 to 1986. The preserve was created with a unique partnership between the government and local interests. The land remains mostly privately owned by the Nature Conservancy while jointly managed with the National Park Service. Today, this unique partnership preserves the tallgrass prairie and educates visitors on the role both Native American and cattle ranching had on the tallgrass prairie.

A small herd of bison was relocated from South Dakota to Tallgrass Prairie National Preserve in 2009. More bison have been introduced over the years since, and now visitors can observe 100 bison roaming Windmill Pasture. Our goal for the day was to pushike the Scenic Overlook Trail, which crossed Windmill Pasture for 2.4 miles. Strollers are welcomed on all the trails within the park, but they are discouraged on the Scenic Overlook Trail due to the crossing of the Windmill Pasture.

After discussing our options with the ranger, I felt confident following the Scenic Overlook Trail. The path started by crossing a small bridge to enter a field directly behind the visitor center. We enjoyed a quick snack, and I took advantage of the available cold water fountain to top off my bottles. With that, we were on our way for a late afternoon pushike across the prairie in early autumn.

The Scenic Overlook Trail started by heading south before making a quick loop back to the northwest. There was a small body of water ahead, reflecting the surrounding landscape over its still surface. After admiring the beautiful little lake, my eyes were drawn to the significant incline of the hill directly in front of us. I knew the trail traversed rolling hills, but the grade of this first incline had me a little concerned.

I took a few sips of water before pushing Kellisa to the crest of the hill. There were endless seas of Indiangrass, Buffalo grass, and Canada wild rye blowing in the moderate breeze for as far as we could see in all directions. Immediately to the west, we could see the fence surrounding Windmill Pasture and the cattleguards across our trail.

A sign greeted our arrival to the bison enclosure with the warning that bison are unpredictable and dangerous. There was a picture of a bison flipping a person into the air. We cautiously entered the pasture with great anticipation, hoping to witness the majesty of the once near-extinct bison making a historic comeback in Kansas, although our strong preference was to observe them off in the distance.

Without any bison in sight, my immediate concern was all the remaining rolling hills we still had to navigate. The entire trail was wet from recent rainstorms with a few muddy areas in the low spots between hills where intermittent streams crossed the path. Once the tires get covered in mud, it is like pushing a mobility chair with solid tires. Usually, I would find a stick to clean the mud off the tires, but in an area without trees, I was left doubling my effort to propel Kellisa across this sweeping landscape.

Our first sighting of the resident bison herd happened about a mile into Windmill Pasture. To my relief, the herd was hanging out several hills away to the east. Despite their large size, the bison appeared as small animals in the distance. I decided to continue since the herd was so far off to the side of the trail.

After several uneventful hills, the bison were again out of our view. And, we neared the exit of the enclosure at the bottom of the long descent. I could see a small stream flowing over the path and knew Kellisa would love going through the water. I was hoping it would clean her tires off a little, providing some relief in pushing. One might think I was excited to be at this descent, but I wasn't because I knew we were close to the Scenic Overlook. I could see the final ascent beginning as soon as our descent ended. Since this was an out-and-back trail, I also knew that I would be pushing Kellisa back up the hill we were about to go down.

We exited the pasture with only three-tenths of a mile to our destination. The last push was all uphill to the overlook. Once we reached the highpoint, endless prairie views took on a new meaning as our already impressive views seemed to double in the distance. I stood in awe in the wind as Kellisa giggled from our perch high above the tallgrass prairies. After a few sips from my water bottle, I took customary pictures of Kellisa and myself with the camera on a tripod. The afternoon hour was getting late as the sun was starting to set. We needed to limit our time at the top.

The trail continued as a loop back to the visitor center. Following the loop would add a mile but would eliminate the need to pushike back through the bison enclosure. The extra mile didn't worry me. However, when given a choice while out on a trail with Kellisa, I tend to favor out-and-back over loops. I have a fear of completing 95 percent of the path before reaching an obstacle that we can't safely negotiate, resulting in a complete backtrack. If that happened on this trail, we would be caught out long after dark, and I could feel the temperature already falling. I was hoping the bison were still far off the trail. I decided it was the best and safest option to pushike back to the visitor center the same way we came.

Since we were at the highpoint, I enjoyed our initial descent while trying to block the images of the coming ascents. After a few minutes, we found ourselves reentering Windmill Pasture. I pushed Kellisa through the stream a second time without cleaning her tires before starting another uphill battle between myself and the trail. Kellisa giggled at my now-labored breathing.

Despite the cooler temperatures, I was working up a sweat while I could tell Kellisa was getting chilled in her chair while wearing her fleece. I decided to give her my jacket for added warmth, which she appreciated. As the hour was growing late, I found myself picking up the pace as we wheeled up and over the next couple of small hills. In the middle of Windmill Pasture, we rounded a corner and found we had a perfect view of the entire bison herd. They had migrated to the west and were now completely blocking our forward progress.

Due to our position on top of a hill, we were within the 125 yards distance we were supposed to stay back. Most of the bison acted like we weren't there, but a few had their eyes trained on us. The constant staring us down was a little startling, but not as concerning as the fact that the herd seemed to have stopped moving with several even lying down on the trail.

I knew we were in trouble as I reminded myself of our options, wait, go back, or go around. None of the options were good this late in the afternoon. At this point, going back would add six miles, and I would have to reclimb the most prolonged and steepest hills in the preserve for a second time. It didn't take long to rule out this option. I figured we could wait about an hour before darkness would fall over the tallgrass prairie, making our situation more dangerous. Going around wasn't appealing. We didn't know what was waiting for us in the tall grass—water, mud, rocks, perhaps a poisonous snake?

I was mad at myself for allowing us to be in this position. I didn't mind the bison impeding our forward progress; instead, I was critical of being out on the trail without enough sunlight for a several-hour delay. I had a small headlamp in our pack, but that was for emergencies, and my first rule was to minimize risk to avoid emergencies. We were educated and prepared, so I was able to remain calm as I decided to wait out the herd.

Kellisa was enjoying our front-row view of the now gigantic animals. Two of the bison who were staring at us took a few steps in our direction. I immediately started backing up to give them more room. They eventually lost interest and went back to eating their dinner.

The herd made slow progress in their movement across the trail. After forty-five minutes, most of the bison were still blocking the trail. It was evident unless they started running; the path would not be safe before darkness fell over the prairie. Since I didn't know how to make them run and had no intention of going back at this point, our only option was to go around.

For average hikers, going around the bison isn't a massive undertaking if you go slowly and watch where you step. My problem in the tallgrasses was not being able to see where I was pushing Kellisa. My main concern was the rattlesnakes and copperheads who also call this prairie home. We found our off-trail route filled with good-sized rocks and even bigger bison droppings. My eyes loved playing tricks as each rock and dropping looked precisely like a coiled snake ready to strike. The entire prairie was soggy, and I was sinking to my ankles in the muck.

Knowing that Kellisa was out of striking range high in her mobility chair, I decided to plow through the prairie using brute force. I pushed Kellisa around the herd. I hoped our vibrations, loud giggles, and heavy breathing would alert any snakes of our presence and send them scurrying out of our way. Kellisa was having a blast. Her endless laughs provided the fuel for my powering through our less-than-ideal situation. It took about fifteen minutes to go around the herd and find our way back to the trail.

As I enjoyed a few sips of water, two young men suddenly appeared and high-fived Kellisa. With all my attention focused on safely avoiding the bison, I never noticed them hiking toward us from the other side of the herd. The older of the two explained they had been watching us while we were in the prairie going around the bison herd. They were impressed, resulting in compliments and high fives. After answering a few of their questions, they headed off in the direction we just came, but not before making Kellisa feel like a rock star on the trail with another series of high fives. With my adrenaline still flowing strong, we made excellent time covering the remaining path back to the visitor center and our awaiting rental SUV.

Tallgrass Prairie National Preserve was everything I dreamed it would be and more. Even considering our brush with the bison, I was confident that we were never really in any danger. We knew what to do and followed the instructions given to us by the ranger. While enjoying a few snacks in the heated comfort of our SUV in the parking lot, we reveled in sharing our bison encounter story with our friends and family online. With more than forty miles of trails perfect for pushiking, I'm sure Kellisa and I will be making a return trip to the preserve.

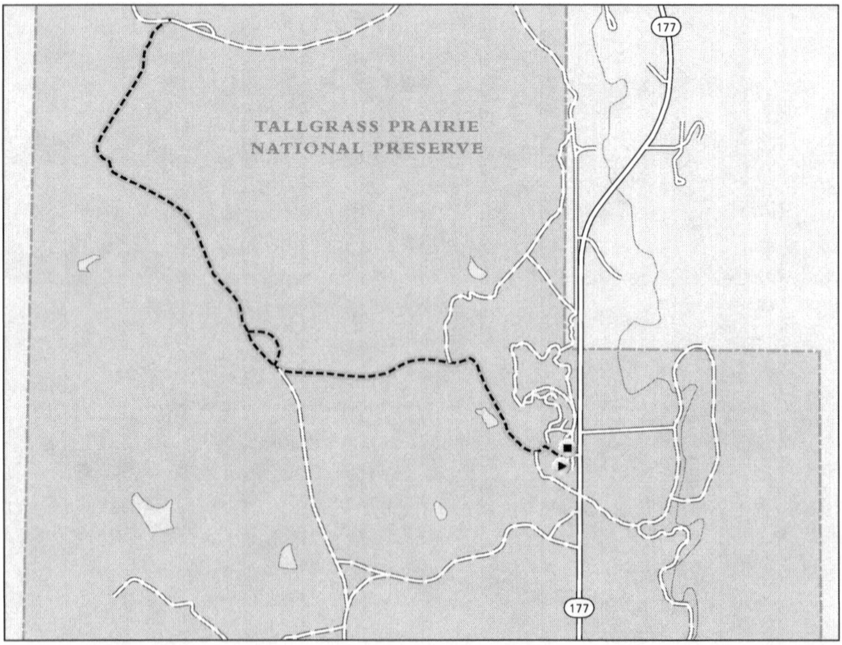

Scenic Overlook Trail, Strong City, KS

19
Kentucky

Trail name: Fitness Loop
Location: Cumberland Gap National Historical Park
Distance: 1.9 mi
Duration (active): 1h 6m
Average speed: 1.7 mi/h
Total ascent: 308 ft
Highest point: 1,343 ft
Difficulty: Challenging

The sky was showing no mercy as it dumped massive amounts of rain during our drive to Cumberland Gap National Historical Park. If it didn't stop soon, we would leave the southeast without completing a pushike in Kentucky. Not pushiking in Kentucky would be a significant setback in writing this book. Kentucky borders seven other states, and Kellisa and I had already successfully pushiked a trail in each of them to use in our book.

Kellisa and I had an afternoon available between a drive from Virginia to Nashville, Tennessee, for our Kentucky pushike. I was getting discouraged during my research because all the trails that weren't too far for us to reach with our limited amount of time seemed too rocky, short, steep, or something else that didn't seem right. I try to plan for more time so we can have a plan B if needed, but for this trail, we would only get one chance, and I had to get it right. All descriptions and pictures of the Fitness Loop Trail checked all the boxes I was looking for in a trail. We would need the weather to hold out.

I was seriously considering turning our rental SUV around, skipping Kentucky, and driving directly to Nashville. We didn't have time to wait out the rain. Even if it stopped, I feared the trail would be too muddy. Pushing Kellisa is always a challenge, and going through deep mud, especially on inclines, is not fun. Still, something told me to keep driving. We had to give it a chance because I did not want to have to fly back to Kentucky from Sacramento when we were already so close.

As the Roman playwright Terence wrote, "Fortune favors the bold"; the rain stopped just as we were approaching the parking lot to the visitor center, which also doubles as the trailhead for the Fitness Loop Trail. By the time I opened my door, I was thrown back by the heat and humidity. The sun was now the one showing no mercy. It was uncomfortably hot.

I loaded Kellisa in her chair and threw the backpack on my shoulders. I wanted to stop inside the visitor center to get a trail map. The ranger behind the desk handed us the park brochure, which included my desired map, without asking any questions. I had selected my trail and would soon find out if it was too muddy for us, so I didn't have any questions for him. I wasn't sure how long the rain would hold off, so I headed back toward the doors to start our pushike. Just as I was about to push the little blue button for the doors to automatically open, I heard a voice from behind us ask, "Are you planning on hiking the Fitness Loop Trail?"

I stopped, and my first thought was, "Here we go again, someone is going to tell us that we can't do something."

I turned around to see an older park ranger approaching us. I answered with a simple, "Yes, sir."

To my surprise, he didn't try to discourage us. Instead, he asked which direction we planned on following the loop. I didn't have a plan but told him we would go in a counterclockwise direction. He strongly recommended going in a clockwise direction to avoid a particularly steep and muddy uphill section. He looked at Kellisa's chair and thought it would be more comfortable and safer going down this portion of the trail instead of up.

He helped himself to my park brochure to point out the steep section of the trail. He handed it back and said, "You should have a great time on the trail; it's not supposed to rain anymore this afternoon."

I thanked him for the tip and encouraging words before heading out to start the trail in the direction he recommended. Over the years we've had rangers discourage us from attempting some trails. I use this as a form of motivation. So far, all the doubting rangers have been wrong. I suspect most of them have never encountered pushikers before. There have been a few rangers who take one look and support us and our goals 100 percent.

Once outside, we were blasted again by the oven-like heat with humidity that had to be approaching 100 percent. I wheeled Kellisa at a walk/run pace to start this trail. I was hoping to find some relief under a thick canopy of trees. Unfortunately, part of the loop was through the parking lot and down a sidewalk along a road before we found what looked like a regular wilderness trail. I was drenched with sweat but welcomed the shade as I felt what appeared to be a ten-to-fifteen degree drop in temperature. But, it was still unbelievably humid.

I took a minute to observe Kellisa. She seemed to be doing fine and was her usual self. I didn't want to proceed if she was showing any signs of lethargy from her exposure to heat. After a few sips of water, we started up the trail. It almost immediately started to ascend the side of the mountain. We found the path precisely as expected from our research, wide and covered with roots. The unknown was the mud, and while wet, the trail was still firm and in good condition.

The trail was relentless in its uphill pursuit to reach the top of the ridge. Some parts were so steep that I was beginning to wonder if the ranger was confused and gave us wrong information. A few sections of the path had rocks in the middle. But we were able to navigate around them without too much trouble. Of course, Kellisa was giggling from the bumps and my huffs and puffs behind her. I stopped for a breather every time we reached a little section of flat ground.

I expected to reach the ridge after every turn in the trail, but the path kept going up. I knew we would climb approximately the height of a thirty-story building in a short distance, but I didn't expect it to seem never-ending.

Finally, we reached the top of the ridge and it was time for a break with water and a snack. The entire trail was nicely shaded, which helped block the sun but also prevented long-reaching views. I continued pushing Kellisa while enjoying this very gentle section of the trail. I tried not to think too far ahead but knew we would have to drop down and lose all the altitude we gained.

We stopped several times for pictures hoping to capture some of the elevation changes along the Fitness Loop Trail. The greenery from all the earlier rain was amazingly vibrant. We felt like we were in a tropical jungle instead of on top of a mountain in eastern Kentucky.

Eventually, the ridge ended, and the trail began its descent back to the parking lot. We were headed down, but it didn't feel steep. It seemed gentle, and again, I found myself questioning the park ranger. After a couple of switchbacks, I finally saw what the ranger warned us about, and the trail went down at the steepest angle of the day.

I double-checked everything before starting—my shoelaces, the tether between my body and Kellisa's chair, and the condition of the trail. I didn't want to proceed if it was too muddy. I was worried about slipping and possibly falling. Once we started down this section, I knew there was no turning back.

I carefully examined what I could see and felt comfortable proceeding. While wet and steep, the trail was never muddy. I was surprised since I knew how much rain had fallen just a few hours earlier. Instead of fighting gravity more than necessary, we just moved steadily without stopping. In the middle of our descent, the trail turned uphill for a short thirty-foot rise. While it may not seem like much, I found it disheartening to be pushing more than 100 pounds up thirty of the feet we just lost on the descent. I was thankful Kellisa's wheels were rolling free and not bogged down with mud as I pushed her to the crest of this small hill before going down the last couple of sections of the Fitness Loop Trail.

In all, the descent from the ridgetop to the parking lot only took a few minutes. I had parked near the place the trail dropped us out. I turned the air conditioning on full blast before loading Kellisa and our gear into our SUV. I am not sure we could have completed the Fitness Loop Trail in a counterclockwise direction. I appreciate the expert advice we were given to have the best experience on the trail and help keep this book on schedule.

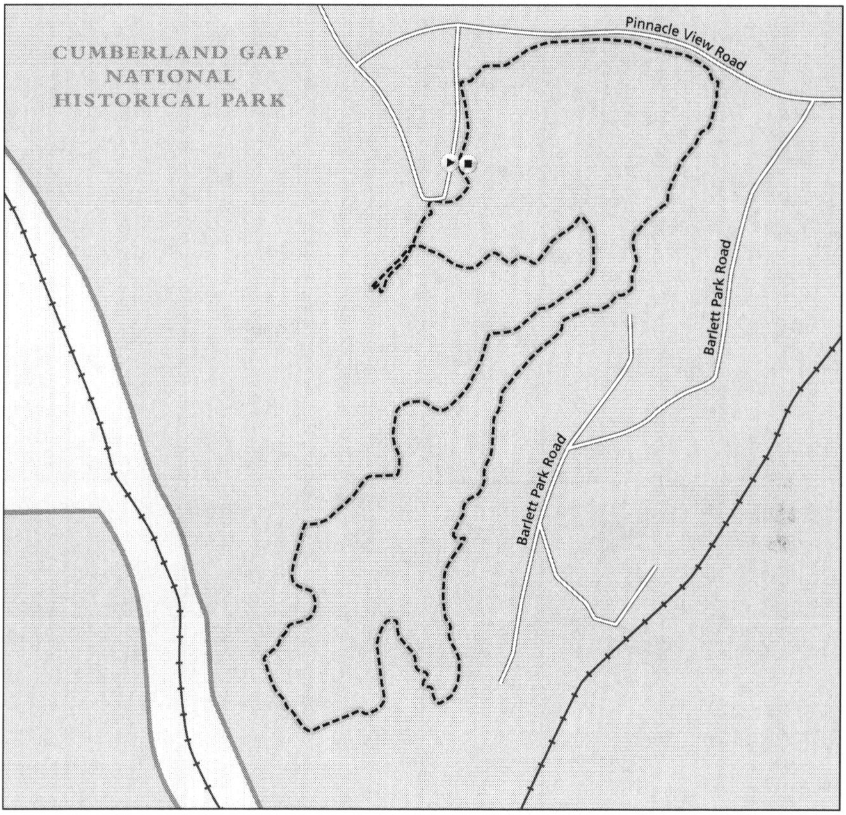

Fitness Loop Trail, Middlesboro, KY

20
Louisiana

Trail name: Alligator Marsh
Location: Fontainebleau State Park
Distance: 1.7 mi
Duration (active): 43m
Average speed: 2.4 mi/h
Total ascent: 10 ft
Highest point: 10 ft
Difficulty: Easy

We selected Fontainebleau State Park for our Louisiana pushike for several reasons. It was close to New Orleans where we landed late the night before. There was a good chance of viewing alligators. And, we got to drive across the twenty-four-mile bridge spanning Lake Pontchartrain. Kellisa loved the ride on the bridge because it was bumpy, and the bridge was surrounded by water as far as our eyes could see. It was an early highlight of our epic summer trip through ten southeastern states.

Despite an early start in the morning, it was already approaching 100°F with uncomfortable humidity. We lived in Florida for sixteen years and grew accustomed to the stickiness. But, after three and a half years in the dry climate of northern California, our bodies were at the mercy of the uncomfortable conditions.

We were planning on pushiking the 3.7-mile Bayou Cane Trail through brackish marshland with the promise of observing birds and alligators in their natural habitats. Due to the extreme temperature, we needed to change that plan to limit our time out in the excessive heat. Being mindful of the increased seizure risk posed by this temperature, we decided to explore the shorter Alligator Marsh Trail. I was hoping we would still see some of the native wildlife while decreasing our sun exposure.

The trail started under a thick canopy of a deep forest. Even though the canopy protected us from the direct rays of the sun, it provided minimal relief from the heat. I expected to have the trail to ourselves but was surprised at the steady flow of hikers out on the last Friday in May. The diversity of the people on the trail was noticeable as we saw families with small children, couples of all ages, and a young woman trail running. Spiders like to cast their webs across paths in the nighttime hours. The first hikers on a trail clear the way for those following them. I was thankful we weren't the first ones on the Alligator Marsh Trail.

Our path was wide, with minimal roots to push over. As always, Kellisa giggled every time she bounced around from the uneven ground. The trail reminded me of most of our hikes in the southeast. I concentrated my eyes on the ground directly in front of us because the roots or the occasional downed branches looked like snakes. Louisiana is home to forty-eight snake species, and seven are poisonous. While we do enjoy observing snakes out in the wild from a safe distance, I do not like encountering them along a trail. Despite my eyes playing tricks on me several times as I scoured the leaf litter covering our path, I did not see any snakes. Although, that doesn't mean snakes weren't close to the trail.

After a short push through the forest, we arrived at a boardwalk that would take us out into the marsh. All cover was gone, and we were directly under the brutal sun; I protected Kellisa's head with a buff. I struggled to balance our need to be brief on the trail with Kellisa's interest to take in the sights.

The boardwalk had several viewing platforms with benches for relaxing, but I did not take advantage of them. Instead, I continued to push Kellisa over several bridges to the end of the boardwalk. We were now in the middle of the marsh and could see several open-water areas scattered between the greenery growing up from the water. My eyes are trained to spot alligators from years of kayaking and hiking trails in Florida. An alligator is excellent at blending into its surroundings. They camouflage themselves on a log, in the reeds, or below the surface of the water.

I wanted Kellisa to see an alligator, so I spent a few extra minutes beyond my comfort level looking for one. Unfortunately, I couldn't find any alligators. The Alligator Marsh Trail is an out and back, so we would retrace our steps (and wheel prints) back to the trailhead and the promise of air conditioning in our rental SUV.

I still held out hope that maybe we missed an alligator sighting on our way to the end of the boardwalk, but we ended the trail without seeing any. The temperature seemed to drop a few degrees as we reentered the forest, which was a minor relief. I felt my pace quicken as my eyes went back to scanning for snakes. I wanted to get Kellisa back to our SUV, where we could cool off, and I could fill her stomach with water through her g-tube.

Despite not seeing any wildlife, we still enjoyed the Alligator Marsh Trail. It was bumpy, and just the activity of looking for alligators was enough for Kellisa to have a good time. While we pushiked this trail, I realized how much I loved and missed the swamps of the southeastern United States after being gone for several years.

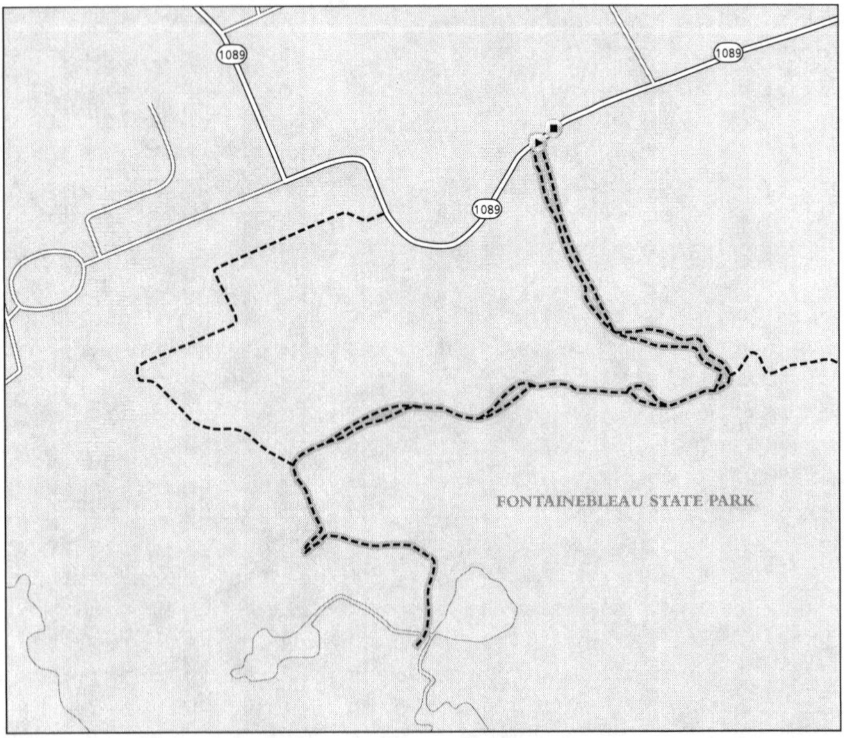

Alligator Marsh Trail and Boardwalk, Mandeville, LA

21
Maine

Trail name: Timber Point
Location: Rachel Carson National Wildlife Refuge
Distance: 1.5 mi
Duration (active): 39m
Average speed: 2.3 mi/h
Total ascent: 49 ft
Highest point: 44 ft
Difficulty: Moderate

When I think of Maine, I can't help but picture the rocky coastline and islands in the Atlantic Ocean. For Kellisa's sixteenth birthday, we traveled to Maine so we could visit the state for the first time, and while there, we pushiked around Mackworth Island near Portland. It was a beautiful trail following the perimeter of the island through a densely wooded forest. I pushed Kellisa in her manual travel wheelchair because we didn't have her mobility chair on that trip. The trail was wide and mostly free from rocks and roots. I was hoping to find a similar trail with just a little more ruggedness to it.

The Timber Point Trail in the Rachel Carson National Wildlife Refuge exceeded my expectations for a trail along Maine's famed coastline. I was worried that we wouldn't be able to pushike the trail on our intended morning. A nor'easter surprised everyone the day before, hitting New England with hurricane-force winds just south of our planned route. When we arrived, the area was still getting pounded by the edge of the system. It was windy, and the waves were violently crashing over the rocks, but it wasn't raining. The weather was a concern and needed to be respected, yet we were prepared, and Kellisa never minds the wind blowing around.

I parked near the trailhead and felt the full power of the wind as soon as I tried to open my door. We were only thirty feet from the ocean's edge with nothing in between to slow the wind. I got Kellisa in her mobility chair, which can be a challenge when she's laughing so hard her knees touch her chest. Because of her cerebral palsy, it can be difficult to straighten them out enough to sit her in her chair, especially when holding her in a strong windstorm. When I placed her in the chair, she was cracking up. Her feet were on the edge of the seat, and her knees were in her face. I was able to pull her legs forward just enough to correct her sitting position. First, the wind and then my struggles; Kellisa couldn't stop laughing. I did a quick double-check of our gear before pushing Kellisa along the narrow strip of land fully exposed to the weather coming in off the ocean.

After a fourth of a mile, the trail entered a heavily wooded area away from the ocean, which buffered the wind and made pushing Kellisa a little easier. Large boulders littered the forest floor off to the side of the trail. There was a backdrop of all the usual fall colors in the far Northeast: reds, oranges, yellows, and a few greens to go with the brown bark tones of the tree trunks and branches. The trail followed an old road, so it was wide, and all the largest rocks had been removed. The path was perfect for pushiking, with only slight elevation changes.

The trail proceeded to go through the forest with a few twists and turns but generally followed a straight course until it opened for a small loop along the coastline. With the protective cover from the trees gone, we were again at the mercy of the wind. A short distance away across a narrow channel is Timber Island, which can be reached by hiking during low tide. I hoped it could also be reached by pushiking. I was looking forward to my attempt to reach the island with Kellisa but knew the conditions would be too dangerous as soon as I heard about the nor'easter.

I held on to a little hope until the last minute when I saw high waves swirling in all directions between our vantage point and the small Timber Island a short distance away. Even without Kellisa and her mobility chair, there was no way to cross the raging water to reach Timber Island. It's always easier when decisions are made for us when out on an adventure. I didn't have to calculate the risk and figure out the safest route. I took pictures of the waves and island then retreated into the forest to get away from the wind.

I took my time pushing Kellisa back toward the trailhead so we could appreciate the beauty and surprising peacefulness of the forest. Once trees surrounded us, the lack of wind was terrific. We could still hear the swirling wind and pounding waves, but the air was still all around us. The difference of just a few hundred yards was striking.

We had passed a wildflower garden with beehives without stopping on the out portion of our pushike, but we decided to explore the area a little on our return. We didn't see any bees, birds, or animals, which didn't surprise us as they were probably all hiding from the storm.

When we emerged from the forest with only the exposed trail along the ocean to pushike, I noticed the wind had slowed down a little, making it more enjoyable to be out. Despite the calming of the sea air, the ocean waters were still battering the rocks. Weather is always a wildcard when pushiking. I was thankful we had our fleece jackets to keep us warm, and our ponchos were in the pack waiting for us in case it started to rain, but it never did. It was hard to tell if we could reach Timber Island with perfect conditions because the ocean was so violent on this visit, but I look forward to returning someday to give the crossing another look.

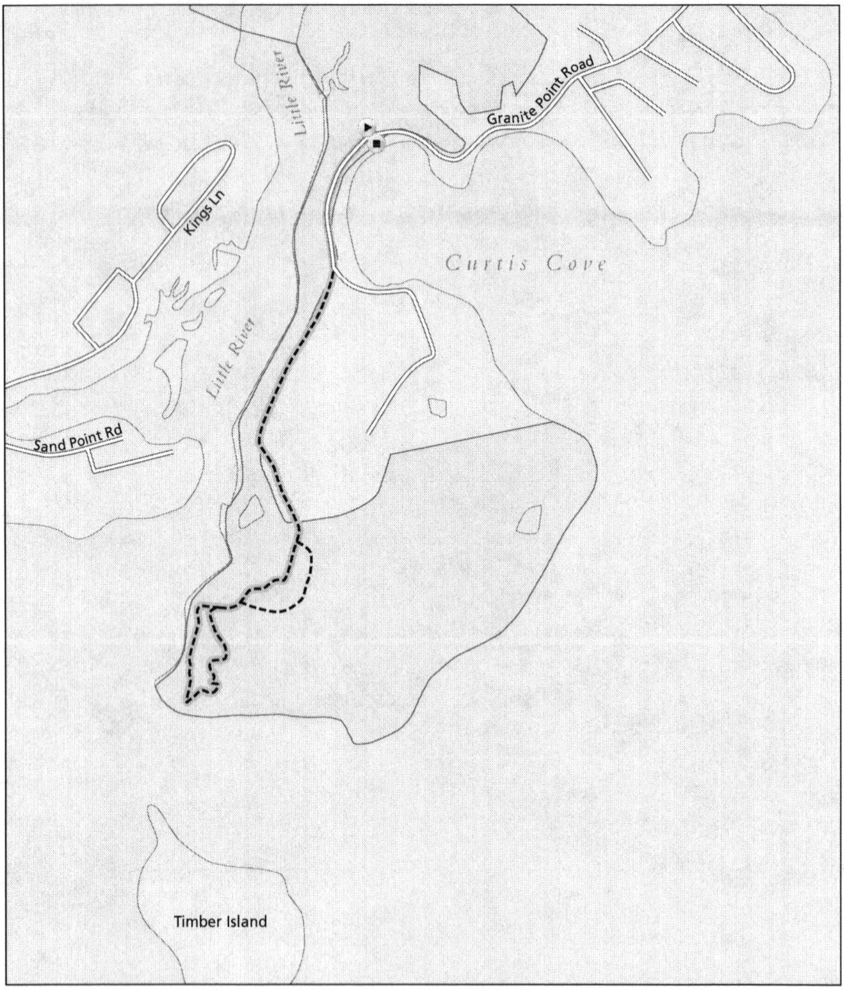

Timber Point Trail, Wells, ME

22

Maryland

Trail name: Deep Pond
Location: Beverly Triton Nature Park
Distance: 2.3 mi
Duration (active): 1h 3m
Average speed: 2.1 mi/h
Total ascent: 52 ft
Highest point: 34 ft
Difficulty: Moderate

It wasn't easy finding a trail to pushike in Maryland. It seemed like every trail was either too rocky, too muddy, or infested with ticks. Maryland, more than any other state in my research, warned about ticks. I've been severely allergic for several years to insect bites and wasn't interested in pushiking in an area where we'd be guaranteed to encounter ticks, even with using repellent. I also don't want to risk us getting exposed to Lyme disease. I eventually selected the Deep Pond Trail at Beverly Triton Beach Park for our pushike in Maryland because I only found one mention of ticks in the several trip reports I reviewed.

We arrived to find a small parking lot surrounded by a fence with a warning about getting locked in if your car remained after the park closed. There were a few parking spots just outside the fenced area. Even though I was planning on finishing our pushike before the park closed, you never know what's going to happen out on a trail, so I decided to play it safe and park outside the fence. There was an opening to walk through, so I knew we would be able to get out even if the park closed.

We planned to pushike the perimeter of Deep Pond. I took the warning about ticks seriously and loaded Kellisa and myself up with the most potent bug spray I could find, which promised to repel mosquitoes and ticks. I made sure to take the bug spray with us in case we needed to reapply before the end of our pushike.

We started down a couple of forest road trails, which reminded me of hiking down fire breaks. Each intersection had posts with color codes and arrows for each pathway. It was easy to know where you were and which way you wanted to go. Once we reached Deep Pond, we had a decision to make since the trail looped around the entire perimeter. We decided to go right, or counterclockwise, because we could see a man with an unleashed dog not too far down the path going left. Leashed dogs on a trail don't bother me, but we've had too many encounters with mean dogs that were not on a leash to know it's usually best to avoid them when possible. I hoped the man and his dog would leave before we reached the end of the loop trail.

The trail became a single track as it twisted through the forest. The path was just wide enough for Kellisa's mobility chair, but a few of the turns between trees were a little tight, although that only added to our wilderness adventure. The path was mostly dry with a few wet sections, yet nothing too muddy. It slowed our progress down a little but didn't cause us to stop or consider turning around. The trail generally followed the shoreline. We could always see Deep Pond, which to me, more resembled a lake than a pond based on its size alone.

The trees reflecting off the water added to our serenity. We encountered some inclines and drops on the far side of Deep Pond, but nothing too challenging. The trail followed the natural contours of the land, and the trail builders didn't put in steps. We've encountered steps many times on smaller and less steep sections on other trails. We usually prefer no steps for safety and general ease of pushing.

We completed the backside portion of the loop trail and started to push away from Deep Pond for the first time since beginning the perimeter trail. A golden forest surrounded Kellisa and me. It felt like we were on a path to a grand palace or castle in a movie, but instead, we were headed toward Chesapeake Bay. Even though we'd eventually reach the shore, I wasn't prepared for how big Chesapeake Bay appeared when standing at its edge. I can only compare it to one of the great lakes or even an ocean.

Kellisa enjoyed the constant breeze coming off the water, and I appreciated the air temperature dropping a few degrees. We were mesmerized by the crashing waves on the sand in front of us. I took a peek and knew a sandy section of the trail was coming up and didn't mind putting that off for a few more minutes.

The sand was deeper than it looked, and it became difficult to push Kellisa in her mobility chair. I was able to maneuver one of her back wheels just off the trail to gain some extra traction in a less sandy area. This process made pushing a little easier, but once I tipped her chair back to raise her front wheel in the air to eliminate it sinking into the sand, we were cruising at a pleasant little clip. Kellisa thought it was hilarious that I was pushing her on only two wheels.

I usually keep my eyes on the trail several feet ahead of Kellisa's front wheel, looking for obstacles and wildlife, mainly snakes. Even though we rarely encounter a snake, we are often pushiking in areas with poisonous snakes, so I always try to remain on high alert. I'm not too worried about Kellisa since she sits up in a chair, but I feel like you can never be too safe or vigilant. I'm more concerned about running over the snake or trapping it under the chair where it will become scared and defensive, which will increase the risk of it striking out while making a quick retreat. This scenario frightens me because the snake would be so unpredictable and hard to see.

We were about halfway through the sandy section when we came to a short spur that led to a rock jetty. Kellisa was still giggling, and the waves were crashing down less than ten feet away when I noticed something directly in front of Kellisa's chair. If I had dropped her front wheel down, it would have landed on what I saw. I thought there was a branch spanning almost the entire width of the sandy trail, but when I looked toward the end of the branch, I saw two eyes looking back at me.

Startled, I took a couple of steps back with Kellisa and her mobility chair. I'm not the best at identifying snakes, especially those without a rattle attached to their tails, but I'm confident this was a black racer between four and five feet long. Once we gave him some space, he quickly disappeared into the brush at the side of the trail. I kept my eye on the area where I thought he was hiding while I got my camera out, but as I carefully searched, I couldn't find him again. I gave up after several minutes, and Kellisa and I continued to finish the beach section of our pushike.

Back in the forest, we came to an intersection, we could turn left to finish our circumnavigation of Deep Pond, or we could continue going straight and take road trails back to the trailhead. My original intention was to follow the path around Deep Pond, but I was a little tired from the sand, and the thought of possibly encountering the unleashed dog caused me to change our plans. We ended up taking the road trails. It was nice pushiking through the forest on a wide trail free of obstacles, and we were back at our rental SUV long before the park closed for the evening. I checked Kellisa and then myself for ticks, and, thankfully, I didn't see any on our bodies. It wasn't easy to select a suitable trail in Maryland, but we found and pushiked an incredible trail.

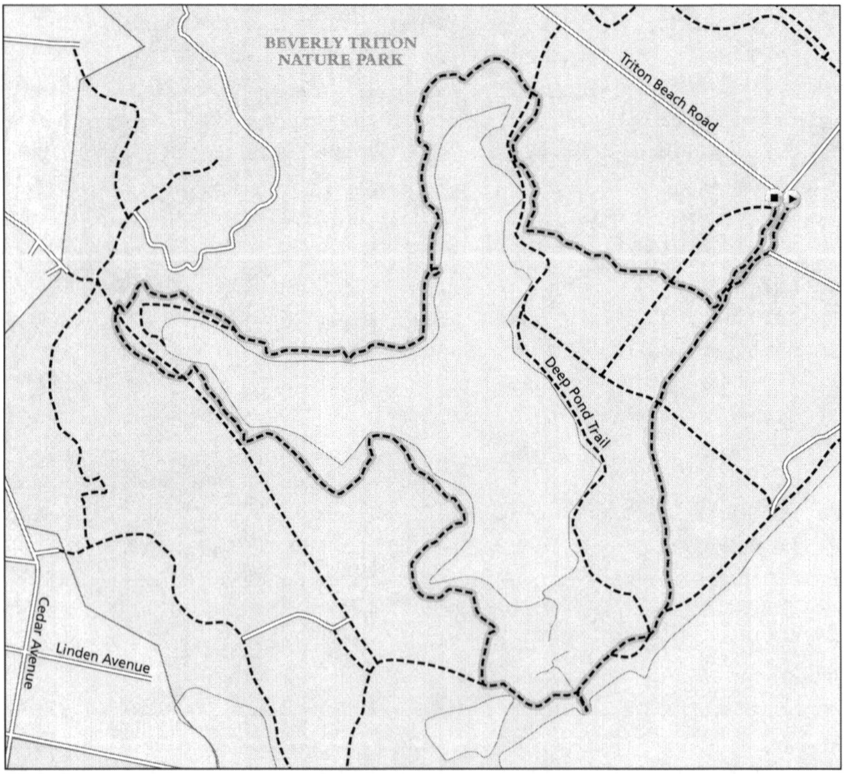

Deep Pond Trail, Edgewater, MD

23
Massachusetts

Trail name: Pond Path
Location: Walden Pond State Reservation
Distance: 2 mi
Duration (active): 57m
Average speed: 2.1 mi/h
Total ascent: 82 ft
Highest point: 213 ft
Difficulty: Moderate

I originally planned to visit Parker River National Wildlife Refuge on the shores of the Atlantic Ocean for our Massachusetts pushike. A surprise nor'easter hitting the coastal area with hurricane-force winds required a change to our plans. I don't mind pushing Kellisa in inclement weather, but we do avoid potentially dangerous weather events if we know about them in advance. Because I was confident in the trails in the refuge, and we had less than twenty-four hours' notice about the storm, I didn't have a backup trail or wilderness area selected.

It wasn't on my radar when I started looking for alternative trails, but I quickly zeroed in on perhaps the most famous pond in America, Walden Pond. I knew the great writer Henry David Thoreau spent two years living in a cabin near Walden Pond and used the experience to write the classic *Life in the Woods*. Thoreau spent his time there in the 1800s, and I had no idea what happened to Walden Pond and the forest surrounding it in the years since.

The land and cabin Thoreau used belonged to his well-known friend, Ralph Waldo Emerson. The Emerson family, along with other landowners, deeded the area to the state of Massachusetts with the guarantee it remained undeveloped.

I wonder how Emerson would feel about the way the state has protected the pond with the creation of Walden Pond State Reservation. The park includes a visitor center, bathhouse, swimming beach, large parking area, along with many daily visitors. I doubt this is what he meant by "remain undeveloped."

Kellisa and I planned to pushike the Pond Path following the perimeter of the water, but the area also has many other trails. We would see more people on this pushike than all the other trails in this book combined. That doesn't mean it felt crowded on the trail, but we did see a steady stream of people making the loop around the famous pond in both directions.

We started our visit by paying our entry fee before finding a parking spot near the pond. We had to cross a two-lane highway before descending a steep, paved access road to reach Walden Pond. We found ourselves just above the beach area. Since it was a cold October afternoon, the beach was deserted. The unobstructed view across the pond from the beach area set a dramatic tone for the rest of our pushike as we could see a wall of the forest surrounding the famed body of water.

I didn't see any signs pointing the way to the Pond Path, so I pointed Kellisa toward the trail closest to the water. We started our loop by going counterclockwise for no reason; besides, it was the first direction I saw the path. About halfway through our circle, this choice would prove by chance to be the best direction for a pushike.

The path was slightly elevated above the pond but was mostly flat, which made pushing Kellisa a breeze. There was a small fence on the waterside of the path that ran most of the way along the course of the trail. It didn't look strong enough to keep people from falling down the slight incline, so I can only guess it was placed to discourage hikers from leaving the path to explore down to the water's edge. The only real concern I had was the path was narrow. We had maybe a couple of inches to spare beyond Kellisa's back wheels. It wasn't a problem for us until other hikers tried to pass.

I would stop pushing Kellisa and maneuver her chair as far to one side as possible whenever someone wanted to pass. Most people went around without incident. However, a few made it known they weren't happy with our presence on the path by letting out sighs or giving us looks that could kill. I was surprised because we are usually welcomed unconditionally with open arms when out on a trail. It might have been because we encountered so many people; simple odds dictated a few would have a problem going around us. I was more worried about meeting a jog stroller or even someone having difficulty walking. Not surprisingly, we circumnavigated the entire path without seeing anyone struggling visibly and needing extra space.

The fence stopped a few times, allowing for controlled access to the pond. These areas were popular resting spots for hikers, and we passed the first few without exploring. We eventually discovered a sizeable accessible area going down to the pond, and surprisingly, no one was around. We took advantage of this opportunity to explore a little and take pictures of the pond and Kellisa without anyone photobombing us. Once satisfied with our photography efforts, we continued our loop, which included a small boardwalk over a wet area.

Shortly after the boardwalk, we saw signs pointing to a trail leading to a replica of the cabin used by Thoreau. Up until this point, the path had a few minor elevation changes, and the trail to the cabin was up a small hill leading deeper into the forest. The cabin could not be seen from the intersection. I considered investigating the cabin, but visitors crowded the area, and I knew it was a small, one-room cabin. Even if Kellisa and I were the only visitors, it would probably be hard to get inside the cabin. The mobility chair's awkward size and lack of maneuverability is a challenge to use in small areas. I decided to continue our loop and bypass the cabin. We were approximately a third of the way around Walden Pond at this point, and people were arriving regularly from both directions.

The trail led away from Walden Pond for a few minutes before making its way back at another access point to the water. I briefly noticed several people congregated on the small beach, a swimmer in a wet suit setting off for what looked like a serious swim, and a kayaker in the middle of the pond. But my attention was drawn to a steep incline just ahead of us with eight-inch cement blocks in the ground preventing erosion while helping hikers navigate the trail. It looked daunting, and I needed a closer look.

Once at the bottom, it didn't look nearly as rough as I first thought. The ground was dry, and the concrete formed significant step-like surfaces to aid in the climb. I was able to tip Kellisa back while pushing until I could place her front wheel on the first step. I then lifted her back wheels off the ground and put them on the same level as her front wheel. The steps in the trail were deep, and Kellisa's mobility chair easily fit on each one. I took my time going up the six steps. I wasn't worried about meeting other hikers because the trail was wide at this point. We even had enough room for two different wheeled chairs to meet and pass on these steps.

Once we reached the top, we saw a young family approaching in front of us. I waited until they arrived, and they could see the steps descending behind me. I asked if we would encounter any more areas like this as we worked our way back to the beach area. I was relieved when they told me these were the only steps on the Pond Path. I thanked them before continuing on our way.

It wasn't long before the trail was narrow again with a hill rising to our right and a drop-off to our left. The fence on the pond side was still present, with a few more gaps providing water access. The last section of the trail was downhill with a fence on both sides. The path was almost a trench at this point and was just wide enough at ground level to accommodate Kellisa's back tires. We were in the middle of our descent when a middle-aged man and woman started their climb up this section. I thought it was odd they would continue after seeing us already on our way down.

When we met on the trail, they couldn't go around us because the fences prevented anyone from stepping off the path. They both looked at me surprised before they leaned into and over the fence. They moved to the side as much as possible instead of retreating to the bottom. I carefully made our way around and tried not to run into them with Kellisa's wheels. As we passed, I thanked them for moving to the side. I didn't hear any words from them and didn't sense any anger or ill feelings, just the initial surprise. When we reached the bottom, I looked back, and the couple already reached the top and were out of sight.

I pushed Kellisa above the still-empty beach area and looked out across the water for the kayaker and swimmer but couldn't see anything except gentle ripples working their way across the open water. I had forgotten about our steep descent along the paved access road, which I was now looking up at from the bottom. I decided to push Kellisa to the top without stopping to get it over with as quickly as possible. Once at the top, I was able to rest and finish the water in my bottle.

Sometimes the best outdoor experiences are surprises. I didn't even know this recreation area and path existed two hours before our arrival. Despite encountering many hikers, it was one of the most scenic and enjoyable trails we would find. I can only imagine the level of peace Thoreau experienced when he spent his two years alone in the cabin above Walden Pond.

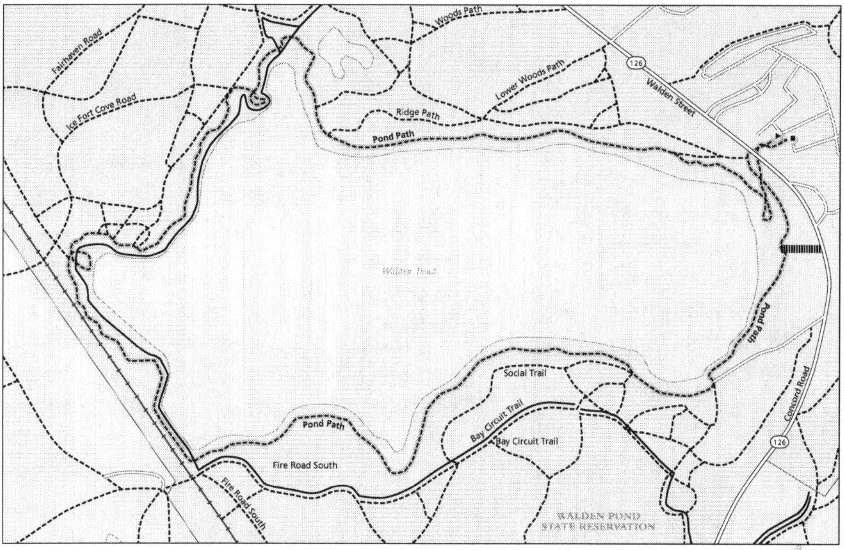

Pond Path, Concord, MA

24
Michigan, Lower Peninsula

Trail name: Old Growth Forest
Location: Hartwick Pines State Park
Distance: 1.7 mi
Duration (active): 39m
Average speed: 2.5 mi/h
Total ascent: 92 ft
Highest point: 1,252 ft
Difficulty: Moderate

Michigan has an upper and lower peninsula separated by the 3.5-mile-wide Mackinac Straights, where two great lakes, Michigan and Huron, merge. You can drive between the two peninsulas on the five-mile-long Mackinac Bridge. The bridge alone is a significant tourist destination. Since Michigan is divided into two distinct sections, I decided to feature a trail from both peninsulas.

The lower peninsula offers many options for pushiking, and it was difficult to narrow it down to just one trail. We ended up selecting the Old Growth Forest Trail in Hartwick Pines State Park for a variety of reasons. First, there's nothing better than the smell of pine while out on a pushike, and one of Michigan's most extensive virgin stands of white pines is in the park. Some of the towering trees are more than 400 years old and reach heights over 150 feet. Second, the trail passes by a chapel and logging museum. Lastly, the trail features a raised boardwalk and a paved trail circling through the forest with some elevation changes. At just over 1.5 miles in length, the trail is also on the longer end of paved trails, which added to its appeal.

We arrived at the park in the morning on an early fall day. I parked in a disabled spot and noticed we had the parking lot to ourselves. It looked like it might rain, so I didn't waste any time getting our stuff together and starting to pushike on the raised boardwalk. The wooden path worked its way through the pines toward the closed visitor center. It continued around to the side of the building before ending where the paved trail began. It was a unique experience passing through the trees, maybe ten to fifteen feet above the ground. I didn't see any water or dried bodies of water, so it was a mystery to us why they built the elevated walkway.

Once on the pavement, it didn't take long to disappear into the beautiful white pine forest. To my surprise, I could see stairs a short distance ahead of us. It didn't make sense because I wasn't expecting any barriers or significant challenges on this path. As we approached the stairs, I could see an alternative paved sidewalk switchback up and around the stairs. It wasn't a huge detour but made our pushike not only easier, but safer for us to proceed.

We reached the intersection where we had to decide whether to go right or left, and we selected right for no particular reason. The scent from hundreds of pine trees filled the air. The pavement disappeared under the pine needles making it easy to forget we were on a fully accessible trail. Another nice touch from the trail designers we appreciated was the fact the path only had one brief straight section. The builders opted for twists and turns reminiscent of traditional trails made over natural surfaces.

The trail had a few minor changes of elevations adding to the authentic wilderness atmosphere. Kellisa and I often stopped to gaze at fallen trees remaining where they fell, offering new life to other animals and plants on the forest floor. Some were entirely covered with a bright green moss, while others seemed to be slowly rotting. Our attention was drawn upward from the sounds of a woodpecker knocking on a white pine tree a little farther down the trail. I pushed Kellisa slowly toward the hardworking bird, and she instinctively became silent as she went into her observe-wildlife mode.

I stopped as close as I thought we could get without disturbing the woodpecker. We just watched the knocking for several minutes before I attempted to get my camera in position to snap a photo or two. Unfortunately, my hand movements caught the woodpecker's attention, and it quickly flew away to another tree. I tried to follow, but the bird was spooked and disappeared out of our view.

As we were continuing down the winding path, a chapel appeared perfectly camouflaged in the forest. It looked like the perfect setting for a nature-loving couple to get married and start a life together in a magical forest setting. I placed a light jacket on Kellisa as a slight breeze began to whistle through the tall pine trees. I was still concerned about rain, so I continued to push Kellisa without lingering in any one spot too long. A few turns later and we were at the logging museum. Nothing was open. We didn't see anyone else around but still enjoyed some of the large equipment displays near the trail.

It wasn't long before we were back at the beginning of the trail and used the elevated boardwalk to return to our rental SUV. Despite not seeing or hearing anyone else on the trail, the parking lot now had five or six other vehicles in parking spaces. It was a perfect trail to take our time to immerse ourselves in the relaxing calm of an old-growth forest. Kellisa and I would return to explore the longer trails in the park if we were ever in the area again. We would have no hesitation in pushiking the Old Growth Forest Trail again.

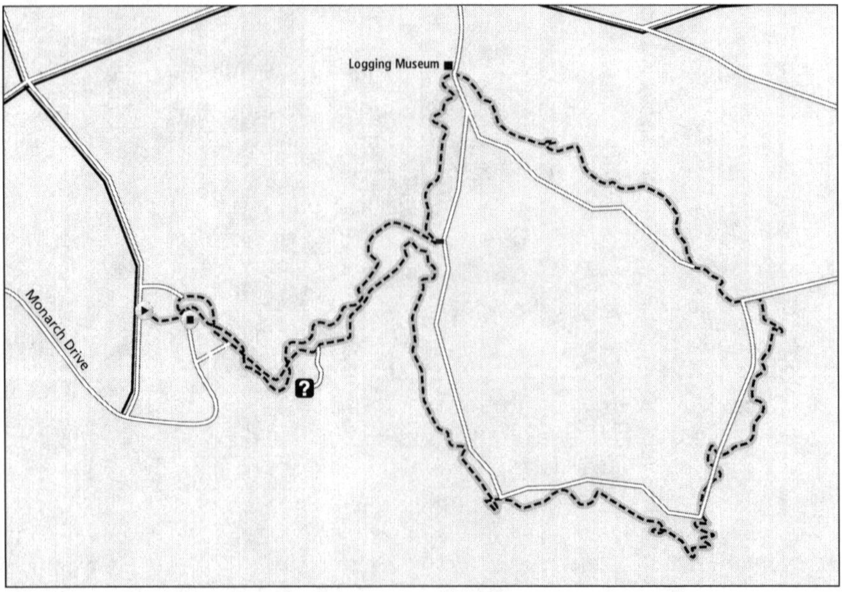

Old Growth Forest Trail, Crawford County, MI

25
Michigan, Upper Peninsula

Trail name: Au Sable Light Station
Location: Pictured Rocks National Lakeshore
Distance: 3.3 mi
Duration (active): 1h 24m
Average speed: 2.3 mi/h
Total ascent: 79 ft
Highest point: 646 ft
Difficulty: Moderate

"Do you have a favorite part of the country to visit?" is a question people often ask. Outside of maybe large sections of Alaska, Kellisa has been to most parts of the country, and we love them all. But, if forced to pick only one place to go, it would be the UP (upper peninsula of Michigan). The UP has just about everything from beaches to mountains to everything in between. It's an outdoor lover's paradise. There are almost 200 named waterfalls to be found and explored. Moose and bears roam the UP for wildlife observers, and birds love the many miles of lakeshore provided by two of the great lakes, Michigan and Superior. The one thing the UP doesn't have is hordes of tourists. Compared to other comparable wilderness areas across the United States, the UP is still a well-kept secret.

As much as we love the UP, it is hard finding a suitable trail for pushiking because many trails are too rocky. I wanted to find a path near Lake Superior to feature in this book because it's my favorite of the Great Lakes. Kellisa and I love pushiking with a constant breeze, and the soothing sound of waves crashing is always a welcomed companion on our lakeshore adventures. I was delighted to find the Au Sable Light Station Trail in Pictured Rocks National Lakeshore. The trail is a rough rocky access road that follows Lake Superior for its entire route. It is also part of the 4,600-mile-long North Country Trail.

We were driving to the trail from following H-58 from Munising. The trees were blazing in hues of gold and orange as the gorgeous road twisted and turned through the wilderness. H-58 would be a beautiful drive at any time of the year, but it's hard to imagine a prettier time to visit than when the trees are so alive with color. We can say the drive was one of the most beautiful we've ever experienced and would be worth a visit to the area by itself.

In our pretrip planning, I read horror stories of the mosquitoes and flies making life miserable for hikers on the Au Sable Light Station Trail. When we arrived at the trailhead parking lot, I made sure the bug spray was ready to go and didn't wait for an attack to cover our bodies. I kept the repellent in our bag just in case we would need to reapply at some point during three-plus mile pushike.

The trail starts next to a raging waterfall where the Hurricane River empties into Lake Superior. After taking a few pictures and cooling off in the misty breeze coming off the waterfall, we started following the trail toward our destination, the Au Sable Light Station. The National Park Service provides the upkeep of the lighthouse complex while the Coast Guard is responsible for the running of the light. Despite the beauty of this coastline, it is one of the most dangerous for passing ships. You can see a couple of shipwrecks down on the beach near the trail.

After navigating between the parking lot and Lake Superior, we continued through an adjacent campground before joining the access road. The wide trail consisted of gravel and sand, which made pushing Kellisa relatively easy. The forest was impenetrable to our right, and a narrow strip of trees and a sandy beach were all that separated us from Lake Superior on our left. The lake was gentle the day of our visit, but we could still hear the waves falling over on the sand and rocks.

Despite being deep in the forest, the trail was just broad enough to be pushiking under the full power of the sun. It wasn't a hot day, but I could feel the sun slowly draining my energy. Kellisa was full of water from her last g-tube feeding, and I made sure to keep myself hydrated.

The trail had just enough minor bends to break up the feeling of pushiking in a straight line. This feature added to a trail feeling instead of just following a road. We encountered a surprising number of hikers out enjoying the trail but didn't see a single vehicle, which made for a more pleasant experience. Scattered along the path were informative displays and access points down to the beach. I wasn't interested in getting sand in my hiking boots, and pushing a wheeled chair in the sand certainly adds to the difficulty level. We were content enjoying Lake Superior from the trail since we could see, hear, and smell all its beauty.

The Au Sable Light Station Trail is an out and back with the lighthouse our destination and, therefore, the halfway point. The National Park Service keeps the station open during the summer as a museum for visitors. I pushed Kellisa around the grounds and imagined living and working at the lighthouse before it became automated. The lightkeepers would have lived through raging storms and long winters from the relative safety of their quarters. I can only imagine natural beauty in such an isolated location.

You can explore on your own or, for a small fee, visitors can join scheduled ranger tours of the lighthouse and grounds. The buildings were built in 1873–1874 and haven't been updated to meet ADA requirements, so Kellisa and I just enjoyed ourselves from outside the buildings. After we were satisfied with our little grounds tour, we started back down the trail.

I didn't notice any elevation changes in our pushike out to the lighthouse but seemed to feel them on our return pushike. I wouldn't call any of the inclines steep or prolonged along the access road. Perhaps I was feeling a little tired. Kellisa was excited to see three dogs on the trail, and each owner was kind enough to stop, so Kellisa could say "Hi" while petting them. One lady was even pushing a small jog stroller while walking her dog. I looked inside and didn't see a child, and the lady was alone. I can only guess the stroller was for the dog. It's kind of ironic that the only jog stroller we would see on our pushikes on all the trails for this book was empty and used for a dog.

We took several of the beach access points down to the sand on our return to see if we could see any of the shipwrecks. We saw one that consisted of weathered boards half-buried in the sand. I would have liked to explore the beach areas a little more, but I did not want it enough to struggle to push Kellisa through the deep sand, so our beach adventures were short.

Kellisa and I were close to reentering the campground, which signaled the end of our pushike was near. A family stopped in front of us. The father asked, "How much farther to the lighthouse?"

I hesitated to answer because I thought he might be joking. When he stopped to wait for my answer, I honestly said, "You're just at the beginning, and the lighthouse is at least a mile up the trail." Their reaction would have been more appropriate if I answered, "You still have about twenty miles to go."

They thanked me and continued their way up the trail while Kellisa and I finished our pushike. We enjoyed a few last minutes near Lake Superior and visited the waterfall one last time before leaving the area. It wasn't until we were driving away that I realized we didn't see or hear any mosquitoes or flies on the trail. I'm not sure if they were not around or if our bug spray did its job. Either way, we completed a memorable pushike along the mighty Lake Superior.

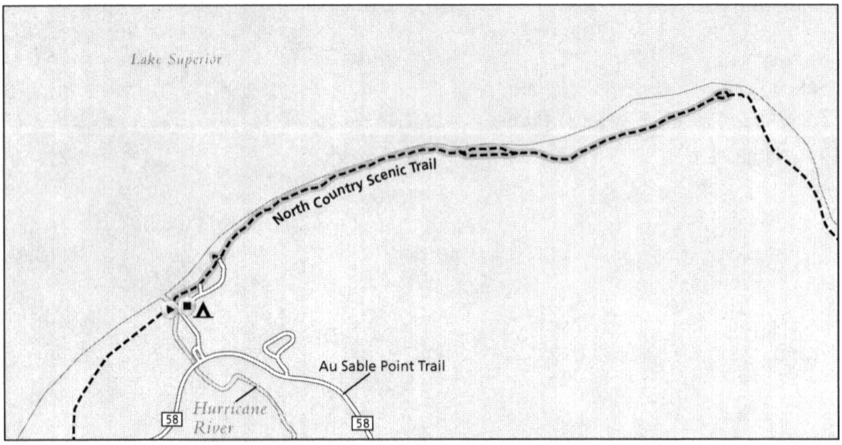

Au Sable Light Station Trail, Alger County, MI

26
Minnesota

Trail name: Big Island Loop
Location: Myre-Big Island State Park
Distance: 1.8 mi
Duration (active): 50m
Average speed: 2.1 mi/h
Total ascent: 52 ft
Highest point: 1,242 ft
Difficulty: Moderate

Minnesota proudly boasts right on the state license plates of their 10,000 lakes. When it was time to pushike in Minnesota, we knew we needed to pick a trail near one of these lakes. We would have loved to find a trail along Lake Superior in northern Minnesota, but I knew from previous trips that we would likely find those trails too rocky for a pushike. Our desire to experience a trail with a lake view drew us to Myre-Big Island State Park near Albert Lea in southern Minnesota.

I selected a trail that looped around an island that was attached to the mainland by a narrow strip of land barely wide enough for the park road. We arrived early in the morning and had the park to ourselves. The trailhead wasn't well marked, so I drove around searching while consulting our map of the state park. Eventually, I picked a corner in a lot to park, and we started down a trail we hoped was the loop around the big island.

We weren't sure because it was paved. In my research, I didn't read anything about pavement on any portion of the trail. The sidewalk led toward a building, but I saw a natural surface trail leading closer to the edge of the lake. I veered off the concrete and pushed Kellisa on the muddy trail. I was confident we found our intended path as we ventured deeper into the forest with the lake on our left. The trail passed through an empty amphitheater for ranger-led programs before continuing its course through the woods.

The trail was wet from the recent rains in the area, and the surrounding forest displayed vibrant green trees from the early fall rains. Kellisa's tires became covered in mud, making the pushing a little more challenging. The path was mostly level, which was appreciated since even the slightest elevation change would be a struggle with so much mud. It's difficult to push more than 100 pounds up an incline if you can't get any footing on the ground. Many times, it's one step up before sliding back three steps. Roots and rocks are usually our nemesis on the trail, but they can be our friends on a muddy incline. Leaf litter and pine needles on the ground also help.

Going downhill can be just as tricky because once you start pushing on a decline without adequate traction, gravity has a way of working against you. It's essential to think out a few steps ahead and always have a plan in case you start sliding out of control. My number-one rule is to have Kellisa and her chair tethered to my body, but I also like to have an additional option or two. Sometimes it can be as easy as turning her chair sideways. Even a little turn helps to stop the pull of gravity. A large rock or root can stop her wheels instantly, and then I can use her chair to stop my slide. And as a last resort, if it looks too dangerous, we turn around, saving that part of the trail for another day.

Our first real challenge was a spur trail leading down to the water with a few muddy steps cut in the trail. The steps were just deep enough for the chair and were flat enough that I felt confident in our ability to go down the steps to explore closer to the water's edge. This descent gave us our first chance to be right on the water. Some of the morning haze was still floating above the calm waters of Lake Albert Lea, and there was a slight chill in the air. Birds were flying in the air and floating on the water, and we enjoyed hearing their songs.

As the birds ended their show, we retraced our route up the few stairs and returned to the main loop trail. Up to this point, the trail had been mostly free from roots, but that would change fast. Kellisa was cracking up as she bounced up and over significant-sized roots spread out across our path.

The path eventually became mostly clear of the roots, which made the ground muddier. As we pushed clockwise around the island and reached the far southwestern portion of the trail, another spur broke off to our left. Our wide trail shrunk to a single track on this spit of land. Kellisa giggled as some of the foliage overhanging the path tickled her face as I pushed her toward the end. I think we startled a mother with her young daughter playing in the mud where the water from the lake met the land. Kellisa greeted them by blowing kisses, and I smiled while offering a "Good morning."

Despite our pleasantries, they promptly stopped their playing and headed back up the trail to move farther away from us. I was a little curious as to why we scared them since I had Kellisa with me, but I don't blame the mother for playing it safe and relocating to another area. Kellisa and I went on our way, and the narrow track eventually opened a little providing us with a gorgeous view across a more extensive section of the lake. I took a few pictures of Kellisa with the lake as the backdrop.

Not surprisingly, Kellisa enjoyed our return through the brush back to the main trail. At the junction with the spur trail turnoff, there was an older man just standing there, and he looked a little confused. He didn't look threatening to me, but I did wonder what the mother we encountered would have thought if she passed this man. As we got closer, I would guess his age to be in the sixties.

He explained that he was camping, went for his morning walk, and got turned around on the island trails. We were at a junction where three trails intersect. Even though there was a sign with accurate information, he wasn't sure which way to go. I was confident in the direction he needed and pointed the way. It happened to be the same direction we were headed.

Even though I didn't think he was a threat, I still had a decision to make. Do we hang back to let him get ahead a little? Do we change our course? Or do we plow forward to put some distance between us?

I made the judgment that we would be faster pushiking then he was hiking, so we decided to get ahead of him once we knew he wasn't lost anymore. Still following the general direction of the lakeshore, the trail was now heading in a northwestern direction toward the campground. It didn't take long for the man to disappear behind us on the trail, and we never saw the mother with her daughter again. Once at the campground, the trail disappeared, and our forward progress was now along a gravel road.

The smell of campfires and the elaborate breakfasts the campers were cooking filled the air. I was tempted to invite ourselves for sunny-side up eggs and bacon but had to settle for the energy bar in my bag.

From the park map, it looked like the rest of the trail would continue to be a road walk. While not ideal, the prospect of a road walk wasn't bad since we were still deep in a muddy forest. The road started moving away from the lake toward the island's interior forests. I noticed a roughly paved path on our right side. The trailhead post even had the familiar blue and white sign with a wheelchair indicating the path was ADA compliant. Since this path was headed toward our rental SUV and away from the campground, I decided to check it out.

It was apparent the paved path was old and neglected. While we didn't have a problem navigating our way, roots were pushing up through the concrete creating jagged peaks with significant gaps from wide cracks. Most of the time, I'm not a fan of pavement, but I must admit it was an improvement over the mud.

We passed a few still ponds as we meandered through the forest. The paved trail eventually led past a large building that appeared out of nowhere. It looked like an event center in need of some desperate love and care. It seemed out of place until we reached the other side of the strange building to see the parking lot suddenly appear. A few minutes later, we were back at our SUV. As I was lifting Kellisa to her seat, we were attacked by mosquitoes in a surprise raid. I had bug spray but didn't apply any while on the trail because we didn't see a single biting pest on our pushike. I was planning to give Kellisa some water through her g-tube but decided to delay that until I could get everything back inside the SUV. Once inside, it took another few minutes to exterminate all the little buggers who became trapped in the SUV. I ended up giving Kellisa her water before leaving, satisfied with our pushike along one of Minnesota's many lakes.

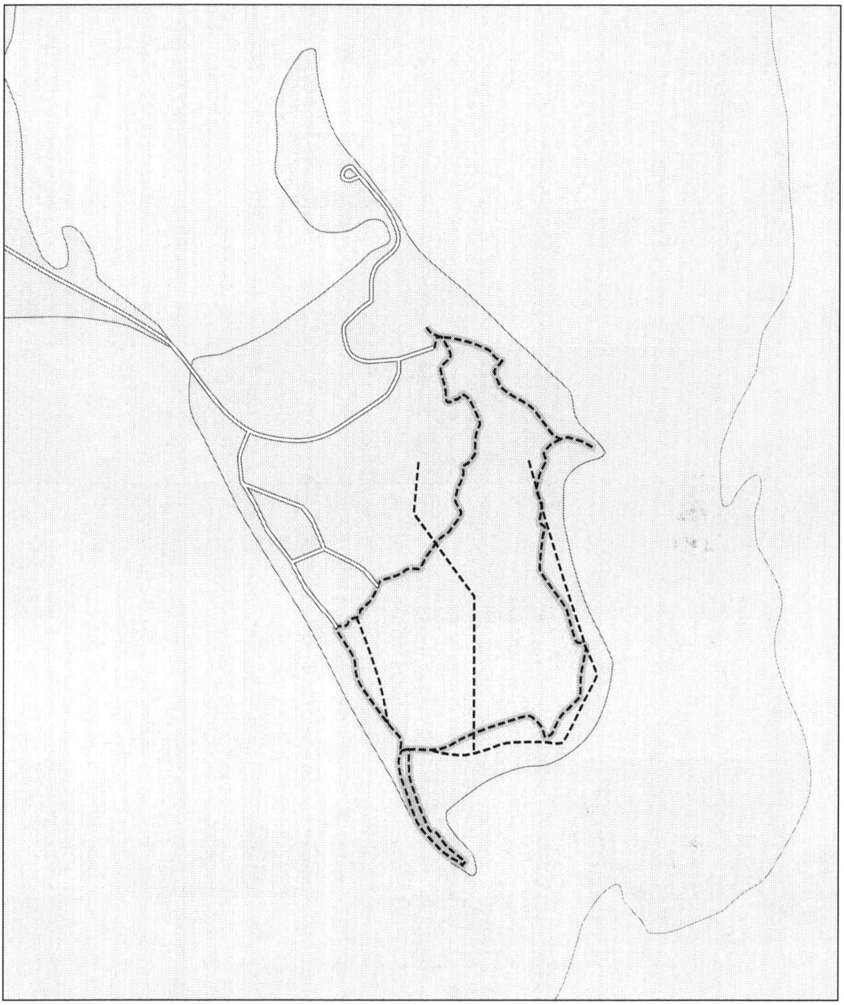

Big Island Loop, Albert Lea, MN

27

Mississippi

Trail name: Fontainebleau
Location: Mississippi Sandhill Crane National Wildlife Refuge
Distance: 1.5 mi
Duration (active): 49m
Average speed: 1.9 mi/h
Total ascent: 49 ft
Highest point: 17 ft
Difficulty: Moderate

While living in Jacksonville, Florida, for sixteen years, I became familiar with the I-10 corridor through southern Mississippi. I would make the drive several times a year for work and another half dozen or so round-trips over the years when we went to visit family in the Houston area. You drive through Mississippi Sandhill Crane National Wildlife Refuge as soon as you enter Mississippi heading west from Alabama. Over the years, we have found national wildlife refuges to have great pushiking opportunities. I had always wanted to stop for a visit and pushike, but we never had the time. We finally had the chance while driving from New Orleans to Jacksonville to pushike trails for this book.

It was a hot and humid afternoon in late May when we visited the refuge. We arrived a couple of hours later than planned due to a severe accident that had all lanes of I-10 closed for several hours. Even after we managed to get off the expressway, the driving remained painfully slow due to the traffic backup along the adjoining roads. Although frustrating, the delay may have worked in our favor as the sun was just beginning its descent on the horizon as we arrived at the trailhead, providing some relief from its afternoon onslaught.

I was drawn to the Fontainebleau Trail because the first 300 yards to an overlook promised to be ADA compliant. My research left me confident that we could complete the entire trail beyond the short, fully accessible section. As soon as we started down the path, we were met with a haphazard boardwalk-type decking across the trail in several sections that weren't connected. To make it worse, piles of gravel filled the gaps. I was able to push Kellisa with minimal trouble, but I doubt someone in a motorized or standard wheelchair could navigate this section.

Once back on natural ground, we found the trail to be wide and comfortable with a bed of pine needles lining the way and minimal roots. We reached the overlook after only a few minutes and were surprised at the elevation difference as we looked out over Davis Bayou. Despite only being sixteen feet above the bayou, we had extensive, sweeping views bordered by tall pines giving the illusion of being higher than we were.

After taking a few pictures, I pushed Kellisa beyond the accessible section down a narrower trail to the same level as the bayou. The bird activity near the water drew our attention as we meandered our way deeper into the forest. Another surprise greeted us as the trail made a turn, and we found ourselves on a steep section that I would have never expected to find in southern Mississippi. Even though it was starting to cool, the elevation changes had me working up a good sweat and got my heart rate going.

The Fontainebleau Trail is a loop with an out-and-back section leaving from the backside of the circle. We decided to explore the dead-end portion of the trail. After a few twists and turns, the trail dropped back down at a steep and surprising angle. I could see a small creek running through our path with a couple of stepping-stones for hikers to stay dry. I had a decision to make: turn around before completing this section of the trail, or push Kellisa through the water, which would muddy her wheels. Muddy tires would make the rest of our pushike more difficult.

It was an easy decision. We pushed forward, and Kellisa loved going through the water while bouncing around as I tried to push her down the path, through the mud, and up the other side without losing any momentum. My plan worked, but I couldn't keep my feet on the stepping-stones. My trail shoes were squeaking from being filled with water as I navigated our way up to the top of the slight incline. While I caught my breath, I looked forward, and to my amazement, the trail dropped back down again with another creek flowing across our path.

I knew we were close to the end and wasn't going to let another minor obstacle prevent us from continuing. Even if I wanted to turn around, Kellisa was having too much fun and wouldn't have allowed us to backtrack. After repeating the process of dropping down, crossing through the mud, and barreling our way up another incline, we were at the end of the trail. The setting was tranquil, and we would have preferred to linger awhile, but the mosquitoes were coming out for their evening feast. If we remained still, we would have been devoured.

I was not looking forward to the two hills and creek crossings in front of us, but Kellisa was giggling with great anticipation. I was motivated to get out of the area to avoid being eaten alive, so I found an extra gear to proceed back toward the loop trail swiftly. Once we were away from the open water of the creeks, the mosquitoes seemed to leave us alone. We continued with the rest of the loop at a more leisurely pace while enjoying the bird activity high in the pines above us.

We were completing the loop in a clockwise direction. The trail was a little narrower than the ADA section, but we found the entire loop to be on the easier side, especially after I cleaned most of the mud off Kellisa's tires with a broken pine branch. Removing the mud made pushing her a lot easier. There were several informational boards on this side of the loop, and we enjoyed learning about the Wet Pine Savannah we were pushiking through.

We were fortunate to reach our rental SUV with plenty of sunlight remaining. From what I could see, we both made it off the trail without any mosquito bites. I had several hours to drive to our next hotel and felt this trail was the perfect therapy to relieve the anxiety and frustration I felt earlier due to the extended traffic delays.

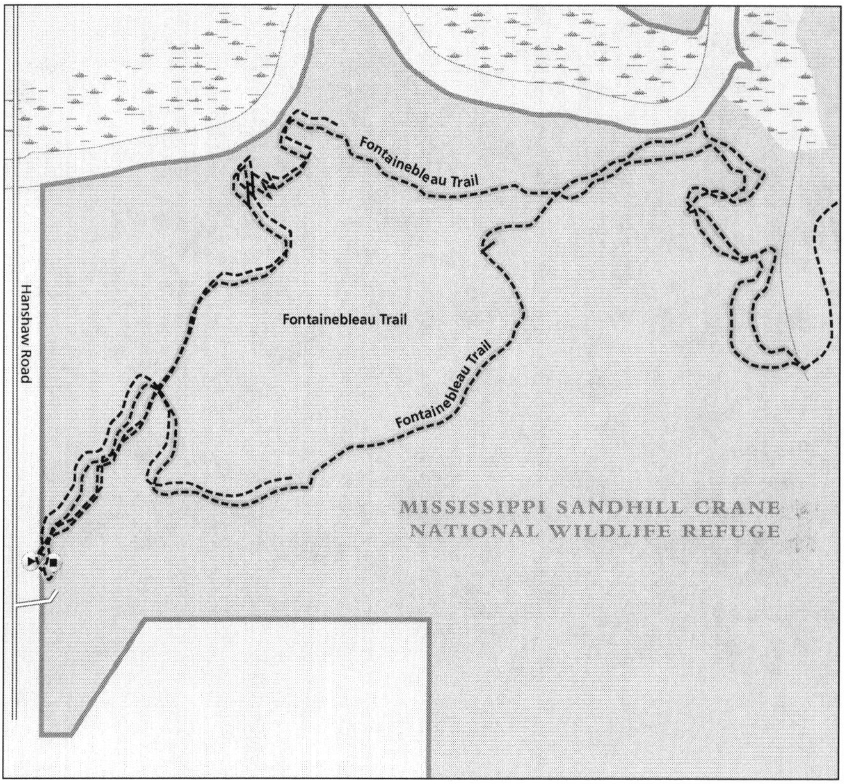

Fontainebleau Trail, Ocean Springs, MS

28
Missouri

Trail name: Path of the Sky People	**Average speed:** 1.7 mi/h
Location: Prairie State Park	**Total ascent:** 43 ft
Distance: 1.7 mi	**Highest point:** 993 ft
Duration (active): 59m	**Difficulty:** Moderate

Tallgrass prairies once covered more than a third of Missouri. Sadly, less than 1 percent remains today, and most of the existing prairie can be found in Prairie State Park. We were drawn to the park because the online pictures we found while researching trails were vastly different from the tallgrass prairies in neighboring Kansas. Before our visits, I thought all prairies were the same.

Our destination was the 160-acre TZI-SHO Prairie and, more specifically, the Path of the Sky People loop trail. We chose this trail because it gave us the highest chance of seeing the resident bison herd. I worried about another close encounter with the wild animals, but it was worth the risk because I knew how much Kellisa would enjoy seeing these magnificent creatures up close again.

We were driving through a slight, but steady drizzle on our way to Prairie State Park. We knew rain was in the forecast and were hoping to complete the trail before any severe downpours. As we approached the trailhead parking area, we saw a herd of bison lounging in the damp prairie grasses. We stopped to observe and take a few pictures. Kellisa was excited at our sighting, but we had a trail to hike, so we didn't stay long.

We were the only vehicle in the parking area, and I immediately saw our first obstacle of the day. There was a wooden border around the parking spaces with a narrow entrance to the actual trail. This is all too common on trails not meeting ADA requirements. These small openings are designed to keep motorized ATVs and motorized wheeled vehicles off the trails despite them already being illegal. While not a problem for nondisabled hikers, these do present an issue to us because Kellisa's mobility chair does not fit. Fortunately, I was able to park close, lift the chair over the barrier, and then carry Kellisa through before placing her back in the mobility chair.

The light rain stopped, leaving the grassy trail damp. I packed our rain gear just in case the clouds decided to drop some rain on us. I was a little worried about mud and impassable trails, but it felt like we were hiking on a soaked sponge. The chair sunk a little without slowing us down as we followed the path clockwise through the prairie.

The TZI-SHO Prairie was filled with vibrant colors and high growing grasses. It was a stark contrast to the prairies we visited in Kansas less than 175 miles away. While both are tallgrass prairies, it would be difficult for the casual hiker to find similarities. The Path of the Sky People had minor elevation changes with the low-lying areas filled with standing water. Usually, water across the trail slows us down, but we found the soggy ground easy enough to navigate.

At times, we had vast views in all directions of low rolling hills filled with fall coloring on our visit. We wanted to linger to enjoy our surroundings fully, but the gray skies kept us on task, so we kept moving along the path. We found ourselves surrounded by high grasses several times, which felt like we were walking through a winding hallway. I was a little nervous because I knew we were near wild bison that could be around any bend, and I had no way of seeing them. The last thing I wanted to do was spook a herd at close range.

I know you're supposed to make noise when hiking in bear country to let them know you are there. Besides keeping a safe distance from bison, I wasn't sure about the guidelines on noise. It seemed to make sense to make noise, so I started talking and singing with Kellisa as we rolled through the high grasses, which were still damp under her wheels. Slightly disappointed and a little relieved, we didn't see any wildlife on this trail.

We decided to pause for a break overlooking a small pond with hope to see some birds and maybe a turtle or frog, but we didn't see any. After five minutes, we decided to proceed to the car. We still had a long drive to a trail in neighboring Arkansas that we wanted to pushike before dark.

Despite knowing the end was near, the last section of the path had just enough elevation changes that I couldn't see the parking area. I was sure we were close, but I consulted the map because I started to fear making a wrong turn at one of the trail junctions.

Many hikers prefer loop trails over out and back because you don't see the same thing twice, even if it's from two different directions. I can't argue that point, but I do like out-and-back trails when I'm on an unknown trail with Kellisa because I know I won't be surprised. One of my fears when hiking a loop trail with Kellisa is a barrier or challenge of some sort after completing 99 percent of the trail that would require us to turn around to retrace our tracks back to the trailhead. Although I pack and plan for emergencies, that doesn't mean I ever want to backtrack an entire trail unless it's necessary. Even though I may prefer out-and-back trails with Kellisa, we also love a great loop trail.

As we rounded the final bend in the trail, I realized my fears were for nothing when I saw our rental SUV waiting for us. It started to rain while we were enjoying a light snack, and I was giving Kellisa some water inside the SUV at the trailhead. I was thankful we completed our 1.7-mile pushike in between the rain showers.

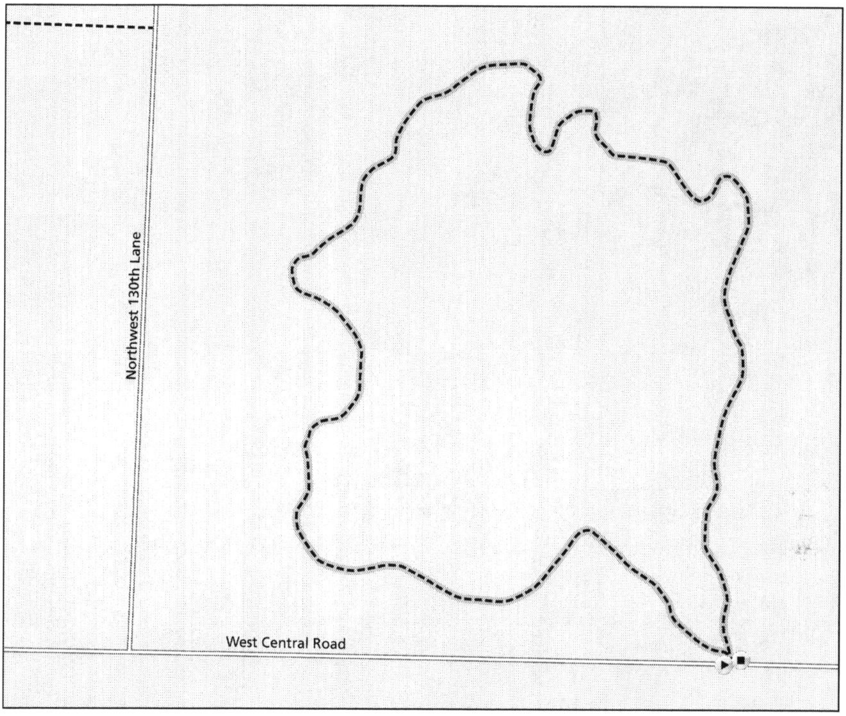

Path of the Sky People, Liberal, MO

29
Montana

Trail name: Sunset Loop
Location: Medicine Rocks State Park
Distance: 0.7 mi
Duration (active): 27m
Average speed: 1.6 mi/h
Total ascent: 39 ft
Highest point: 3,426 ft
Difficulty: Easy

I always try to have a backup plan when traveling to a trail to pushike because I know we can be turned back for many unexpected reasons, such as barriers, stairs, and the weather. In Montana, we wouldn't find success until our fourth trail.

I selected a trail in the Gallatin National Forest above the picturesque town of Red Lodge. Kellisa and I drove from Billings, and when we got close, I realized I left the directions to the trailhead in our hotel room. The lack of cell coverage in the forest made it impossible to use my phone for directions. But, I study and plan for every detail when pushiking with Kellisa, so I had a good idea of where to find the trailhead. When I saw the trailhead, I was relieved to see it looked like a great trail for us. The trailhead did not have the usual sign with a map and information, but I was confident we were in the correct place. The trail was wide and free of large rocks, which is rare for such a mountainous location. It didn't take long before I was pushing Kellisa on the trail past a picnic area and disappearing into a forest.

Soon we were surrounded by towering pines, and I knew something was wrong. The path became very narrow, filled with large rocks, and was moving away from the river instead of following it. It didn't match the descriptions I had read so many times. We continued forward because I was hoping the trail would get better. I thought even if it wasn't the trail I selected, it was still a trail in Montana.

Instead of getting better, the trail turned into a boulder field. We followed the path a little deeper into the forest before turning around. I was confused because it seemed like we were in the right place and frustrated for forgetting the directions at the hotel.

After loading Kellisa and our gear back into our rental SUV, I drove around determined to find the correct trailhead. While I managed to find several trailheads, none of them appeared to be the one we were planning to pushike. When it started to rain, we drove back to Billings. To stay on schedule, we should have left the area the following day, but with the directions in hand and a backup trail selected, we headed back toward Red Lodge and the Gallatin National Forest.

It's incredible how easy it was to find the correct trailhead using the directions. We were within a couple of hundred yards of it but turned around due to the rough road going from bad to almost impassable. Determined to pushike this trail, I attempted to reach the trailhead. I could see it, but the road was just too difficult and dangerous to proceed. I thought about leaving the SUV parked on the side of the road and pushing Kellisa up the rocky road, but I decided reaching this trailhead was not worth that level of effort. I was also concerned about the condition of the trail given how bad the road leading to it was. It was on to plan B for our second day in Montana.

We drove the scenic Beartooth Highway, which has steep switchbacks up to an elevation of 10,947 feet. I selected a trail on a high plateau near the border with Wyoming. I was excited to be driving this scenic highway. It's tough to imagine a more dramatic road in the United States. The drive made it seem like you were a mountain climber inching your way upward to a lofty summit. After every tight switchback, the view was more magnificent and far-reaching than the previous view. The road led high above the tree line. We reached the plateau shortly after passing a rest area.

There wasn't a place to park because the shoulders were still covered with eight feet of snow. I knew we might find snow patches but wasn't expecting this much snow during the last week of June. I drove a little farther, looking for a safe parking spot when snow began falling. I wasn't too worried about the snow because I had fleece jackets and gloves, just in case. I like to be prepared in the mountains. I turned around and drove just past the trailhead again before finding a spot large enough for several cars. I noticed the snow was falling even harder now and was blowing sideways. As soon as I opened my door, we were slammed with cold air and covered in snow. Kellisa thought it was hilarious. She was ready to go play out in the cold and snow. I, on the other hand, was very concerned. While prepared for some mildly bad weather, we weren't ready for a blizzard above 10,000 feet.

I decided to wait to see if the snow would pass. After a half-hour, and with about an inch of new accumulation on our hood, we drove down to the rest area to wait it out a little longer. I pulled into a parking spot with great views that were hampered by the rain pouring down at this slightly lower elevation. I knew this was our last chance for a pushike in the area. We were already a half-day behind schedule and had a long drive waiting to take the rest of our afternoon and most of the evening. After approximately thirty minutes, the rain slowed to a blowing drizzle. I was hoping this was the chance to pushike in Montana.

I drove the short distance back to the plateau, but it was still a raging blizzard at the higher elevation. While it was incredibly cool to be in such a late-season snowstorm, it was disappointing that we would have to leave the area without finishing a pushike. While turning around, a van full of snowboarders arrived and enthusiastically headed up the now snow-covered trail I wanted to explore.

Kellisa and I planned to pushike in North Dakota the following day and had a long drive ahead of us. While researching trails in Montana, I did find a couple in eastern Montana that looked interesting. We would be passing near one of them in Pirogue Island State Park. If everything went exactly perfect, we might make it to the park with just enough daylight remaining to pushike on an island in the Yellowstone River.

Fortunately for us, Montana has high speed limits, which helped us cross the state quickly. We did drive through a few brief rain showers, but they were not bad enough to slow us down. During and after each shower, we would see three or four rainbows off in the distance. They weren't the brightest, clearest, or most colorful, but we've never seen so many in one day. To our amazement, just ahead of us, there was the endpoint of a rainbow. The colors of the rainbow rose from the pavement in the lane of our travels. I didn't know you could see the end of a rainbow. I slowed the SUV down and grabbed my cell phone. I just started snapping pictures as we drove toward the rainbow. I expected it would disappear before we passed through, but I was going slow enough to see the colors move through the windshield. I was confident I had captured a picture or two, but immediately wished I had a video of this amazing event. I thought about turning around, but we drove another seventeen miles before reaching an exit. I figured the rainbow would be gone or at least in a different location by the time we returned, so I continued with our plan to reach Pirogue Island.

We reached our new destination at dusk. We had the park to ourselves, and I had to overpay our entry fee because I didn't have exact change. It was a small price to pay to be on a trail in Montana finally. With my earlier frustrations behind me, I was looking forward to exploring the island trails. I double-checked our headlamp just in case we got caught out after dark.

Kellisa was excited to be freed from the SUV and back in her mobility chair. I pushed her down a small incline through a forested area. I could see a raging river in front of us and an island not too far away. We followed the trail to the water's edge and looked in both directions for a bridge. To my shock and surprise, I did not see any way to cross the river. I retraced my steps back to the trailhead and proceeded to walk around the small parking lot looking for another trail, but there wasn't an alternative. I couldn't believe it, the trail crossed through the river. With it flowing so fast and high, I could not even consider continuing on this trail. I loaded Kellisa and our gear back in our SUV and headed toward our hotel for the night. We were now a full day behind schedule, and we were zero for three when it came to finding a suitable pushiking trail in Montana.

Our hotel was near Mahoshika State Park, where we pushiked with Egypt back in 2015. The trail was great. It was wide and grassy, with moderate elevation changes. It had one major drawback; it was next to the park road. Although we didn't encounter more than a few cars passing by, it was hard to feel like you were out in the wilderness a few feet away from the park road. I quickly ruled out a return.

We were left with one final option for this trip, and it was Medicine Rocks State Park. To say Medicine Rocks is remote would be an understatement. I can't imagine another trail (not counting anything in Alaska) so far from everything. The small towns we passed through didn't have gas stations or general stores to buy even necessary supplies. It felt like we were driving on a different planet as we made our way to Medicine Rocks.

I had been interested in Medicine Rocks ever since I read a quote by Theodore Roosevelt declaring that Medicine Rocks was "as fantastically beautiful a place as I have ever seen."

Since this lofty statement came from the "Conservation President," who visited the Grand Canyon and Yosemite in addition to many other wild places, it was a state park I wanted to visit and hopefully pushike with Kellisa.

Fortunately for us, there was a pump at the entrance station with drinkable water. Having this water saved the pushike since we drove the previous ninety minutes without finding a store near the park. I paid the entrance fee and then filled up our water bottles. We were hoping to pushike two short trails in the park. The drive through the park went between interesting rocks with all kinds of holes and small caves. The rocks looked like hardened Swiss cheese. At times, we were only a few feet from the rocks on both sides of the SUV. I didn't have a park map but continued following the park road passing by one of the trailheads before parking in a small lot near the end of the road, which served as the starting point for the Sunset Loop Trail.

We started down the trail in the early afternoon under a blistering sun. The area was barren of large trees, so I protected Kellisa's head with a buff. The path was wide and mostly flat surrounded by blowing grasses in many colors. The yellows and bright greens popped under the intense sunlight. It was fun taking photos of Kellisa lost in a sea of swaying grasses that stood taller than her seated in the mobility chair.

We were surrounded by the Medicine Rocks, which are sandstone pillars rising sixty to eighty feet above the surrounding land. I'm not sure I would call the area as beautiful as the Grand Canyon and Yosemite, but it was spectacular and well worth the effort to reach this magnificent little park. It was hard to focus on the trail in front of us because I was constantly looking with amazement at the rock formations. Some of the compositions were lit by the intense sunlight, while other areas were hiding in the dark shadows.

Despite being called the Sunset Loop Trail, it's an out and back with a very short loop at the end after cresting a small hill for a closeup of one of the most majestic rocks in the park. This trail had views spreading to faraway horizons between rock outcroppings. I would love to return when we could camp in the park to witness what must be spectacular sunsets and sunrises. Being so isolated, I'm sure the moon and night sky would be just as dramatic.

While returning to the trailhead, we took a short side trail to an area close to the rocks with a bench placed perfectly for reflection and close-up viewing. As we closed in on the sandstone pillar, it was sad to see it was tagged with recent graffiti. It was hard to tell using my untrained eye if any of the markings visible were from Native Americans or if they were the predictable "Bobby loves Sue" in a heart shape and "Jolynn was here" type of defacing.

I mention Jolynn because that was carved in one of the rocks. I have an amazing Aunt Jo, short for Jolynn. She and my Uncle Jack were great influencers in my life and helped guide me as a child toward a future of enjoying and appreciating the great outdoors. I knew my aunt would not have carved her name in a rock, but I took a picture to tease her about it once we returned to a place with cell-phone coverage. When I did, she assured me she had never carved her name in rock.

While looking closely at the rock carvings, I couldn't help but wonder if sometime in the distant future, a person or some other being would be in this very spot studying what is now considered vandalism. Will it be regarded as prehistoric art in a billion years and baffle the great minds of the day?

At less than a mile in length, the Sunset Loop Trail was short by our standards. I had planned on hiking a second trail but decided to save it for another trip because it was starting to get dangerously hot, and we were still behind schedule. I left the park with many deep thoughts stimulating my brain, including the fact that we were in a full-blown blizzard in western Montana, and, less than twenty-four hours later, we were pushiking in temperatures near 100°F in eastern Montana. With wind chill and heat index figured in, we were approaching a temperature difference of a hundred degrees.

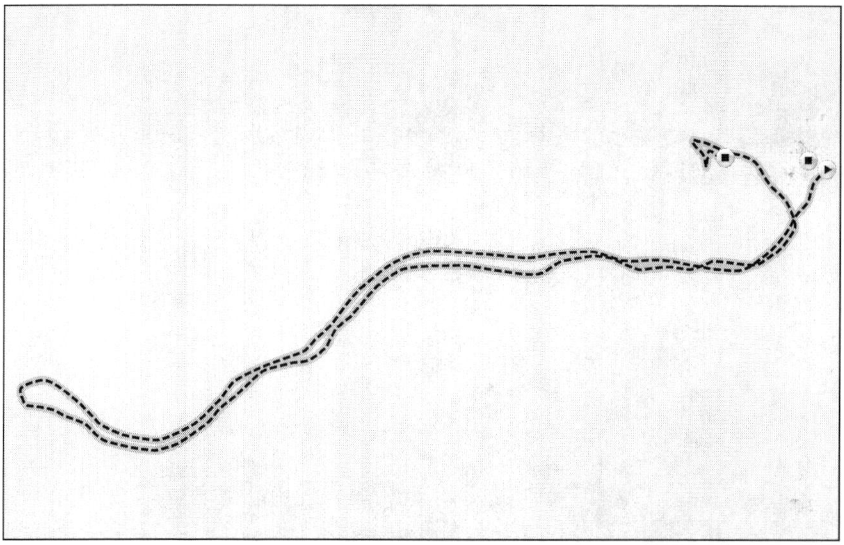

Sunset Loop, Carter County, MT

30
Nebraska

Trail name: Overlook
Location: Ponca State Park
Distance: 1.4 mi
Duration (active): 1h
Average speed: 1.4 mi/h
Total ascent: 272 ft
Highest point: 1,360 ft
Difficulty: Challenging

Kellisa and I originally planned to pushike a trail in Scottsbluff National Monument in western Nebraska for this book. A late-season snowstorm in Montana followed by a couple of days of thunderstorms canceled those plans. We decided to add Nebraska to our trip to pushike Iowa and Minnesota. Therefore, I needed to find a trail in eastern Nebraska. It took a few hours of research, but we finally selected Ponca State Park along the Missouri River. The park is in the far northeastern section of Nebraska as the location for our featured pushike and is known for a wide variety of landscapes, from wetlands to prairies to dramatic cliffs rising from the river's edge. With more than twenty-two miles of trails, I was confident we could find an exceptional trail.

The entire region around Ponca State Park was inundated with rain for days before our arrival. Many of the surrounding low-lying areas were flooded. I called the park to confirm it, and all the trails were open before our afternoon pushike. I selected the Overlook Trail because it seemed to be the highest as it followed a bluff above the river. I hoped it would be the driest trail in the area. I love the challenge of elevation changes on a trail, so I was hoping for long, stretching views of three states from the main overlook area.

Driving through Ponca State Park seemed more like a resort than a wilderness area; it has a modern aquatic center and many lodges which resemble luxury vacation houses. Once past the developed area, the park did take on a feeling of being deep in the forest. It wasn't obvious, but we found the trailhead for the Overlook Trail behind a shelter and playground. I knew mosquitoes would be a problem with so much standing water in the park, so I didn't wait for them to descend upon us to liberally apply bug spray to every inch of our exposed skin.

There wasn't a sign, but it appeared the trail started with one significant step down off a sidewalk to a narrow and muddy path. I could see that the trail widened after twenty-five to thirty feet. I decided to take my time, lowering Kellisa down this step. I hoped this was the right trail and not just a side path from the park into the forest. I was careful not to lose my footing and slip back from the mud. Once the trail widened, I was mostly confident we were on the correct path.

I had to push Kellisa over and around some minor branches that had recently fallen across the trail. The entire trail was muddy with continuous elevation changes. After just a few minutes, we arrived at the overlook platform with views out across three states. The decking was fully accessible, which made pushing Kellisa easy. Park visitors can drive up to the overlook, making it a popular stop. Several families were taking up all the prime viewing locations. Kellisa and I waited patiently for our turn, but we decided to leave when we realized these people were acting like they were the only ones on the platform. I knew we could return later after our pushike, even if it meant driving to the overlook.

The Overlook Trail left the platform with a quick descent back into the forest. Despite many cars in the park, we had the trail all to ourselves. We enjoyed several views from within the forest through the trees out and over the Missouri

River, but none were as good as from the platform. I continued to push Kellisa as the trail lost and gained elevation. I had an overall feeling that we were losing altitude. After following the ridgetop, the trail switchbacked down and away from the river and spit us out on a park road.

I wasn't expecting to find ourselves on the pavement. I decided to consult the park map in my pocket, which confirmed that we would have to navigate a short distance along the road. We found ourselves at a confusing intersection with several connected parking lots. I couldn't see any trail markers or signs pointing the way. I pushed Kellisa in the direction I expected to find the trail but couldn't find it. I went a little farther, but the road went up a steep hill, which didn't interest me since it seemed like it was taking us farther than we needed to go. I decided to turn around, thinking maybe we just missed a narrow opening in the forest leading to the trail. When I got back to the point where we exited, I was thoroughly confused. With no one around to ask, I had a decision to make. We could backtrack along the trail, making it an out and back. I continue searching to see where the trail started again. I decided to push Kellisa along the road I thought would lead back to the overlook and eventually our rental SUV.

The idea of pushiking Kellisa down park roads as an alternative to trails has been bouncing around my head since our visit to Zion National Park back in 2010. Zion restricts personal vehicles on the Zion Canyon Scenic Drive during the busy seasons. Instead, visitors need to ride shuttle buses that stop at seven locations along the drive every seven to ten minutes. Kellisa and I waited in line for about thirty minutes at the visitor center for one of the shuttles. At the time, we were using a jog stroller for children with special needs. It was just a little larger than jog strollers off the shelf at your local store. Most people probably couldn't tell it was anything special.

The bus was ill-equipped to handle a chair of any kind. We were herded in with the masses. The driver did not attempt to strap Kellisa down or clear a spot for her. Kellisa blocked the entire aisle and was surrounded by tourists on all sides. The bus was packed to the point where you couldn't move because you were touching at least four or five other people. I was initially worried that Kellisa's jog stroller wasn't strapped down. There were many people to cushion the impact of any kind, but I was more concerned about people on the bus falling and landing on her.

We eventually got off and pushiked a couple of trails under the towering red cliffs. We didn't have any ambitious trail plans for this trip, and we were taking in the beauty of our surroundings. When we were done exploring, I pushed Kellisa to the nearest shuttle bus stop to wait for the next bus. We were the only ones there. I didn't have a concern until the bus pulled up, and I could tell it was packed. Only a couple of visitors exited the bus, and it was apparent there wasn't enough room for us and the jog stroller. Over the next half hour, this frustrating process happened two more times.

It was midafternoon, and I was feeling my anger levels rising. I was getting concerned this could go on the rest of the afternoon and into the evening. When it happened a fourth time, I asked the bus driver if he could call and let someone know that we've been stranded for forty-five minutes. He recommended we wait, and he'd let someone know when he got back. I wasn't hopeful anything would change and decided to start pushing Kellisa back to the visitor center along the Zion Canyon Scenic Drive.

I knew the road was closed to cars but didn't know the policy for people walking down the pavement. Since there wasn't much of a shoulder, I figured there was a chance walking along the road was against the rules, but I wasn't worried. I just thought the worst thing that could happen is a ranger would stop us and be forced to drive us back to the visitor center.

I started our walk with outrage. We had the road to ourselves deep in a restricted canyon, and I felt better in no time. We only had to deal with an occasional bus, and we always moved as far over as possible, giving the bus plenty of room to pass us. You don't notice it as much when packed on a bus, but the road is filled with many elevation changes and curves. I doubt you'd have the same views from inside the shuttle buses.

Thankfully, Kellisa and I had extra water and snacks for this bonus pushike. After going about three miles, a ranger pulled up in a national park pick-up. He heard about us from a bus driver and came to offer us a ride back to the visitor center. I'm not sure if it was the original driver or one who passed us on the road. I asked how far it was back to the visitor center, and he said another two to three miles. I wondered if I could pass on his kind offer and continue pushing Kellisa. He said, "Sure," before telling us to be careful, especially as we neared the visitor center because tourist cars and campers were allowed on the road.

We thanked him and completed what turned out to be a highlight of our time spent in Zion National Park. I realize there will always be trails where it's too dangerous or just impossible to pushike with Kellisa. I started to think there might be a real possibility to push Kellisa along a park road or maybe even a dirt road through a national forest or across Bureau of Land Management lands. A whole new opportunity appeared from a flaw in the shuttle-bus system at Zion National Park. I don't know if families with jog strollers or visitors in wheelchairs have it any easier since our first visit. We've only returned once since then, and I received a special permit from the chief ranger to drive our rental SUV in Zion Canyon. I called and explained the issue on our previous trip.

Since I first came up with the idea of using roads as trails, Kellisa and I never had a need or opportunity until the afternoon we were pushiking in Ponca State Park in September 2019. I decided to push Kellisa along the road back to our trailhead with a quick stop at the overlook. The muddy condition of the Overlook Trail and frustration from not being able to find the trail led to my decision.

The road was wide enough that I wasn't worried about not having enough room to move over to allow an occasional vehicle to pass us. The pavement was surrounded by forest, and the road was narrow enough for the trees to keep us out of the sun for portions of our road walk. The road had curves and enough elevation changes to provide a real workout. I think the return was more difficult because the road seemed steeper, but I was thankful not to be pushing Kellisa through the mud. Even though the park seemed crowded at the visitor center, aquatic center, and around the lodges, deeper in the park we had the road mostly to ourselves. Only two cars passed us the entire time we spent on the park road.

The parking lot for the overlook was empty when we returned for our turn to enjoy the views. With the Missouri River flowing far below, Kellisa and I had the platform to ourselves. I enjoyed reading the informative signs, which included pictures explaining what we were seeing. The signs educated us on controlling the river with dams and Lewis and Clark. From our high vantage point, we could see wooded bluffs in Nebraska and farmland in South Dakota and Iowa. After enjoying the views and taking a few pictures, we ended our afternoon in the park.

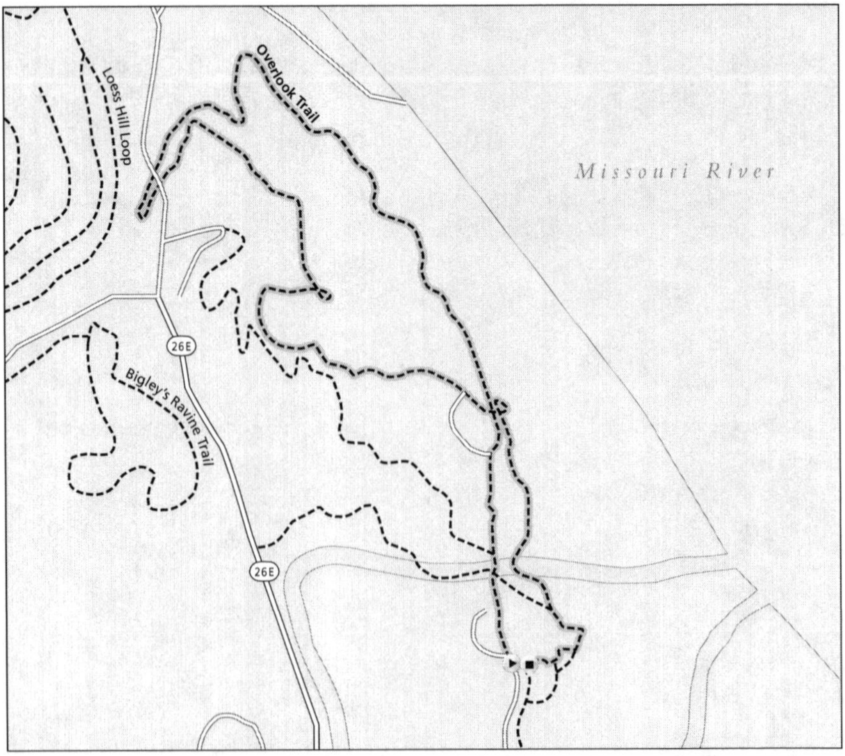

Overlook Trail, Ponca, NE

31
Nevada

Trail name: Tahoe Meadows Interpretive Loop
Location: Mount Rose Wilderness
Distance: 1.4 mi
Duration (active): 49m
Average speed: 1.8 mi/h
Total ascent: 82 ft
Highest point: 8,726 ft
Difficulty: Moderate

High above Lake Tahoe on the Nevada side sits the Tahoe Meadows Interpretive Loop Trail. The trail is only two hours from our home in Roseville, California. We are fortunate to live so close to one of the great resources for people who hike with jog strollers or mobility chairs. The Tahoe Meadows Interpretive Loop Trail is fully accessible, which means it's designed for wheelchairs. While I consider myself an expert in pushing a person in a wheelchair, I prefer using Kellisa's mobility chair designed explicitly for trails instead of her wheelchair. Kellisa can wheel herself in a wheelchair, but it needs to be on solid ground with minimal elevation changes and for only short distances. We are not experts in wheelchair hiking, where the person in the wheelchair propels him- or herself along a trail. There is also another category of wheelchair hikers who use motorized wheelchairs, and again, we don't claim to be experts in either activity.

That said, in my opinion, this trail would be a considerable challenge for motorized wheelchairs and manual wheelchair users, even with some help. I would never say impossible because I hate when people say that to us, but I'd rate this trail as one of the more challenging trails we've pushiked with an accessible trail rating. I'm sure the trail is wide enough with gentle grades to meet the ADA requirements. However, we found the ground to be soft in places and covered in snow in others during our early October visit. The soft areas would be my most significant concern for wheelchairs. A wheelchair's narrow tires tend to sink, making forward progress difficult, and if they sink enough, they become stuck. I'm sure people in wheelchairs have completed this loop many times over the years with proper planning and possible assistance. Even though this is far from a remote trail, I'd still hate to hear about someone getting stuck out on this beautiful trail.

Kellisa's mobility chair was designed perfectly for trails like the Tahoe Meadows Interpretive Loop because its wide tires don't sink. Probably the biggest challenge for me was not being used to the altitude at the Tahoe Meadows since it sits at 8,700 feet above sea level. While we live close, our house sits at only 264 feet above sea level. I felt myself getting winded from lack of oxygen and having to take the trail slower than our usual pace. Kellisa has been to higher elevations without any issues, but that doesn't mean she is free from all risk of altitude sickness. It's essential to stay hydrated when traveling to higher elevations. Thankfully, I was able to control a little extra water intake through Kellisa's g-tube before and after our pushike. I kept my eye on her looking for any signs of difficulty while keeping myself well hydrated.

It was a warm afternoon in early October when we visited the trail. Earlier in the week, it had snowed at higher elevations. We found several short segments with snow covering the trail several inches deep in the shaded areas. The snow was full of footprints from other hikers and even a few animal tracks. Kellisa's wheels were the first wheel impressions in the snow.

The Tahoe Meadows Interpretive Loop Trail is a lollipop configuration. Once you reach the loop portion, you can turn right over a short bridge leading to a boardwalk above the meadows or continue straight on what appears to be an old roadbed. Since it was our second time pushiking this trail, and we went straight for the bridge the first time, we decided to continue forward on the roadbed. The trail gained a little elevation during this section through rock outcroppings and scattered trees with views over the meadows to our right.

This first portion of the path is part of the 165-mile Tahoe Rim Trail that circles Lake Tahoe through California and Nevada. Since it's in our backyard, I would love to attempt the entire trail someday, preferably with Kellisa. Even though we only pushiked a tiny portion, it was still cool to complete a brief section before turning off the longer trail to continue our short loop. Just a few feet beyond this turnoff is a short side trail to a bench and viewing area. I pushed Kellisa to the end of this out-and-back path to take a few pictures before returning to the main trail. The trail crossed several bridges passing over small running creeks as they emptied into the broad meadows. The trail entered more of a forested area with scattered pine trees swaying high above us in the mountain air. A mountain rose to our left, and we found the most snow in this sheltered area.

With the warm daytime temperatures, we found the conditions perfect for making snowballs. I would make a snowball and hand it to Kellisa. She would giggle as soon as she gripped the snowball. She didn't hesitate to throw them at me while her giggles turned to full-blown laughter echoing through the valley. I would gently throw small snowballs back at her, which she found equally hilarious. Kellisa could have spent all afternoon engaged in our snowball fight, but I was ready to continue down the trail after five minutes.

Some sections of the path were narrow with the wet meadows on one side and rising terrain on the other, but it was always wide enough to keep the wheels on the trail. We exited the forest area and found ourselves surrounded by the meadows. A raised boardwalk helped to keep my feet dry, but it was a little icy. Not wanting to slip, I proceeded while slowly pushing Kellisa. The views were far and wide from the boardwalk, and once I found solid footing, we paused to admire the view and take a few photographs in all directions. Dramatic snow-covered peaks rose in the distance beyond the meadows and towering pine forests. We even had a small view of Lake Tahoe in the distance.

The wind seemed to pick up now that we were in an exposed low-lying area. After our impromptu snowball fight, we were slightly chilled, so we didn't stay too long on the boardwalk. After one more short bridge, we were back at the intersection where a left turn would lead us the short distance back to our SUV. I was satisfied with our pushike and was tempted to complete another loop, but Kellisa had school the following morning. We still had a two-hour drive home and needed to pick up dinner along the way, so I decided to end our afternoon adventure with one completed loop.

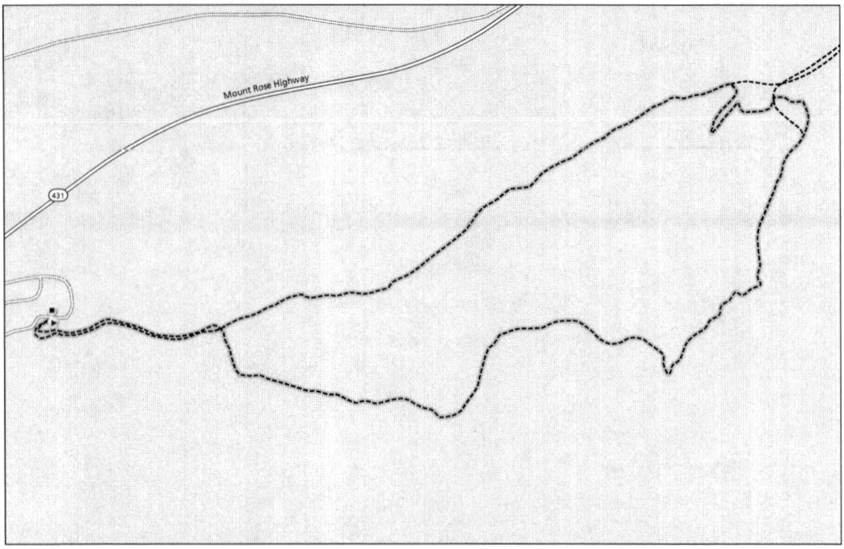

Tahoe Meadows Interpretive Loop, Incline Villiage, NV

32
New Hampshire

Trail name: Sewalls Falls
Location: Sewalls Falls Recreation Area
Distance: 1.6 mi
Duration (active): 49m
Average speed: 2.0 mi/h
Total ascent: 52 ft
Highest point: 286 ft
Difficulty: Moderate

I found a couple of promising trails in the far northern part of New Hampshire deep in the Northwoods with an excellent chance to observe moose. When I started figuring out the travel logistics, I realized how far off the beaten path these trails would be, and while not a deal breaker, it was a concern. I wanted to have a backup plan in case the trails were flooded or too rocky for a pushike. The mighty Presidential Range of the White Mountains separates the northern from the southern part of New Hampshire. I knew from a previous trip and my research that it would be tough to find a suitable trail in the mountainous terrain. The next closest trails would be a considerable drive, so I focused my attention on the area south of the major mountains to find a pushiking trail. The Sewalls Falls Trail in Concord grabbed my attention for two reasons. First, the promise of a waterfall was unique. Second, the Sewalls Falls Trail would count as an urban trail. Concord is the capital of New Hampshire even though it isn't a significant population center, with just under 150,000 residents in the metro area.

The parking lot was large, paved, and had bathrooms big enough for flush toilets and sinks (I didn't verify). All of this would be unusual for our typical trail out in the middle of nowhere, but not surprising considering the park's location in an idyllic residential area along the Merrimack River. I parked in a disabled spot directly in front of the trailhead. I could also see a lot of people walking around, many out for a walk with their dogs.

The combination of a fast-flowing river and towering pine forest made me forget how close we were to civilization as we started down the trail. We often find pine forests great for pushiking because the floor is often free of obstacles and brush. The Sewalls Falls Trail didn't disappoint, with a beautiful bed of pine needles covering our path. The trail generally followed the river upstream but had enough twists and turns to keep it interesting. We noticed many joggers enjoying the trail along with the dog walkers. Kellisa enjoyed seeing the dogs, and many of the owners approached so she could get a closer look and a few wet kisses, which made her giggle. This socializing slowed us down a little, but it was all good since Kellisa was having a great time.

We came to a small overlook area at the edge of the river, and I could see a small set of rapids. I wasn't sure if these rapids were Sewalls Falls. This vantage point gave us the best views of a dense forest hillside on the other side of the river covered in fall foliage. A man with his dog approached as I took pictures of the views. While his dog gave Kellisa some attention, I asked, "Is this Sewalls Falls?"

His answer surprised me because he told me it wasn't, and there wasn't a Sewalls Falls. I was curious, and he explained that a dam across the river created a waterfall, but the dam had been removed. So far, the trail and river were gorgeous, but it was a little disappointing to learn we wouldn't see a waterfall. I thanked the man before pushing Kellisa deeper into the forest.

There was a short break in the forest where several power lines passed through, went over the river, and continued up the hill on the other side. I was glad to quickly pass under the power lines and enter the forest on the other side. The trail started to have some roots to push over, which made Kellisa happy. The path crossed over a wooden bridge above a small creek. A lady passed us just after we crossed, and she told us the river area was a prime habitat for Atlantic salmon, raccoons, minks, and otters. I thanked her for the information before pushing Kellisa up a short, but steep section. Once on top, the trail became difficult to follow as most of the ground was open under the trees. It looked like the area saw fewer people, probably because it was so deep in the woods and required a short climb.

The Merrimack River was always close on our left side, so I was never concerned about getting too far off the trail and wasn't at all worried about getting lost. Now that we were at a higher vantage point, I knew we wouldn't see a waterfall.

It was Sir Isaac Newton who said, "What goes up must come down" due to gravity, and this would be true for our trail. To continue following the path, we needed to navigate a steep descent. While the trail wasn't muddy, it was slightly damp. I took a step back to study the trail and consider our options. I wasn't too thrilled with the idea of attempting this downhill portion due to a risk of slipping, and it was so steep that a fall would likely lead to a tumble. Even with Kellisa tethered to my body, it just seemed a little too dangerous. I decided to make this the turnaround point after I looked around for safer descent routes but didn't find any.

We still had a descent on our return, but it wasn't as steep or slippery. Once back on the lower ground and past the power lines, we started to see dog walkers again much to Kellisa's delight. All the playtime with the dogs made for a slow pushike, but it was worth it since Kellisa made at least a dozen new friends along the way.

Over the years, we've had several scary encounters with dogs out on a trail, and they've always been off leash where dogs weren't allowed or were only allowed on a leash. Due to these close encounters, I usually don't get too excited to see a dog out on a trail, but every single dog we encountered on this trail was on a leash and well behaved. Dogs in the wild still make me a little nervous, but I was glad to see Kellisa have such a great time in their company.

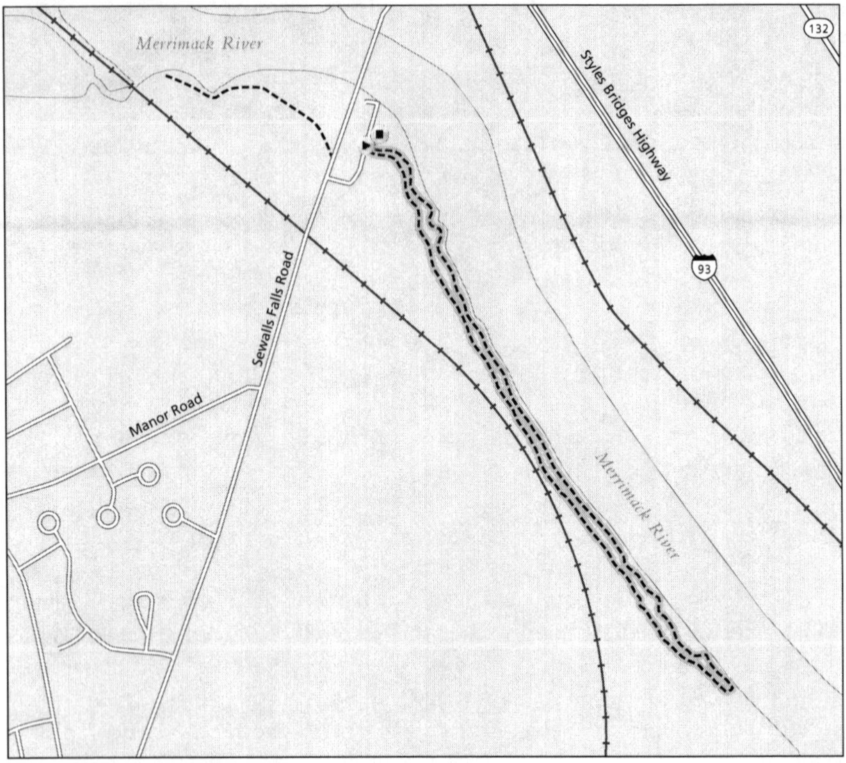

Sewalls Falls Trail, Concord, NH

33
New Jersey

Trail name: Grassland
Location: Supawna Meadows National Wildlife Refuge
Distance: 1.4 mi
Duration (active): 35m
Average speed: 2.4 mi/h
Total ascent: 16 ft
Highest point: 18 ft
Difficulty: Easy

Kellisa and I had unfinished business in New Jersey. I have a hard time getting past trails we don't complete for reasons beyond my control. For instance, if we turn around on a trail I'm enjoying because of rain, I will always want to return someday to complete the trail. Back in July 2015, when I was in New Jersey push-iking with Kellisa and Egypt, we visited Supawna Meadows National Wildlife Refuge. I planned to pushike both trails in the park. We completed the Grassland Trail but couldn't even find the trailhead for the Forest Habitat Trail. The map for the refuge doesn't show the trail connecting to a road or parking lot. It just starts in the middle of the sanctuary. The refuge does not have a visitor center, and we were the only ones there, so we didn't have anyone to ask for directions.

More than four years passed, and I was still thinking about the Forest Habitat Trail and selected it for inclusion in this book. I did my advance research, and we left with what I felt like were the right directions to the trailhead. Without any signs, it was still tricky to find, and we drove right by the turnoff several times. The road to the trailhead looks more like a driveway, and I was initially hesitant to turn down a stranger's private drive, but it turned out to lead to several homes and tucked a short distance back from the road was a small parking area.

We could see a gate blocking most of the trail, but I could tell there was enough room to get around. A short distance down the path, a large tree was down across the entire trail. Beyond that, from what I could see, the trail looked wide and free from other obstacles. Since I'd been thinking about this trail for so long, I decided to give it a try. I pushed Kellisa around the gate with ease, but going over the fallen tree wasn't an option. Going around was our only option, and that wasn't appealing since we would have to push through the considerable brush. I was worried about insects, especially ticks. We probably should have turned around, but I loaded us up with a strong insect repellant and went around the tree. I was careful pushing Kellisa. I didn't want her to get any scratches, and I didn't want any branches snapping back from the mobility chair and hitting me.

Once around the obstacle, we continued deeper into the forest. I had a feeling no one had been on this trail for a very long time. The path was heading in almost a straight line with little or no elevation changes. I noticed the trail started getting narrower the deeper we went in the woods. The trees and shrubs were left to grow wild and were stretching out to the trail. I was again careful to avoid scratches.

We came to a second tree across the trail, blocking forward progress. The dense forest overlapped the edges of the path. The only way forward was going over the tree. I was determined to pushike this trail, so I carefully lifted Kellisa up and over the tree. I scouted the ground where I set her mobility chair down beforehand to make sure it was safe and free from snakes. I followed Kellisa over the tree before continuing down the Forest Habitat Trail.

The forest started closing in, and the trail was barely wide enough for Kellisa's mobility chair. I continued hoping our path would eventually open a little, but it soon came to a point where it was difficult to tell if we were even on a trail. I stopped to look around to assess our situation. Looking forward and to both of our sides, I couldn't make out a trail. I had been following the path of least resistance from the forest, and now the trail was gone. I looked behind us and could see where the trail last resembled a real trail.

I slowly and carefully backed us out of our entanglement with the overgrown forest until I could turn Kellisa around back on the trail. I looked around again to see if maybe I missed a turn, but all I could see was a dense forest with no option other than backtracking to our rental SUV. I wasn't looking forward to dealing with the two trees blocking our route. I ended up lifting Kellisa in her mobility chair up and over both trees on our return pushike.

I felt defeated once back at the SUV since we didn't complete the trail, and I felt like I couldn't include the almost mile we did complete in this book as our New Jersey trail. In the end, we did pushike nine-tenths of a mile and gained seven feet on the Forest Habitat Trail. Since we pushiked the Grassland Trail back in 2015 and enjoyed it, that was our backup trail for New Jersey, and it was conveniently located just a short drive from where we were parked.

Less than five minutes later, we were at the parking area for the Grassland Trail. Fond memories of my first visit with both girls came flooding back. I felt a little sad that Egypt wasn't joining us on our second adventure to pushike a trail in all fifty states for this book. I had to remind myself that Egypt was content doing it once and was happy to be home with mom, where she could continue her singing, dancing, acting, and art class extracurricular activities.

Before pushiking the main Grassland Trail, we started with the short spur trail through a forest to an observation platform at the edge of a marsh. Back in 2015, we found the view to be spectacular as we looked out over the expansive marsh swaying in harmony to the rhythms of a summer breeze. Visiting in October this time, we found the platform completely gone. It wouldn't have mattered because the wall of marsh grasses facing us was so high that it was all we could see.

We returned the way we came and passed our SUV before starting on the main lollipop trail. I pushed Kellisa through a small upland forest before coming to a small historical cemetery protected by a fence. The trail turned right down a rough road before turning back into the forest a short distance later. After another short distance, the path emerged where the forest met the grasslands. The trail remained wide as it followed the edge of the forest with the grasslands spreading out in front and to our right.

We had a decision to make. We could follow the perimeter around the grasslands or take a shorter loop through the interior. It was getting late in the afternoon, so I selected the shorter loop. Back in 2015 with Egypt, we took the longer route, and I thought it would be cool to experience the trail in the middle of the grasslands for our second visit to add a little variety.

I think we made the right decision. Being surrounded by swaying grasses taller than Kellisa in her mobility chair was a unique experience. The muted colors of autumn were in full effect, adding to the trail's ambiance. The sun was hiding behind a layer of clouds adding to our picturesque setting. If there were a bench in this area, I would have been tempted to sit down and take it all in for a prolonged period. Instead, we continued to finish our loop after I took some pictures to try to capture the moment.

I forgot my frustrations from our struggles to find to pushike the Forest Habitat Trail by the time the loop ended at the road trail leading back through the forest and past the cemetery before reaching our SUV.

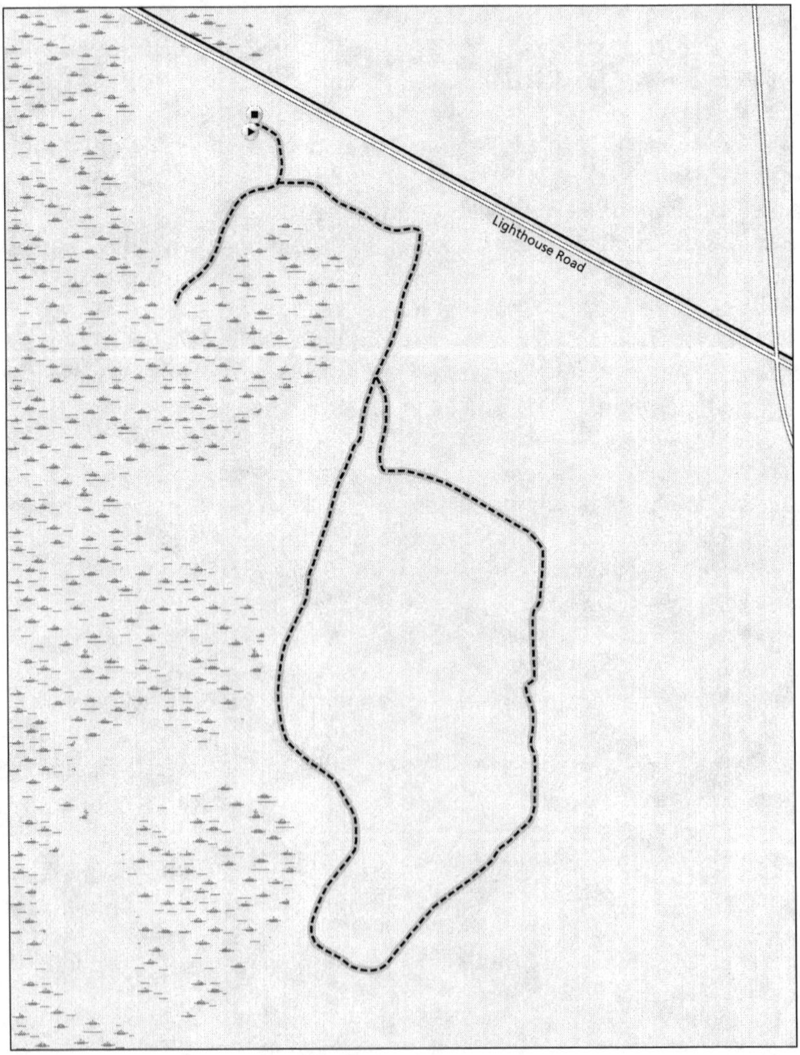

Grassland Trail, Pennsville, NJ

34
New Mexico

Trail name: Canyon Rim
Location: Los Alamos
Distance: 5.0 mi
Duration (active): 1h 54m
Average speed: 2.6 mi/h
Total ascent: 325 ft
Highest point: 7,287 ft
Difficulty: Moderate

I've taken Kellisa to White Sands National Monument in southern New Mexico several times over the years, and it's one of our favorite places to pushike because it has a surprising variety of options. There's a short, fully accessible boardwalk trail, and sand covers the park road, so while you are technically on a paved road, there's an inch or two of compacted sand below your feet and wheels, which makes it seem more like a natural trail. The sand of the dunes is unusually smooth to pushike. The wheels don't seem to sink as much as they do on ocean beach sand, making pushing up and over towering dunes possible. As an added thrill, you can bring your plastic snow sled or rent one from the visitor center to go sledding down the sandhills. Sledding on the sand is a favorite pastime for Kellisa because it's an adventure, and I think she enjoys getting out of her mobility chair now and then. I also like to pull Kellisa across the sand while she's on a sled. Sometimes she falls off, and we both find it equally hilarious.

I was looking forward to taking Kellisa to White Sands National Monument for the New Mexico chapter because it had been several years since our last visit. But I wanted to do my due diligence and at least research other trails in the state.

While looking for trails, I stumbled upon the Canyon Rim Trail in Los Alamos. It was paved but ran along the rim of a canyon. I looked at a few pictures and felt an attraction. I wanted to push Kellisa on this trail. I read how the path had two trailheads: one was across the street from a major chain hotel, and the other was in the parking lot of a large grocery store and famous coffee shop.

As I drove through Los Alamos, we passed the first trailhead across from the hotel, but I wanted to drive to the second trailhead to scout it out. We found the grocery store, and sure enough, the other end of the trail started from the parking lot. I was able to park directly in the space in front of the path, so I decided we would start from this direction.

As soon as I got out of our rental SUV, I was surprised at how windy it was outside. I had to tighten the strap from my hat below my chin to prevent it from blowing away. It was also a little colder than I was expecting, so I unpacked Kellisa's fleece jacket for her. I carried Kellisa to her mobility chair, grabbed my pack, and locked the car before pointing us in the direction of the trail. There was a short and steep section on a small connector trail. The Canyon Rim Trail ran next to the large grocery store building, and the canyon was just off on the other side. There was a fence preventing hikers from venturing too close to the edge. The views, in the beginning, were a little disappointing. While they stretch to distant snowcapped mountains, we could see industrial buildings directly on the other side of the canyon.

Once past the grocery store, the paved trail turned away from the canyon. It started to head to what looked like the main road through this part of Los Alamos. Instead of making the turn, we had a choice to proceed straight on a rugged dirt road, which continued along the rim. I paused for a few minutes as I was thoroughly confused, and we were only minutes into our pushike. I was sure the entire trail was paved, but I was equally confident the trail followed the rim of the canyon for its whole length. From where we stopped, both couldn't be accurate.

While we paused, I hoped a walker or jogger would pass by our position so I could ask for information, but no one appeared. I decided to take the dirt path in front of us and see where it led. Yes, it followed the rim, but it also had a feeling of being across private property despite the lack of fences and signs warning as such. I continued forward while looking around. There was heavy equipment parked and large piles of earth debris. I wasn't sure if we were in an excavating company's yard or on the trail. After a couple of minutes, the dirt road curved away from the canyon. Again, I paused to assess our situation. We were still all alone, and I was growing more confident we should have stayed on the pavement. The dirt road seemed to circle back toward the paved trail, so we continued to follow it, and after another few minutes, we were back on the pavement.

Knowing the dirt road wasn't the correct route, we followed the paved trail toward the main road, but first we crossed a street leading into an industrial park. I knew we had to be on the Canyon Rim Trail, but so far, it was nothing like I was expecting.

Instead of reaching the main road, the trail curved to skirt the edge of another canyon. This one was narrow and deep. It was filled with pine trees and reminded me of our pushike in Coquihalla Canyon Provincial Park in British Columbia, Canada, back in 2013. A short distance later, the trail turned to cross the canyon by way of a bridge spanning to the other side. Once across the bridge, there were apartment buildings on one side and more industrial buildings on the opposite canyon rim. Still a little confused and surprised, we continued and passed a large fire station.

Once past the fire station, the trail finally entered a real wilderness area. The canyon to our right opened, and we could see mountains towering in the distance with snow covering their upper slopes. To our left was a gentle-rising scrub area with a few trees scattered around adding some color and height. The trail also started to go uphill in this area and followed the sweeping curves of the canyon rim. Now fully immersed in the beauty of the nature around us, I forgot about my early disappointment on the Canyon Rim Trail.

We passed a couple of women out for their afternoon jogs; both said "Hello" as they went by, and Kellisa blew them kisses.

A few men were walking along the path dressed for business, so I guessed they were on their lunch hour. To our surprise, we started seeing patches of snow on the ground in the shaded areas. I knew we were at an elevation over 7,200 feet above sea level because I could feel it with every breath. But it was the middle of October, and I wasn't expecting to see snow. I had to pick some up to verify it wasn't white sand or rocks, and since it was cold, it was snow. I made a few snowballs for Kellisa, which she promptly threw in my direction, causing her to laugh at her actions.

The Canyon Rim Trail continued to twist and turn as it seemed to be getting deeper into a wilderness area. Some of the trip reports I read complained that road noise is a distraction. I could see taller vehicles as they passed by higher up on the hill to our left, but I could only hear the occasional motorcycle or loud truck. The wind was howling pretty good through the canyon and might have been drowning out some of the road noise.

As we went farther along the canyon, I was starting to notice the trail was changing in elevation more often. Nothing too steep or complicated, but at a higher elevation without acclimating, I could tell even the smallest change in my exertion levels from how I was breathing. I checked on Kellisa, and she seemed to be doing fine without any apparent adverse effects from the altitude.

The views continued to be far-reaching and outstanding, except for a few industrial buildings and towers in our view. The canyon continued to get broader and more impressive. We crossed a second bridge as it passed a side canyon off the main canyon. We stopped to take in the views and snap a few pictures. It was extra windy at this spot, and Kellisa was enjoying it whipping into her face.

Just past the bridge, we passed a mother and her daughter out for an afternoon walk. The little girl had an ice cream cone in her hand, which reminded me how close we were to civilization. Next, we passed another man out for a walk while on a break from work and then an elderly lady who seemed to be struggling from exertion. I asked if she was alright, and she assured us she was, so we continued on our way and reached the trailhead across from the hotel.

Unlike the grocery store parking lot, this trailhead had a bathroom and kiosk loaded with trail information. There was a large sign warning hikers they were in mountain lion country and what to do if you encounter one while out on the trail. I knew we were in prime mountain lion habitat, but the reminder helped to bring it to the forefront of my brain so that I would be on more alert for our return on the out-and-back trail.

After I read the sign, I turned Kellisa around for our return pushike. The trail seemed to go uphill in both directions. It's funny how that appears to happen; maybe because every inch of incline is more noticeable when you are pushing another person in a jog stroller or mobility chair against gravity. It didn't take long before we caught up to the elderly lady. I felt tempted to ask again if she was alright, but at the same time, I didn't want to insult her.

I'm not sure if she sensed us or heard us approaching from behind, but she turned around and acknowledged us with a smile. I believed she was in control and knew her capabilities.

It didn't take long to see the mother and daughter returning to their trailhead. The mom stopped to chat because she thought we were traversing the trail a second time and wanted to tell us how impressed she was with us. I explained how we parked at the grocery store, and she became less impressed with our accomplishments, but she did tell us we were doing better than they were since they had to turn around after only going a half-mile. I wished them well before pushiking Kellisa back toward our endpoint, which was still a couple of miles away.

There was quite a bit of bird activity on our return. I wasn't sure if the birds arrived in the last half hour or if they were there when we passed by the first time since I didn't remember seeing any birds. Either way, Kellisa and I enjoyed watching them fly from bush to bush while chirping at each other. They didn't seem to mind us passing through their backyards.

As we were nearing the fire station, we saw a young lady who gave us quite the scare. She was still a few curves ahead of us on the trail, and I could see she was looking down while holding her hand out. I thought she was looking at a handheld device. She was wearing dark sunglasses so that I couldn't see her eyes, but it seemed like she wasn't paying attention to the trail. She continued to look down. When she was just one curve ahead of us, I started to move to the far side of the path to allow extra room for her to pass. I was worried about her walking into Kellisa and falling, but before that could happen, she took a step off the pavement. It was clear she wasn't intending to step down and off the pavement, as evidenced by her tumbling forward. She did a little dance, which prevented her from falling and quickly returned to the pavement. As we passed, I was going to ask if she was OK, but her face was still looking at her phone, and I'm not sure she even saw us standing a couple of feet away.

Where she went off the pavement wasn't near the edge of the canyon, but she would have landed on rocks if she hadn't kept her balance. It would have been a hard landing, and, at the very least, would have left some bruises. There were other sections of the Canyon Rim Trail where a fall could have been a lot worse.

Because I've been in the disabled world since Kellisa was born, I loved seeing the next person we encountered out on the Canyon Rim Trail. He was a young man out for a walk with his mother. It wasn't obvious, but he had subtle signs of having cerebral palsy and maybe developmental delays. He was walking on his own and looked great. It was clear that he was on a mission and didn't stop as he passed us. I just exchanged smiles with the mother, so I can't be positive he was disabled. In the end, it doesn't matter. I was just excited to see him outside, enjoying the natural world.

We had the trail to ourselves for the last section, including the bridge over the narrow canyon and through the industrial area leading back to the grocery store parking lot. I wanted to run into the coffee shop to get a fresh cup, but I was a little extra sore after pushiking Kellisa on five miles of pavement. Although I prefer natural surfaces, the Canyon Rim Trail is by far one of the best-paved trails we've ever experienced, even with the confusing and unappealing section through an industrial area.

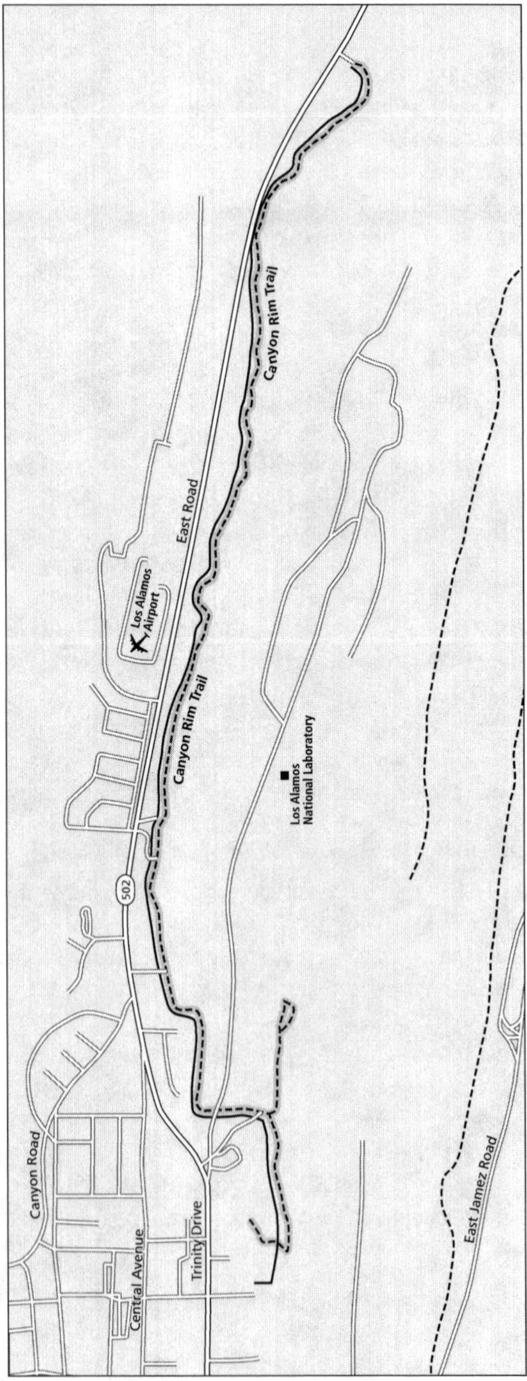

Canyon Rim Trail, Los Alamos, NM

35
New York

Trail name: Bloomington Bog
Location: Saranac Lakes Wild Forest
Distance: 2.5 mi
Duration (active): 1h 8m
Average speed: 2.2 mi/h
Total ascent: 79 ft
Highest point: 1,709 ft
Difficulty: Moderate

The Adirondacks have held a place in my imagination since I was a child. I would look at a map of the United States and see a large green circle covering most of northern New York designating Adirondack Park. I took Lisa to the Adirondacks on our first-ever weeklong vacation. Many times, reality doesn't live up to dreams, but the Adirondacks were everything I expected and more. I was impressed with the high peaks, waterfalls, lakes, and the endless forests of the region. At the center of the park is Lake Placid, home to the 1932 and 1980 Winter Olympics. Besides hiking many trails on our vacation, Lisa and I walked out on the ice in the rink where the United States won the 1980 men's hockey gold medal.

Kellisa and I attended a conference in Lake Placid in 2013, and we added a few adventures in between seminars. One of them was pushiking on the excellent Bloomington Bog Trail. The out-and-back trail follows an abandoned railroad corridor. On the early autumn day of our pushike, the trail was flooded from a nearby beaver dam, causing the bog to overflow from its edges. I pushed Kellisa through some of the ankle-deep water, but we had to stop short of pushiking the entire trail so I could clean up before returning to the conference.

I knew I wanted a trail in the Adirondacks for this book and knew the Bloomington Bog Trail would be an obvious and safe selection, but I thought we should try a new trail. I was concerned because I remember all the trails Lisa and I hiked were very rocky. Even though we vacationed there before Kellisa was born, I knew we wouldn't be able to use any of the same trails. In my research, all I found were trail descriptions and pictures of rocky terrain. I was having a difficult time finding an alternative trail when I saw a trail that sounded promising.

The Spectacle Pond Trail is three miles long while gaining 314 feet along its course. I immediately thought of rocks with that kind of elevation gain, but I couldn't find any mention of rocks in the few trip reports I read, and I didn't see any pictures that would prevent us from trying. I knew if it didn't work out, we could always fall back on the Bloomington Bog Trail.

There were a few cars in the parking lot when we arrived. I decided to check out the beginning of the trail before unloading the mobility chair and Kellisa so I didn't waste time and effort lifting if I didn't think we could even start the Spectacle Pond Trail. I could only see the first fifty yards or so, and the path looked perfect, wide, flat, and, most important, I didn't see any large rocks forming an impenetrable barrier for us.

I start pushing Kellisa up the trail with confidence, but as soon as we turned around the first bend, the path started to become rocky. Not too bad, but still a little concerning. We started gaining elevation while the trail became more and more covered with large rocks and tree roots. I found a few of the inclines to be a test of all my strength. We crossed a wooden bridge, which provided a brief reprise from the uphill battle I was fighting. The voice inside my head was telling me to turn around, but another voice was telling me, "Continue since we've made it this far, and maybe it will get easier."

The trail wasn't dangerous; it was just very hard navigating a route through and over the many boulders while going against gravity. I found myself lifting Kellisa and her mobility chair up and over too many boulders for my liking. I probably would have turned around if the thought of descending wasn't as daunting as continuing to Spectacle Pond.

After crossing a second bridge, the trail went up a series of rocks that formed a stairway-like passage on the side of a hill with Shanty Bottom Brook cascading below, providing a comforting soundtrack for our slow progress. Once at the top of this section, I stopped for a breather while surveying the trail ahead. It was at this point I knew we were defeated. I couldn't see any sign of Spectacle Pond, and the path looked like a narrow boulder field spread out in front of our perch. Going down wasn't much easier or faster despite now having gravity on our side.

For the entire descent, I was trying to talk myself into accepting that this pushike was enough of a success to publish. I knew it was borderline, and I didn't like the idea that we didn't make it to the end of the trail to see Spectacle Pond. That we worked hard and this trail would be one of the more difficult that I would write about were arguments for its inclusion. I know we had a backup trail nearby, but I was tired and worn-out after covering an ascent and descent of 164 feet in just 1.2 miles. But was that enough for a chapter?

As I was driving away, I was still undecided when we passed another trailhead with an almost full parking lot. It was the Gull Pond Trail. I didn't research this trail and didn't have cell service to look anything up, so I decided to check it out. The trailhead was lacking an informative kiosk, but the sign by the road indicated the Gull Pond Trail was just over a half-mile in length. Again, I scouted the beginning, and it looked promising.

Like the Spectacle Pond Trail, our path quickly turned to rocks and boulders once we made our way around the first bend. I proceeded a little farther, but the trail turned into another rock scramble. I turned around after just one-fifth of a mile and an elevation gain of only 26 feet.

I wasn't satisfied with either trail and was kicking myself for using so much energy on trails I should have known were filled with rock barriers. My tired self was telling me that I should have just started with the known Bloomington Bog Trail.

Our drive through the High Peaks region to the Bloomington Bog Trail was one of the most spectacular experiences of my life. The northern forest was ablaze in its full spectrum of autumn colors. Coming from dry California, I was not expecting the many vibrant shades of orange, red, and yellow covering the mountainsides. Despite being in a hurry to reach the Bloomington Bog Trail, I couldn't help but take my time to enjoy our immediate surroundings.

I remembered having a hard time finding the Bloomington Bog trailhead on our first visit because it's just off New York Route 86 on what looks like a long private driveway through the forest without any signs. Once you find the right road, the trailhead and small parking lot are tucked in the trees not far from the busy highway. I remembered the turnoff and didn't drive past it this time. I knew I didn't have to scout the beginning of the trail before loading Kellisa in her mobility chair and grabbing our gear.

The Bloomington Bog Trail passes through a dense forest before reaching the abandoned railroad bed. All the rails and ties have been removed, leaving the trail a perfect combination of gravel and dirt for flat pushing. Once on the old corridor, the path is a straight line through many different environments. We passed a lake on our left with large boulders and cliffs on the opposite shore set below a hillside covered in the colors of fall. I knew from reading trip reports that this was a prime location for spotting bald eagles. Kellisa and I paused with the hope of observing one, but we didn't see any.

The trail enters a forest area with a dense canopy where I reminded myself to make some noise with Kellisa since we were in black bear country. After exiting the tunnel of trees, Bloomington Bog appeared with mountains rising over it on the far side. This area is where the trail flooded in 2013. And perspective is everything when I was glad to find the trail just muddy instead of covered in six to eight inches of water. I was able to push Kellisa through the mud without too much trouble. I did slip and slide a little while gaining my traction. Kellisa thought this was hilarious, and I thanked her for being our natural bear deterrent.

Once past the long, muddy section, we entered another dark forest area filled with the familiar scent of pine. The trail was in perfect condition, so I took my time pushing Kellisa so I could savor one of my favorite scents. As we were nearing the exit of the pine forest, I could see the trail was flooded a short distance ahead of us. I pushed Kellisa up to the water, now blocking our forward progress, to think about our next move.

I wanted to pushike the entire out-and-back trail, but not if it meant a long slog through cold water. It wasn't deep enough to get Kellisa wet, so I decided I was willing to give it a try. Back in 2013, when I pushed Kellisa through the water, the hard surface below was gravel, and I was hoping to find the same this time. As soon as I pushed Kellisa into the mud, I felt her mobility chair sink. I knew she was in the mud, but still hoped it would only be for a short distance.

It wasn't long before I started sinking to my ankles, which required a great deal of effort to break the natural suction made by the mud each time I went to lift a leg. I was afraid I was going to lose a hiking boot in this battle. Kellisa was doing a great job of keeping the bears away with her now uncontrolled laughter when I decided it was time to turn around. It wasn't easy as we sunk deeper in the mud, but we eventually made it the short distance back to drier land. I knew we had pushiked enough of the Bloomington Bog Trail to include in our book, which made the idea of returning to the trailhead that much easier.

I was trying to clean some of the mud off my boots and Kellisa's wheels when I noticed something running through the forest toward us on the trail. I had a difficult time focusing since we were in the sun, and whatever was running was covered in shadows created by the forest canopy. It looked too large to be a dog, plus I didn't see an owner. As it got closer, it looked more like a black bear.

Usually, bears tend to shy away from people and run away, so this wasn't fitting my understanding of a bear encounter on a trail. I was thinking through the options in my head. Then I noticed it looked like a person was running alongside the bear. As they emerged from the darkness, I could see a young woman out jogging with a bear.

A minute later, they slowed down as they approached us. I probably still had a look of sincere concern on my face when the woman smiled, said "Hello" to us, and asked if we thought her dog was a bear.

I answered, "Actually, I did think it was a bear."

The jogger apologized and said that most people make that mistake. Even up close, this dog still looked like a bear. I asked what kind of dog, and she said, "He's a Newfoundland male who weighs 180 pounds."

With that, they continued down the trail through the water and mud like it was nothing while Kellisa and I headed back to our trailhead. We didn't encounter any more animals and look forward to a day when we can return to the Bloomington Bog Trail and pushike its entire length without having to go through a beaver-created flood!

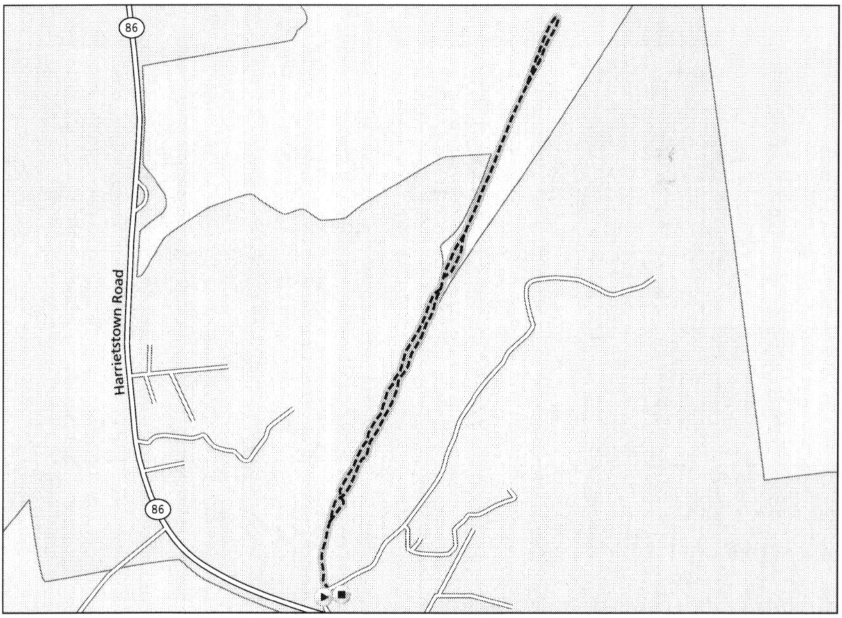

Bloomington Bog Trail, Saranac Lake, NY

36

North Carolina

Trail name: Max Patch	**Average speed:** 1.4 mi/h
Location: Pisgah National Forest	**Total ascent:** 318 ft
Distance: 1.7 mi	**Highest point:** 4,640 ft
Duration (active): 1h 16m	**Difficulty:** Challenging

Kellisa has attended several presentations given by Jennifer Pharr Davis over the years. In case you don't know, Jennifer is arguably the most famous long-distance hiker in the world with several speed records on her hiking resume along with a National Geographic Adventurer of the Year award to her credit. After getting to know each other a little better, Jennifer included Kellisa in one of her books. She suggested joining us on a pushike to the summit of Max Patch in North Carolina. We planned an overnight backpacking trip with Jennifer and her young son. We purchased our airline tickets and were packed and ready to go in October 2018 when Tropical Storm Michael decided to disrupt our plans. The storm promised to dump record amounts of rain and damaging wind to the Max Patch area. Even though the storm would be gone when we arrived, we reluctantly canceled the trip. We knew the trail would not have time to dry out before our trip, and there was a possibility of trees being down blocking our path.

Max Patch is a bald mountain found deep in the Pisgah National Forest. The trailhead is about ninety minutes from Asheville in western North Carolina. On the summit of Max Patch, hikers have a 360-degree views of distant mountain ranges from the Smoky Mountains to Mount Mitchell, the highest peak east of the Rocky Mountains. Jennifer knew we could make the summit, and that was all the confidence I needed to schedule our attempt in June 2019. I knew from the pictures online that this would be an epic pushike.

Unfortunately, Jennifer couldn't join us, so we planned to do the short hike as a day trip instead of a backpacking adventure. Kellisa loved driving on the bumpy gravel road as it traveled around the mountainside in a dense forest before we arrived at a clearing where the parking lot at the trailhead was located, just below the summit of Max Patch. I was worried at the sight of parked cars lining both sides of the road in both directions from the small lot. It's hard enough pushing Kellisa on a trail, and I wasn't looking to add distance to our pushike by adding a gravel road walk to get to the trailhead. I decided to check out the parking area, hoping to find a spot. It was packed with cars, but just as I was ready to give up and find a place down the road, I noticed an older couple leaving the trail and walking toward their car. I was hoping they were leaving and wouldn't be picnicking at their vehicle for an extended amount of time. I hung around watching them and was excited to see them go, which opened a spot for us.

It didn't take long to get Kellisa in her chair and my backpack on. While I was looking for a parking spot, I missed seeing the gate blocking the trail from the parking lot and the wooden steps up to the trailhead kiosk. Sadly, this isn't a rare occurrence. We often find obstacles blocking our path at trailheads. I've been told it's to prevent ATVs from riding on the trails, but it also prevents hikers like us from quickly accessing the trails. Since the trail isn't ADA, it doesn't have to be a certain width, and we must figure out a way past the barrier.

Fortunately, I'm able to maneuver Kellisa under most gates. On a few occasions, I set Kellisa on the ground before I lift her mobility chair over the gate. I return and then carry Kellisa to her mobility chair. I'm thankful I have this ability so we don't have to turn back, but I suspect these barriers prevent some from accessing trails they could otherwise enjoy. For Max Patch, I was able to tilt Kellisa back and push her under while she giggled. I left her at the bottom of the stairs while I conducted some last-minute research at the informative but not-at-all-accessible kiosk. I knew from my planning that the loop trail was easier to ascend if we started going clockwise. Nothing at the kiosk changed my mind, so after a minute, we started climbing Max Patch.

We found the trail steep and rocky, but it was wide enough that I could push around the largest rocks. The views were outstanding right from the beginning. There was a steady breeze that kept us comfortable on our climb. Our view became limited as we entered a dark forest area. We quickly encountered several root systems, yet nothing significant enough to slow us down. It wasn't long before we exited the forest and found ourselves just below the summit in a grassy area. We could see several campsites with hikers off on short side trails setting up, and I wished we had our backpacking gear so we could spend the night in this paradise.

The trail was in excellent condition as it continued toward the actual summit. Pushing more than a hundred pounds made it feel like I was pushing Kellisa straight up the path for a short, steep pitch before the ground leveled out, and we were on the summit. I could see a family at the summit marker posing for pictures. I took a few sips of water while waiting for our turn for photos.

I snapped a few pictures of our feet at the top with the marker before moving back a few feet to focus on just Kellisa on top of the world at 4,629 feet above sea level. Kellisa's face was smiling. There was a steady flow of people arriving, so I didn't want to occupy the prime spot for long. I pushed Kellisa along as we started to explore the vast grassy area of this bald mountain.

The views were breathtaking in every direction. It was mountain range after mountain range with colors varying from greens to blues, all under a picture-perfect blue sky with puffy white clouds. Despite the many people on top, we never felt crowded and always had an area to ourselves. I did approach a family to ask if they could take a few pictures of me with Kellisa. The mom agreed, and afterward, I returned the favor for her family.

I had a decision to make: continue the loop or go back the way we came? I had been thinking about this long before we arrived at the summit. I knew going back was the easiest choice because finishing the loop would include some steep and narrow descents. The weather was perfect, and we had plenty of time. I decided to continue our loop with the thought that we could turn around at any point if I felt uncomfortable proceeding.

We enjoyed new views as we headed down the other side of the mountain. The trail stayed above the tree line, and we could see the parking lot far below. After a few turns, I was surprised by what I saw just in front of us. The trail dropped almost straight down a set of stairs carved into the mountainside. The stairs curved around a bend and disappeared. I locked the wheels on Kellisa's chair before leaving her to descend several stairs to recon the situation. I also turned her chair sideways, so even if it rolled a little, it wouldn't go down the stairs.

I was facing a difficult decision. Turning back was a real option. The stairs were wide with deep enough landings that I knew I could safely proceed with Kellisa, but since I didn't read a single mention of stairs or see a picture with these stairs in the many trip reports I read in advance, it was impossible to know if this set of stairs was the crux of the loop. I knew Kellisa would love going down the stairs, and I also knew I would always wonder if we turned back. I decided we would continue with a descent of the stairs. I was right, Kellisa giggled as she bounced down each step. Even though I was tethered to her chair, I always kept a firm grip on it with both hands and paused on every level to carefully plan our next move.

Once we were at the bottom of the stairs, I was hoping we were done with the hard parts because I did not want to have to push Kellisa up the stairs in retreat. It was possible but would have been a backbreaker since I go backward, pulling Kellisa up one stair at a time!

The trail continued its downward march, and before long, we entered another forested area. Just as I thought we were in the clear of all obstacles, we came to another small set of stairs. This time it was only five stairs, and they were not too steep. The trail turned back toward the parking lot as we exited the forest. A few minutes later, we were back at the trailhead, feeling proud of our accomplishment.

I was glad we completed the loop, but it elevated the difficulty of this pushike by a considerable amount. While possible, I would never want to complete this loop in a counterclockwise direction. I do wish we would have camped out near the summit, and I have a strong feeling we will be back with a heavily loaded backpack.

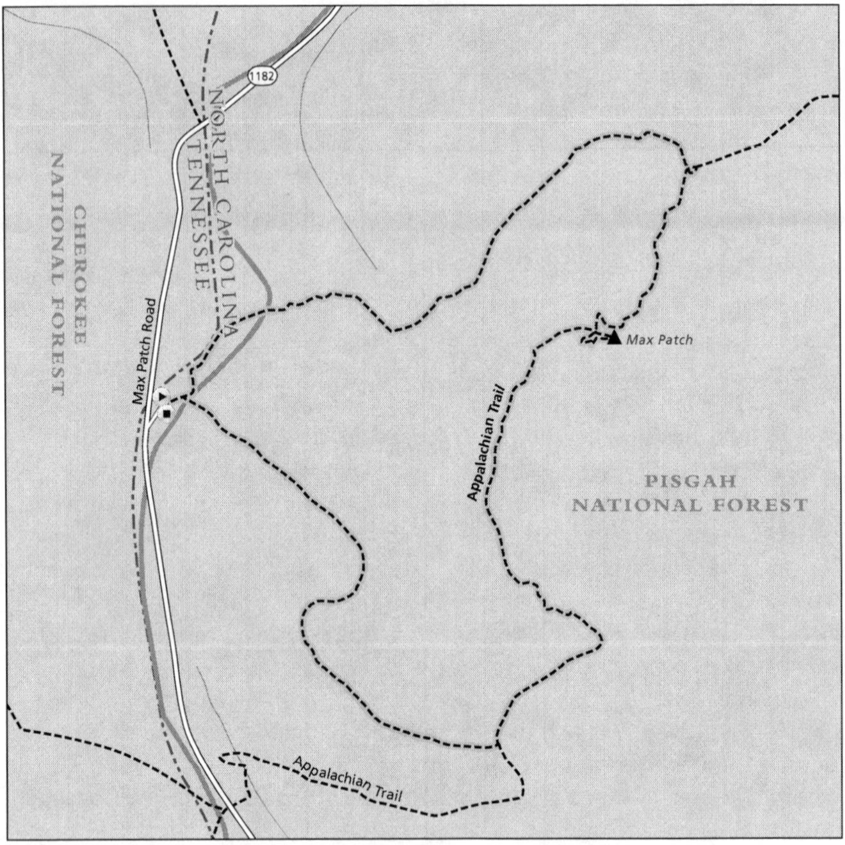

Max Patch Trail, Hot Springs, NC

37
North Dakota

Trail name: Prairie Dog Town
Location: Theodore Roosevelt National Park (North Unit)
Distance: 2.3 mi
Duration (active): 1h 34m
Average speed: 1.5 mi/h
Total ascent: 108 ft
Highest point: 2,108 ft
Difficulty: Challenging

Years ago, while researching trails, I stumbled upon a trip report from a father backpacking with his two sons on the 144-mile Maah Daah Hey Trail in western North Dakota. From what I read and saw in the accompanying pictures, I thought there was a chance Kellisa and I could pushike the entire trail. I consumed everything I could find about the trail and concluded that yes, it was possible for us if we had a foolproof plan and at least two weeks to complete the trail. Most of the path passes through one of the least-visited national parks in the United States and the only one named for one person: Theodore Roosevelt National Park. I've been a fan of Roosevelt ever since I read about his adventures on the River of Doubt in Brazil.

So far, the stars haven't aligned for an epic thru-hike of the Maah Daah Hey Trail, but Kellisa and I pushiked a portion of the trail back in the summer of 2015 with Egypt when we were on our first quest to visit and pushike in all fifty states by Kellisa's eighteenth birthday. We planned to camp the night before our pushike. While I was setting up our camp, Kellisa and Egypt were dancing. Kellisa was in her travel wheelchair. The girls were having a little too much fun, and Kellisa fell over sideways. Unable to brace herself, she landed on her forehead with a hard impact. Egypt started crying and yelling for help. I saw what happened, and it was just an accident. Most kids fall and scrape their knees when they are playing. Unfortunately, when Kellisa falls, she usually lands on her face.

I ran over, and Kellisa had a nervous look on her face. She was fighting back the tears and looking for reassurance. I started laughing and saying stuff like, "You crazy sisters having too much fun dancing around the campsite."

Egypt caught on to my ploy and joined in, and before long, I was picking small rocks out of Kellisa's skin while she started smiling and eventually giggling. Egypt grabbed a bottle of water and one of my clean T-shirts from the van so I could clean the wounds. I was a little startled by how bad her forehead looked and made the decision it would be better if we found a hotel for the night. We abandoned our camping plans. Once we found a hotel, I cleaned the scrapes and gave Kellisa some pain reliever to help her rest.

After everything settled down, Egypt started crying. She was overcome with guilt. I explained to her that Kellisa was fine, and it was just an accident. Egypt still felt terrible, but I told her that Kellisa would want to dance with her again. I didn't want Egypt to hold back because that would be denying Kellisa the opportunity to have fun with her sister. I asked if Egypt would want to deny Kellisa fun, and she answered, "No."

The following day we pushiked a short section of the Maah Daah Hey Trail, and I knew I wanted to return someday. Since pushiking the entire trail is beyond the scope of this book, I researched segments and nearby trails for our North Dakota pushike. I found the Prairie Dog Town Trail located inside Theodore Roosevelt National Park. It was a two-mile out-and-back section of the Buckhorn

Trail. As its name suggests, the path leads to the middle of an active prairie dog town. I knew Kellisa would love it.

It was sunny and hot on the afternoon of our visit in late June, but it wasn't brutal. The entire pushike would be under the direct sun without any trees, so I made sure we lathered up in sunscreen before starting. The beginning of the trail was wide and flat. It was perfect for pushiking, and I thought I found the perfect trail.

After maybe 100 yards, the trail made an abrupt right turn. I was quickly returned to reality. The path was narrow and a little overgrown, but not enough to stop us. We continued. The trail would drop down a little embankment before going back up a short distance later. Kellisa enjoyed all the bouncing around, and the path was just wide enough for her back wheels. My only real concern was to keep an eye out for rattlesnakes. I knew it would be easy to see them if they were sunning themselves across the trail, but I worried they might be lurking just off to the side of the trail. I had to push Kellisa at a slower rate to be safe. I would also stop every twenty-five feet to listen for their distinctive rattle to warn us that we were trespassing.

I pushed Kellisa up the fourth little rise of about five feet, and there he was hidden in some short grass, a coiled-up rattlesnake directly in our path. I slowly moved backward until we were at the bottom and a safe distance away. Even though I saw him before we were in his striking range, never in any real danger, my heart was still racing as sweat poured from my forehead. I have to admit, I am not a snake person.

I kept my eye on the serpent the entire time, and he was holding his ground. I was hoping he would slither away, leaving our path unblocked. I didn't want to go around him in the tall grass where it would be difficult to see his friends. I also didn't want to disturb him in his home. Wanting to capture this moment, I got out my camera and zoomed in to get a detailed picture. I was hoping for an award-winning photo showing fangs and tongue, but I struggled to find his head within the coil. I stopped taking pictures so I could look closer to see if I could find his head. I had my prescription glasses on, and I moved closer and closer. Not only was the head missing, but it wasn't moving at all. It took another few seconds before I realized I was staring down a bison "pie."

I couldn't help but laugh at myself, and Kellisa soon joined in. I would have felt silly, but knew I was playing it safe. We continued on our way, careful not to wheel through the bison dropping.

From this point on, we would encounter many bison droppings that all looked like coiled snakes. We approached each one slowly with careful observation before proceeding. I didn't want to assume they were all harmless droppings. We were making our way through the badlands when I saw a bison blocking the trail directly in front of us. We stopped and decided to try and wait him out. He was alone, so I was hoping he would walk off to catch up to his herd before too much time passed.

Twenty minutes passed, and the bison didn't move an inch. I had a decision to make: we could make our way around as we did in Kansas, or we could cut the pushike short and return to the trailhead. I didn't like either decision, especially since we were still short of the prairie dog town. I didn't know what to do when suddenly, I saw a couple approaching from the other side of the bison. They didn't hesitate and went around the bison. They ended their little detour by rejoining the trail where we were stopped.

They explained that the bison had been in the same spot for at least forty-five minutes. The man told us we were close to the prairie dog town, and it was full of the adventurous little guys popping up from their holes and running around. The woman said, "You'll love it," and they went on their way.

I decided to follow their lead and go around the bison. Since the couple matted down the grass just enough so I could follow in their footsteps, I felt relatively confident we wouldn't surprise any rattlesnakes. Instead of taking my time, I decided to plow through this area as quickly as possible to limit our time off-trail. Other than following us with his eyes, the bison wasn't budging. A few long minutes later, we were safely past the bison and back on the trail headed toward the prairie dog town.

After just a few more minutes on the trail, including a couple more downs and ups, we could start to see prairie dogs popping out of their little holes and looking at us while others were running around. When we would get too close, they would drop down and disappear underground. We continued following the trail until we were in the middle of the town surrounded by its residents.

Kellisa had a great time watching them as I was taking pictures in all directions. They were a riot to watch. I was so focused on the little prairie dogs that I didn't realize the multicolored badlands surrounding us. It would have been worth the hike to have this view. When I started to feel a little hot from standing in one spot under the sun, I decided we should probably start heading back. It wasn't easy pushing Kellisa away from her many new friends, but she would return to enjoying the trail as she bounced around while we negotiated the downs and ups on our way back.

With the prairie dogs behind us, I started thinking about the bison again. I was hoping the bison had moved on so I wouldn't be faced with another decision. After a few turns in the trail, there he was again, blocking our forward movement. We had passed the bison at least thirty minutes earlier, and it appeared he was in the same location. It was apparent he wasn't moving, and I made a quick decision to go around. I wanted to go through the grasses as quickly as possible again to have this experience behind us. I was able to follow our previous path around the bison. Before long, we were back on the trail.

I continued to keep my eyes on the trail as we returned to the trailhead without encountering any rattlesnakes. Kellisa would have loved to see one at close range in the wild, and I would have loved telling that story at a later date, but I was glad we avoided a real encounter. We left Theodore Roosevelt National Park with a unique experience of pushiking through a prairie dog town, and I had a renewed interest in pushiking a more extended section or maybe attempting the entire Maah Daah Hey Trail.

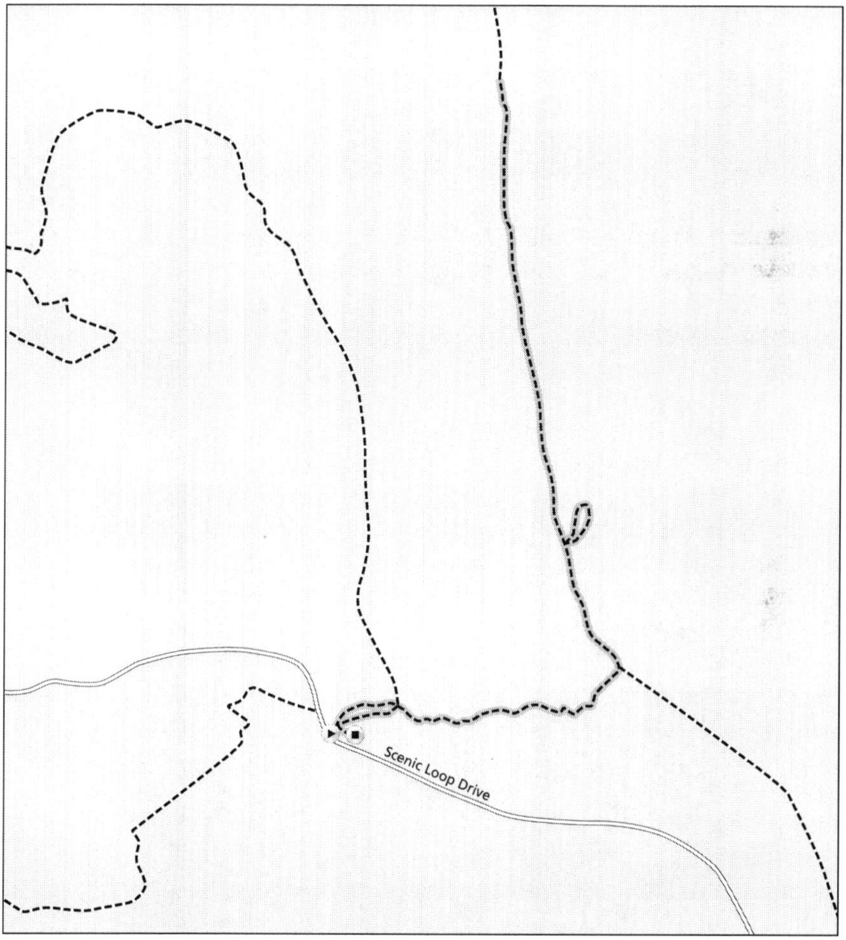

Prairie Dog Town, Theodore Roosevelt National Park (North Unit), ND

38
Ohio

Trail name: Woods/Boardwalk/ Butterfly Meadows
Location: Sheldon Marsh State Nature Preserve
Distance: 2.0 mi
Duration (active): 54m
Average speed: 2.2 mi/h
Total ascent: 23 ft
Highest point: 651 ft
Difficulty: Easy

Sometimes the most rewarding trails are short in length. One such combination of trails can be found at Sheldon Marsh along a narrow strip of undeveloped land on the shores of Lake Erie. We completed the Woods, Boardwalk, and Butterfly Meadows trails while pushiking portions of the paved Old Cedar Point Road, NASA Road, and Pond Loop Trail. Despite the many trails, it all added up to precisely two miles of what was mostly an out-and-back stroll on a freezing late-fall day in northern Ohio.

Sheldon Marsh's 472 protected acres represent one of the last remaining natural tracts in the Sandusky Bay area and offer protection to the many plant and wildlife species that use the area for survival, including more than 300 species of birds. A great deal is packed into this small space, including meadows, ponds, forests, marshlands, and a breathtaking experience from a secluded Lake Erie beach.

We started our adventure on the Old Cedar Point Road before taking a left turn on the Woods Trail, and Kellisa enjoyed the twists, turns, and bumps over the roots. She will always choose rugged over paved. Even though paved is easier for pushing, I agree with Kellisa and prefer a more rugged trail. The Woods Trail was narrow and filled with leaf litter but was easy to follow. The wind was whipping through the bare trees, so I was glad Kellisa was wearing her gloves and headband, keeping her ears warm. I even had to break out my fleece to cut the bite of winter creeping into the air. We learned later that it was snowing less than fifty miles away.

The trail was high and dry during our visit. There were a few wooden bridges over low areas that probably flood during wet weather but were still fun to cross. The Woods Trail ended at a marshy area that surprised us since it was reminiscent of the swamps you might find in the southeastern United States. We found ourselves back on the paved trail. There were several beautiful overlooks where we took a break to observe many birds taking flight over a small lake.

We found the short Boardwalk Trail at the end of the pavement. After a short distance through a forest, the boardwalk ended at a sandy beach. After a brief push through the sand, we were on the shores of an angry Lake Erie. The wind was fierce in our faces, and the waves were violently crashing just beyond our position. We were pleasantly surprised at the beauty of this section of Lake Erie. The winter atmosphere added to the grandeur we felt, but also made it difficult to linger.

We followed the Boardwalk Trail back to the paved Old Cedar Point Road and began our push back toward our waiting rental SUV. To make the most of our little adventure along a Great Lake, we took the paved NASA Road for a short distance before jumping off on the pleasantly unpaved Pond Loop Trail. We didn't complete the loop as we switched to the Butterfly Meadows Trail because it led us back to the trailhead. Usually, we would have completed the Pond Loop, but the chill was starting to penetrate our clothing. Despite its name, we didn't see any butterflies in the meadow but enjoyed the short path that concluded our fantastic visit to Sheldon Marsh. It's nice to know that a peaceful pushike to an unspoiled section of a Great Lake is still possible in such a highly developed and industrial area.

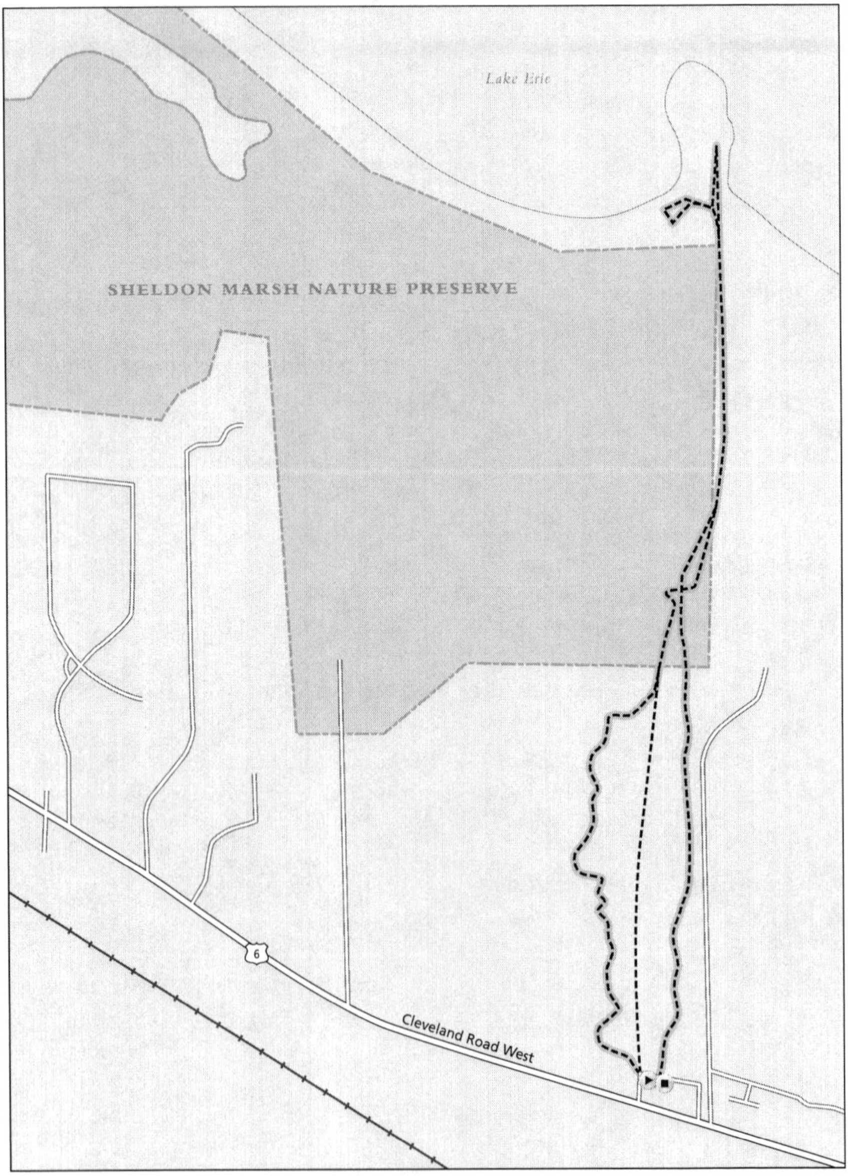

Boardwalk, Huron, OH

39
Oklahoma

Trail name: Antelope and Buffalo Springs
Location: Chickasaw National Recreation Area
Distance: 2.5 mi
Duration (active): 1h 9m
Average speed: 2.1 mi/h
Total ascent: 75 ft
Highest point: 1,088 ft
Difficulty: Moderate

When Kellisa and I arrived at Chickasaw National Recreation Area in Oklahoma, I didn't have a backup trail in mind. I stopped researching the area once I found the 2.8-mile paved path circling Veterans Lake. Rarely is a paved trail my first and only choice, but it is equally rare to find a paved trail of this length in a mountain setting next to a large body of water surrounded by forests. Since the loop trail is paved and fully accessible, I knew we would be able to complete it without any surprises. That's why I didn't take the time to research other trails. I knew from the pictures this would be a beautiful wilderness area just off the expressway connecting Oklahoma City and Dallas, Texas. I had no idea we would be blown away from the second we entered the park.

The forest was dense and packed with a diverse variety of green shades. The mountains were more impressive than expected, but my real surprise came when I saw the rushing creeks with falling cascades and majestic waterfalls found along their journeys. All this was visible from the road. I was eager to hit the trail as we drove toward Veterans Lake. The lake was spectacular with mountains rising from near the shores. Most of the path was exposed to the sun, and it was an unseasonably hot and humid day in early October when we visited the park. I was worried about pushiking a longer trail with Kellisa, considering how sunny it was. At the same time, I felt drawn back to the waterfalls. They were completely unexpected due to my lack of research.

Instead of venturing out on our intended trail, I drove around the entire park before pulling over to do some on-the-spot trail research. I ended up selecting a trail that started near Little Niagara Falls before following a cascading creek to and around a couple of the natural springs that initially made the area a destination for health-minded tourists. I learned from the park brochure that the springs area was designated as Platt National Park for seventy years between 1906 and 1976.

Cars filled the parking lot on Travertine Island, but this lot was near the start of the Antelope and Buffalo Springs Trail. Little Niagara Falls appeared within a minute of starting our pushike, and we quickly realized why the parking lot was so full. Besides being a beautiful waterfall, visitors were swimming in the large pool area at the bottom of the falls. I wanted to take a picture of Little Niagara Falls, but I didn't want our photographs to be filled with strangers. I decided to wait until we returned to the area after completing our out-and-back pushike.

Along with all the people, it was also apparent mosquitoes were out in full force. Before leaving the falls area, I sprayed Kellisa and myself to provide a coat of repellant protection. I knew we needed it for our entire pushike.

The trail crossed a park road before passing a nature center and eventually disappearing deep into the forest. The trail was wide and mostly composed of crushed gravel with a few roots to navigate. There were only a few gentle grades as the trail followed the winding creek with a few small cascades breaking up the gentle flow.

A couple of short lollipop trails branched off the Antelope and Buffalo Springs Trail. When we reached the first intersection, we decided to investigate the side trail. The trail was a little narrower than the main path, but we were feeling confident for the minute or so it took us to reach the creek. Boulders were placed across the creek instead of a bridge. This alternative bridge necessitated jumping from one stone to the next to cross the water and stay dry. The creek didn't appear to be too deep, and it looked like I could get Kellisa across, but I decided to play it safe and dry. We returned to the main path.

When we reached the second intersection, we decided to check it out. We found another boulder crossing. This one appeared to be even more sketchy, which made our decision to turn back easy.

After a few more minutes along the main path, we came to an open pond where the trail turned into a small loop around the natural springs. To our right was a picturesque bridge spanning the creek. We stopped so I could take a few pictures of Kellisa perched on top of the short span. Despite being covered in bug spray, the water surrounded us and the mosquitoes started landing on us, which cut our photo session short.

I applied a second coat of repellent, which helped to keep the mosquitoes at bay before we continued to Buffalo Springs. There were signs telling visitors not to go in the water. We weren't planning on soaking or swimming, so we weren't disappointed. We continued toward Antelope Springs, where we found another short bridge directly over a small waterfall and surrounded by native foliage. I could see this was a perfect place to take pictures of Kellisa. With the freshly applied bug spray, we could squeeze in a few shots without getting eaten alive.

I found the perfect place to take the pictures across a small pond that would frame Kellisa, the bridge, and a waterfall perfectly. I locked the wheels on Kellisa's mobility chair and jogged to the spot. It was a little more challenging to reach than I had expected because I had to crawl between some bushes. Once I made it through, I knew it was worth my effort. Kellisa was looking at me with a smile so big I could easily see it from my vantage point. I didn't want to leave her for too long, so I snapped pictures horizontally and vertically as fast as I could push the button. Once I was satisfied, I worked my way back through the bushes and hustled back to Kellisa, where I found her giggling.

Antelope Springs was our next destination. The spring emerged from a small rock pool with crystal-clear water. It was a hot afternoon in Oklahoma, and I was tempted to relax in the water for a few minutes to cool off. But again, signs were warning against my idea. I wasn't prepared to get wet and probably wouldn't have submerged myself anyway.

I pushed Kellisa to complete the short loop and started back toward Little Niagara Falls. Despite so many people at Little Niagara Falls, we only saw a group of three people out on this beautiful trail. When we made it back to the falls area, there were fewer people, but it was still a popular spot. I noticed a trail on the far side of the falls and swimming area. I decided to push Kellisa over there to check it out, and I'm glad we went there. The angle was perfect. I was able to take a few pictures of Kellisa with the falls in the background and not a single stranger in the frame. I even had time to take a few pictures of just the falls.

We fell in love with Chickasaw National Recreation Area. Besides our initial Veterans Lake paved trail, I'm confident we could complete several other trails in the park, including one that circles a buffalo enclosure. I know we will be back to explore the park when we have more time. And I look forward to swimming at Little Niagara Falls after completing a challenging trail or two.

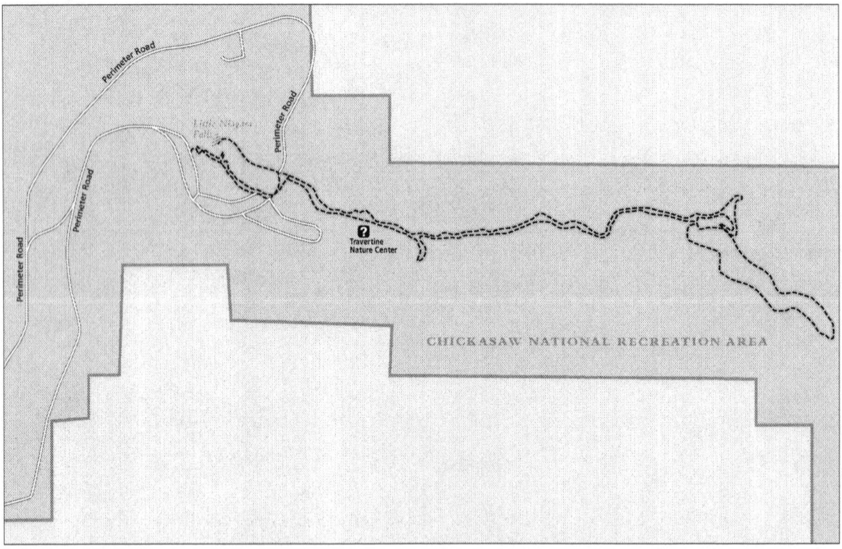

Antelope and Buffalo Springs Trail, Sulphur, OK

40
Oregon

Trail name: Discovery Point
Location: Crater Lake National Park
Distance: 1.3 mi
Duration (active): 59m
Average speed: 1.4 mi/h
Total ascent: 210 ft
Highest point: 7,200 ft
Difficulty: Challenging

I received a book from my Nana, when I was nine or ten, about the most beautiful places in the world. As a kid growing up in Chicago with parents who never traveled west of the Mississippi River, the vivid pictures contained in the book seemed like a world away. Longing for the wilderness, I would get lost in this book for hours at a time. The book was my constant companion for years as I imagined myself in all the captivating landscapes.

Out of the hundreds of pictures, one touched my soul more than others. It was a picture of Crater Lake so vividly blue that it didn't look real. Towering cliffs surrounded the lake with snow-covered peaks rising in the distance. The description explained how an ancient volcano exploded the top off a mountain, and the remnants collapsed on itself, creating a sizeable bowl-shaped feature. This impression would eventually fill with rain and snowmelt to form Crater Lake, the deepest lake in the United States.

If I could only see one of these beautiful landscapes, I knew it would be Crater Lake in Oregon. But Oregon was a world away for a young boy living in Chicago. I would be almost thirty-eight years old before I made my first visit to the lake of my dreams. Kellisa had just turned ten, and we were about two years into really creating this concept of pushiking. Kellisa was small for her age, and I pushed her in a jog stroller made for disabled children. It was just a few inches bigger than a standard jog stroller. I was determined to push Kellisa on new trails. I was looking for longer, higher, steeper, and so forth.

While planning our vacation to Crater Lake, I knew we had to pushike down the only trail to the shores of Crater Lake. The Cleetwood Cove Trail steeply descends more than 700 feet in just over a mile from the crater rim to the water's edge. Once at the bottom, you could take a scenic boat tour of the lake. I studied every picture I could find of the trail and read countless trip reports. I was confident that I could push Kellisa to the bottom and, just as important, back up again after taking the boat tour.

I was determined to pushike the Cleetwood Cove Trail by the time I read the description on the park's website. I learned the park and concessionaires use ATVs on the trail to supply the lakeside operations. The ATVs could also be used for emergencies. Any path wide enough for ATVs would be more than wide enough for me to push Kellisa and presumably free from significant obstacles. I was so excited; I would be able to visit the park and take Kellisa down to the lake for the boat tour.

Then I read the asterisk note at the bottom of the online trail description. It clearly stated that only park-approved, wheeled vehicles were allowed on the trail. I didn't think anyone would call a jog stroller a wheeled vehicle, but since we were traveling across the country from Florida, I wanted to know for sure before we arrived. I called the park to talk to a ranger and ask for the definition of a wheeled vehicle. To my surprise, the ranger said, "Anything with wheels is strictly prohibited."

I was still hopeful and asked for more clarity. Surely, he didn't mean a jog stroller, so I explained our situation and asked if a jog stroller would be allowed. He reinforced his interpretation of the rules: "No wheeled vehicles, including jog strollers."

The ranger told me the park had a few accessible overlook areas, and wheelchairs were allowed on the sidewalks. I was surprised, but not in shock after hearing his answer. My ace up my sleeve was mentioning the ADA, wheelchairs, and equal access for disabled people. The ranger wasn't intimidated. He repeated that under no circumstances would any wheeled vehicle be allowed. I shared our resume of pushiking accomplishments from summiting Black Mesa in Oklahoma to descending and climbing back out of Canyon de Chelly in Arizona, but his answer remained unchanged.

Frustrated, I said, "I wasn't calling for permission, I just wanted to be prepared before I push my daughter on the Cleetwood Cove Trail."

His response caught me by surprise, "You will be arrested if you attempt to push any wheeled vehicle on the Cleetwood Cove Trail."

"You can help me or arrest me," was my comeback, as I asked if there was a way to receive a special-use permit or a waiver I could sign before hiking the trail.

The ranger ended our phone call by repeating, "Any wheels on the trail will lead to an arrest."

I hung up with a sick feeling in my stomach. I felt like I was punched in the gut. I had a decision to make: Did I want to see Crater Lake enough to be happy just looking at it from the viewpoints along the park road? My answer was easy—absolutely not! I knew if we went, I would pushike the Cleetwood Cove Trail with Kellisa.

The real question I had to answer was, am I willing to get arrested? I didn't hesitate and knew I wouldn't let Kellisa be discriminated against by a national park. Even if it meant being arrested for continuing to push the limits of our sport, I was more than willing to take the chance.

As the trip approached, I decided to take an under-the-radar approach. I never called again hoping to talk to a different ranger with the intent of getting a different answer. I didn't want to alert the park of our arrival to prevent any preparation on their part to meet us. I had a cabin rented inside the park for five nights with a plan of blending in with all the other tourists for a couple of days while doing a little reconnaissance before attempting our outlaw-style pushike.

Approaching Crater Lake for the first time leaves a person searching for words. Majestic, breathtaking, and all similar grand words fall hopelessly short of describing the view. The old cliché, "pictures don't do it justice," is as accurate with Crater Lake as it is with the more well-known Grand Canyon. The deep blue color of the water is forever engrained in my memory. At the first overlook on the north end of the lake, I placed Kellisa in her travel wheelchair and wheeled her toward a short stone wall high above the water. I stood there speechless with Lisa as Kellisa giggled from the slight breeze hitting her face.

We stopped at every overlook on our route to where we needed to check in for our cabin. Our little cabin was small with one bed, a private bath, a small table with two chairs, and no TV. It would make for a tight but perfect base for our visit. We stopped at the visitor center to buy the typical souvenirs, books, trail maps, and obtain a Junior Ranger Book for Kellisa.

We spent several days pushiking the more accessible trails in the park and enjoyed driving the park's road that circles Crater Lake. I left Kellisa and Lisa in the cabin so I could hike a couple of the more challenging trails in the park. Crater Lake has limited services, so we had simple breakfasts and picnic lunches before dining on cheese and fruit plates at the Crater Lake Lodge built near the edge overlooking the lake far below.

We purchased our boat tour tickets in advance. I scouted the top portion of the Cleetwood Cove Trail and didn't see any reason not to attempt our pushike. It was a Thursday afternoon in early August when we arrived at the trailhead several hours before our boat tour was scheduled to begin. I left Lisa and Kellisa in our rental SUV while I walked up to the concessionaire's kiosk at the trailhead to pick up our tickets. I didn't want them to see Kellisa in her jog stroller and alert the park rangers and withhold our tickets, which were paid for in advance.

With the tickets in my pocket, I loaded Kellisa in her jog stroller and grabbed my fully laden backpack, and we were off. The trail was perfect, and it was wide and free of all barriers. I quickly noticed how steep the trail was on the descent. The views through the trees and occasional wide-open sight line made it easy not to worry about how steep the climb back up the trail would be in a few hours.

I had no fear of getting arrested because I was in complete control of our pushike, and I was confident I could convince any ranger that we were more than capable of completing the trail with minimal risk. I was prepared to make the argument that we were safer than many of the other families we saw on the trail with their young children running around near the steep drop-offs. I felt Kellisa was safer because she was tethered to my body with a minimal chance of anything happening.

Since the trail was a constant downhill plunge to the waters of Crater Lake, I was surprised and a little disappointed at how fast we reached the bottom. Our quick descent allowed ample time for snacks, drinks, bathroom stops, and a chance to check in for our boat tour. Up until this point, we didn't encounter any park officials, and I figured we would be in the clear. Would they arrest me at the bottom? They would have to carry me to the top because I wouldn't have walked willingly while someone else pushed Kellisa unless they would remove us by helicopter.

Despite my confidence, I approached the boat tour operator alone with our three tickets to check in. I was told when and exactly where to meet the boat on the short dock. As I was wheeling Kellisa toward the dock, I saw a ranger on an ATV emerge after descending the trail. He was alone, and I hoped he wasn't there for me. I continued pushing Kellisa while acting as if we belonged, and we did belong.

A lady was taking the tickets before the passengers boarded the boat. I handed her our tickets, and without missing a beat, she asked if I needed any help with Kellisa. There was only one way to the lake's edge, and it was a trail that did not allow wheelchairs or jog strollers, so I was a little surprised how natural this lady acted. I told her I was OK and that I would carry Kellisa to our seats. Lisa asked the lady if there was a safe place to leave her jog stroller, and after thinking for a few seconds, she recommended leaving it behind the kiosk.

Kellisa and I settled into our seats as Lisa moved the jog stroller out of the way as directed. I was more worried about someone taking her jog stroller than I was getting arrested. I kept looking for the ranger who came down on the ATV, but he wasn't around. The boat quickly filled, and the last person to board was the ranger.

I couldn't help but feel nervous as he looked around before introducing himself as the narrator of our tour. And just like that, we were off on our two-hour cruise around the perimeter of Crater Lake. The tour boat would pass near Wizard Island and all the other features of the lake while the ranger shared stories and pointed out all the natural highlights from dramatic cliffs to waterfalls cascading down to Crater Lake. We learned that these waterfalls were formed by melted snow working its way through the rock before finding its way out through an exposed crack.

Kellisa and every other passenger sat in awe. Everyone was silent except when they had a question to ask the ranger. All week we had been looking down at the boat tours and were surprised how small they looked, and now we had a better understanding of why. Looking up toward the rim, you couldn't help but feel very small.

Near the end of the tour, the ranger pointed out the Cleetwood Cove Trail, and you could see the steep switchbacks working their way back to the top of the rim. For the first time, I felt some doubt in my abilities. Rarely is there such a vantage point where you can see an entire trail as it climbs over 700 feet. Rarer still is the hiker who must push 100 pounds up that mile-long trail. I couldn't help but think that getting arrested might not be such a bad idea since I planned to go limp to make the rangers carry me.

After the boat was safely attached to the dock, I waited with Kellisa to be the last passengers off. Lisa jumped off to get the jog stroller to limit how far I had to carry Kellisa. The ranger was still thanking every passenger as they exited when I saw Lisa emerge with the jog stroller, relieving that worry. It was our turn to exit, and I figured if anything was going to go down, now was the time. As I approached the ranger, he thanked us and asked if I needed any assistance as I climbed out of the boat with Kellisa slung over my shoulder. I thanked him and said, "I've got it."

I placed Kellisa in her chair and put the seat belt around her waist before pushing her off the dock. While on the boat, the ranger told us the air temperature was around 65°F, not considering the wind, and the water in the lake was 46°F. I wanted to procrastinate pushiking up to the rim. I had one more selfish dream to fulfill. I was wearing shorts that doubled as my swimming shorts, and I carried a small towel in my backpack for drying off.

I couldn't convince Lisa to join me, and the water was too cold for Kellisa since she has a hard time regulating her body temperature, so I went swimming alone. I broke one of my golden rules; I usually don't do anything that Kellisa can't do with me when she's in my presence. I didn't know if I'd ever be back and couldn't resist going for a short but refreshing swim. The water was so cold, and my body felt like thousands of sharp daggers were piercing it. It didn't take long for my arms and legs to feel tingly and slightly numb. I submerged my head as I swam around for a few minutes, just enjoying the moment. I could tell from Kellisa's giggles and how she was watching me that she was more than OK to watch this one time. If Kellisa wanted to join me in the water, she would have been pointing to herself and yelling, "Me."

I stayed in the water for less than ten minutes, but it was more than enough to count as one of the coolest things I've ever done. I dried off and put my shirt, socks, and shoes back on. The fun was over, and it was time to pushike a mile up the trail back to the trailhead. This would also be a serious test for Lisa, who had broken her ankle less than two years before this trip. Her ankle was fully healed with pins and screws, and this wasn't her first hike post-recovery, but this would be by far the most difficult. It was hard for Lisa to stop and start once she got going on the trail, so I told her to go at her pace, and we would meet her at the top.

I hated separating from Lisa on the trail, but since there was only one trail and many hikers, I felt comfortable in the decision since I knew I would have to stop many times to catch my breath. I was nearing the halfway point of our ascent when I saw a ranger hiking down the path toward us. I stopped in case the ranger wanted to talk to us. She did stop but only for a second to tell us, "I've worked in this park for twenty-years, and I've never seen anyone doing what you're doing."

I thanked her, and she continued on her way down toward Crater Lake.

Lisa, now far above us, recognized a bench along the trail and knew it was just a couple switchbacks from the top, so she decided to wait for us there. Lisa was getting a little concerned at the amount of time that was passing when she heard two ladies discussing a man pushing a jog stroller up the trail. They seemed to be in disbelief at what they just witnessed. Lisa asked them how far back we were on the trail, and they informed her that we were maybe two switchbacks below where Lisa was waiting. Kellisa and I saw Lisa above us as we rounded a switchback, and I also recognized the bench and knew that we were close.

As I stopped for a breather, Lisa snapped a picture of me and Kellisa with Crater Lake far below. Ten years later, and it's still my favorite picture of the two of us pushiking. We finally caught up with Lisa and finished the last few switchbacks together. Back at our cabin with Kellisa asleep inside, Lisa and I shared a partial bottle of wine under the dark skies filled with millions of stars to celebrate a day of my dreams coming true.

Over the years, Kellisa and I have pushiked several other trails from the redwoods in southern Oregon to waterfalls in the Columbia River Gorge in the northern part of the state. But when it was time to select a trail for this book, I knew it had to be a trail in Crater Lake National Park. My first thought was to repeat the Cleetwood Cove Trail, but then I wasn't so sure about that idea. I didn't want to recommend a trail that needs to be pushiked in outlaw style. I decided to research the trail on the park's official website to see if anything changed in the decade since our epic pushike, and to my surprise, the park doesn't wholly ban wheelchairs and jog strollers on the Cleetwood Cove Trail anymore. However, they strongly recommend against the idea.

I couldn't help but feel a little sense of pride in this significant change and hoped we were at least a little bit responsible for the new rules. Since I successfully pushiked the trail with Kellisa, I could agree with the decision to discourage others from pushing a wheelchair or jog stroller on the Cleetwood Cove Trail. Kellisa and I had several years and many difficult miles of experience before our attempt, and we had a jog stroller that was fully tested on other trails before our pushike. We also had good weather and were adequately prepared and supplied. With so many variables that could go wrong, I knew I needed to select a different trail for Oregon.

After researching our options, I chose the Discovery Point Trail along the rim of Crater Lake as my recommendation to detail in this book. The trail starts near the parking lot for the Crater Lake Lodge. When we arrived on a Saturday morning in August, the parking lot was already full of people parking and walking around. From what I could see, the trail in this area looked paved and full of tourists standing around taking pictures. I also noticed many had little kids and dogs along the sidewalk. While the views were out of this world, it was evident that a wilderness experience would be fleeting in this area.

The Discovery Point Trail is an out and back, so I decided to drive along the rim to the turnaround point, if you start at the lodge. The trailhead parking lot is also an overlook for Crater Lake, making it challenging to find a parking spot, but we got lucky and were the second spot from where the trail starts. After a few pictures of the lake, I loaded Kellisa in her mobility chair, and we were off.

The beginning of the trail follows the narrow shoulder of the road. The thought of a road walk was a little scary, since I could picture drivers looking at the landscape instead of the road in front of them. There was a drop-off to our left just beyond the shoulder. Thankfully, it was only a short distance before we dropped down on the actual trail.

The trail was a little steep and narrow before it leveled out and headed toward a rock wall. From my research, I knew this would be the apex of the pushike. The trail would work its way up the rock in a series of steps, which we found difficult due to the uneven nature of the rocks and steep grade. We were about halfway up when an out-of-shape man and woman came down from above us. They were huffing and puffing dressed in jeans without a visible water bottle or any other supplies. They stopped to talk and catch their breath. The lady was encouraging and told us that we were near the top while the man was checking out Kellisa's chair. He proceeded to say to us, "If we could make it up there, so can you."

We parted ways, and I continued to struggle to get Kellisa up the trail. The rim of Crater Lake sits at more than 7,000 feet above sea level, high enough to make breathing more difficult for those not acclimated to the higher elevation. I could see the top, and the trail looked a little too steep, jagged, and narrow for my liking, so I decided to turn around and descend back to the trailhead to play it safe.

I didn't have a plan B before entering the park, but as we were driving to the trailhead, I noticed an overlook parking area near the lodge. It looked like it was where the sidewalk ended and the real trail began. I was hoping that we would be able to pushike from this trail entry point to the top of the rock wall just above where we turned around, making for a nice pushike.

This parking area was small, but luck was on our side because I found a spot on our second slow drive-by waiting for someone to leave. As I was loading Kellisa in her mobility chair, I noticed that everyone was taking pictures and selfies, but no one was hiking the trail. I could see the path immediately climbed up and out of the parking area. I was a little worried about how steep the trail appeared, but I didn't see any rock steps, which was positive. I was anxious to start the path to see if we could complete it because I didn't have a plan C. Without stopping for pictures, I started pushing Kellisa up the trail.

We would gain approximately 200 total feet on this segment of the trail, with most of it coming in the first 100 yards after leaving the parking area. We stopped only once as we worked our way up and through the rocky environment. Once at the top, we found ourselves in a forest setting with views through the pine trees of the entire lake. We could see Mount Scott, the highest mountain in the national park, rising directly across Crater Lake. Many cliffs plunging to the lakeshore were visible in all directions. Wizard Island rose from the blue water instantly in front and below our vantage point. We could also see two tour boats circling the lake. I was tempted to find a natural rock or log seat and take in the views before falling into a deep and satisfying nap, but we still had plenty of trail to explore.

The trail generally followed the rim through the forest and a couple of small meadow areas with little elevation change. Most of the time, the trail was a safe distance away from the drop-off, but sometimes we were right at the edge looking down. The path didn't have any barriers, so watching small children closely and keeping the jog stroller or mobility chair tethered is a top priority. With the endless views, it would be too easy to get distracted.

At just over a half-mile, we found ourselves on a rock outcropping that seemed to rise straight up and out of Crater Lake. We carefully posed for several pictures, and I hoped another hiker would come along so I could ask them to take a few pictures of us. This was at the top of the trail where we turned around earlier in the day. I was able to look down and see the exact spot where we decided to play it safe. From this vantage point, I knew we could have made it, but I still thought that we had made the correct decision. No regrets. We lingered while enjoying the views, still hoping for a guest photographer to arrive, but none appeared, so we started our pushike back to our SUV.

A lot of hikers don't like out-and-back trails because you cover the same ground twice. I would argue that there are many trails where everything appears completely different when heading in the opposite direction, and the Discovery Point Trail was a prime example. The lake, mountains, islands, cliffs—everything looked new and exciting from the reverse angle. It felt like we were seeing everything for the first time.

We took our time on the return, just enjoying the views. Near the end of our pushike, I could see our SUV far below parked on the side of the road, approximately 200 feet below where I was standing. Our descent went by without incident, but this would be significantly more difficult and dangerous if the trail were wet. I usually like to pushike an entire trail to consider it a success, but I wasn't at all disappointed to only pushike a portion of the Discovery Point Trail. We avoided the masses on the sidewalk portion and played it safe by skipping the most challenging section, but still enjoyed an excellent pushike while taking in the serenity of Crater Lake.

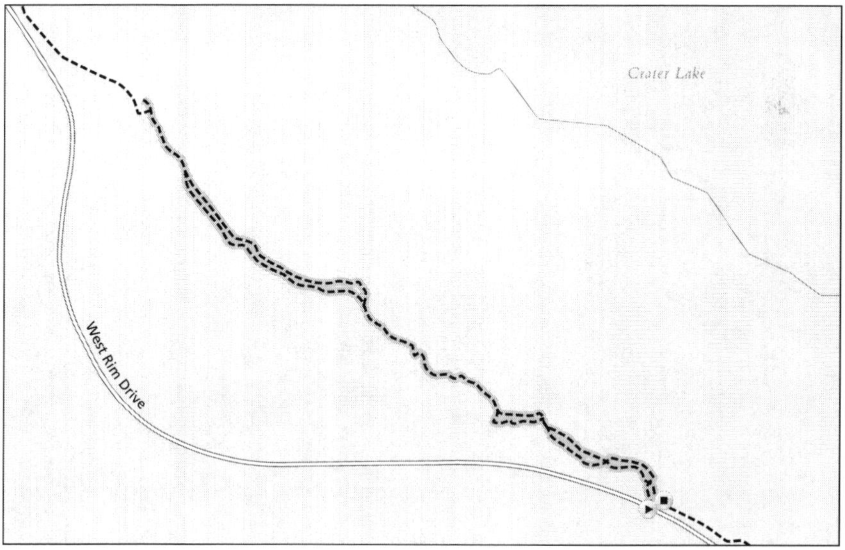

Discovery Point Trail, Rim Village, OR

41
Pennsylvania

Trail name: Front Nine
Location: Cherry Valley National Wildlife Refuge
Distance: 1.9 mi
Duration (active): 52m
Average speed: 2.1 mi/h
Total ascent: 144 ft
Highest point: 459 ft
Difficulty: Moderate

I love it when I stumble upon a unique trail.

To me, a unique trail is one of a kind or, at most, one of a very select few for at least one compelling reason. When I was reading about how Cherry Valley National Wildlife Refuge was created from a former golf course, I was intrigued. With some strategic planning and planting, the old golf course is being allowed to return to its natural state. I was sold when I read that the former golf-cart paths were left intact to serve as trails through the refuge.

Our last house in Florida was near a golf course, and I would see the cart paths every day and think how they would be great for pushing Kellisa. I know the paths are paved, but they're long and twist through a beautiful setting, often near lakes. The problem is that people aren't allowed to walk, hike, or jog on cart paths, and I'm sure safety is a reason in addition to being a distraction to those paying to play a round of golf. I always thought there had to be a compromise to allow others to use the perfect trails but couldn't think of how to make it happen. Now, I had my chance to push Kellisa along a golf-cart path.

It was overcast and chilly when we arrived on a weekday morning in early October. We were the only vehicle in the parking lot. I parked in front of the trailhead kiosk and left Kellisa in the car while I read the information and looked at the maps. The Cherry Valley Golf Course had eighteen holes, and the cart path was divided into two trails, the Front Nine and Back Nine. From the trailhead, I had a great view of the refuge and could see rolling hills in all directions. It was hard to tell which trail would be more difficult. I was hoping to pushike both while we were there. To me, the Front Nine looked more difficult due to a steep incline near the start of the trail. I wanted to get that hill behind us as soon as possible, so I decided to start on the Front Nine Trail.

I got Kellisa in her mobility chair and double-checked our pack. I wanted to verify we had our rain gear because the smell of rain was in the air, and I didn't know how long we would have until it started pouring. It didn't take long, and we were pushiking down the trail. The golf course was filled in with native grasses, flowers, shrubs, and trees. The refuge was created in 2008, and in just eleven years, it was difficult to tell you were hiking through an old golf course.

I pushed Kellisa over a swiftly flowing creek before heading up the hill I could see from the trailhead. I'm not a big fan of pavement, but I was appreciating how nice it was to push Kellisa up a steep incline without having to worry about roots, rocks, mud, or stairs. The only real concern was slipping on the wet leaves scattered across the path, but my hiking boots seemed to have adequate traction. And as always, I had Kellisa and her mobility chair tethered to my body for safety. I wanted to get to the top in one constant push, but I needed to take a break to catch my breath and sip on some water.

It's not easy pushing more than 100 pounds up a steep hill the height of a ten-story building. Once at the top of the ridge, I took a second break before I could enjoy the far-reaching landscape of the valley and its autumn colors, filling my view in every direction. We were close to entering a forested area, and I knew we were in black bear country, so I started talking loudly and singing with Kellisa to make enough noise for any bears in the area to know we were out on a pushike. Even though it's unlikely to meet a bruin on a trail, its good practice to make noise because they will usually run away before interacting with humans.

The former cart path twisted through the forest, and the old fairways now appeared as meadows in the valley. Birds were singing amid the swaying grasses. Most of the time, we could hear them but not see them since they were hiding in the brush. The trail approached and then crossed the refuge road at a point where the view of the valley opened again. It was beginning to look like the rain could start falling at any second.

I was planning to pick up our pace as soon as we crossed the road, but there was a beaver just to the side of the path. We stopped to observe for a minute before I tried to reach for my camera. The movement from my arm spooked the beaver, who disappeared into the grasses toward a water feature. The beaver then spooked many birds out of the grasses. It was thrilling to watch so many birds take flight to retreat at one time. We paused in amazement while looking for any more wildlife before starting back down the trail. A short distance away, we saw a turtle hanging out near a small creek flowing under the path. He watched us for a minute while we looked at him.

A breeze was starting to pick up, which reminded me to stay focused on completing the trail before the rain started. The trail headed toward a forested area on a ridge, but the path made a U-turn just before entering the woods. We saw a beautiful bridge coming up, and I was planning to take a series of pictures of Kellisa on the bridge before I saw a rope blocking our entrance with a sign saying, "Bridge Closed."

I was disappointed, but it was a spur trail, so we were able to continue without a detour or backtracking. The path led back toward the parking area, and I thought we were near the end, but the trail continued across the park road again and headed up a small hill as it disappeared into the forest on the other side. The weather was holding, and we were having a good time. I decided to skip the Back Nine Trail due to the impending rainstorm and appreciated this last segment of the Front Nine Trail.

The hill in front of us was challenging. But it wasn't as high or steep as the hill at the beginning of this pushike. The trail entered a wooded area, and after a few twists and turns, we descended back down the hill that we just climbed. We had one more bridge to cross and a short distance to cover before returning to our rental SUV. Before I loaded Kellisa, her mobility chair, and our gear, I looked up at the weather in all directions one last time hoping for a sign of it clearing to give us the green light to proceed on the Back Nine Trail, but if anything, the weather looked like it was getting worse. Kellisa and I weren't in the SUV for ten minutes before the skies opened with a furious downpour. I was relieved to have completed the Front Nine Trail and would make plans to return the next time we were in the area to attempt the Back Nine Trail.

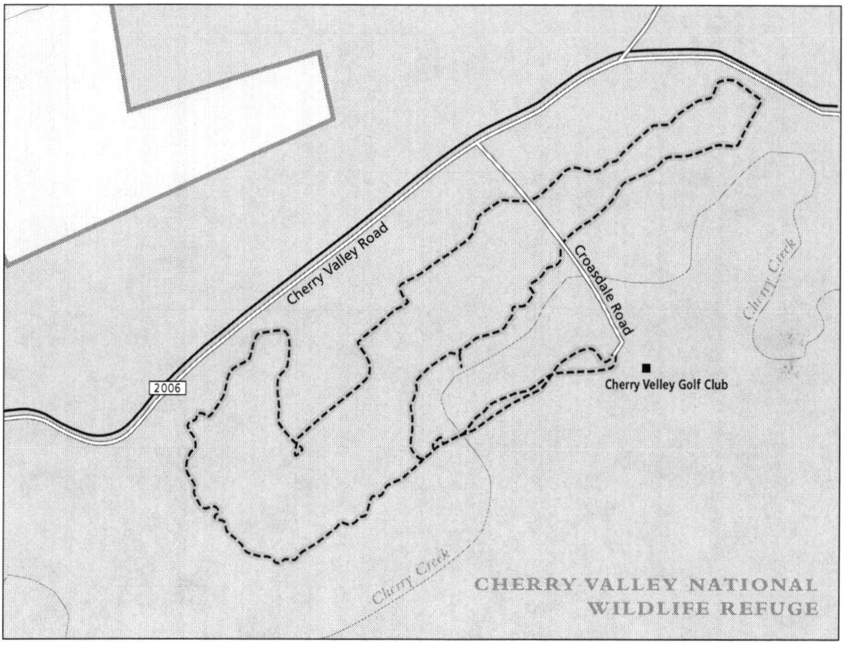

Front Nine Trail, Monroe County, PA

42
Rhode Island

Trail name: Jerimoth Hill	**Average speed:** 1.5 mi/h
Location: Foster, RI	**Total ascent:** 26 ft
Distance: 0.4 mi	**Highest point:** 841 ft
Duration (active): 15m	**Difficulty:** Easy

Rhode Island is the smallest state in land area in the United States. Duval County, where we lived for eleven years in Florida, is roughly the same size and has a similar population. Despite its limited size, Rhode Island has many trails through a surprising number of different terrains. I decided to pushike a familiar path to Jerimoth Hill. Kellisa and I have pushiked to the summit twice: once back in June 2009 when Kellisa and I spent a week exploring New England together, and then we returned with Egypt in June 2013.

Jerimoth Hill is the highest point in Rhode Island at 812 feet above sea level. Because of its ranking as the highpoint of a state, it's a popular destination. While the trail only gains twenty-six feet on the ascent, it is one of the most dangerous highpoints to reach. You don't have to worry about avalanches or altitude sickness, but you do have to be careful crossing Route 101 to reach the trail from the parking area. The danger level is high because you park at the crest of a hill and can't see cars driving up the hill in either direction. The vehicles driving Route 101 travel at a high rate of speed. Hikers can't see the oncoming cars until they reach the top of the hill and have little time to cross or get out of the way. I had several false starts to our crossing on each of our visits before successfully crossing with my heart frantically pounding. Pushing a mobility chair or jog stroller adds to the level of difficulty, and watching over small children on foot would add to the complexity and danger of this crossing.

Once safely across the highway, there's a small opening in the forest. There's a sign marking the beginning of the short trail to the summit of Jerimoth Hill. The path is narrow but just wide enough for Kellisa's mobility chair as it works its way through the dense forest. A few rocks and roots provide minimal obstacles along the way, and I even pushed Kellisa to the top in her manual travel wheelchair when we summited with Egypt. You pass two survey marker rocks along the trail before the path makes a quick U-turn to end at a large boulder with only about a third of it visible above the ground. The top of the boulder is the actual highpoint, and a waterproof canister can usually be found nearby with paper and pencils to record your visit. I often write our names and the date along with how many highpoints we've reached. This time, I also noted how this was our third ascent of Jerimoth Hill.

Kellisa has reached the highpoint in twenty-two states, ranging from easy drive-ups in states like Mississippi to significant pushikes. In Oklahoma, we've pushiked to the top of Black Mesa on an 8.4-mile out-and-back trail with an elevation gain of 648 feet. On our trip to the highpoint of Maryland, the trail became too narrow and rocky. The only way up was carrying Kellisa over my shoulder fireman style the last quarter of a mile before reaching the top of Backbone Mountain. Egypt has summited four state highpoints. I added several of the harder to reach highpoints to my total when Kellisa was younger and before our pushiking career took off. While not a top priority, I believe there's a chance Kellisa and I can pushike another ten highpoints together, including a couple of serious western summits.

The boulder on top of Jerimoth Hill is large and level enough to pose Kellisa in her mobility chair for the customary summit pictures. Sometimes the best part of a trail is the journey, while on other trails, it's the destination. In the case of Jerimoth Hill, it's the highpoint destination more than the short journey along the very average wooded path.

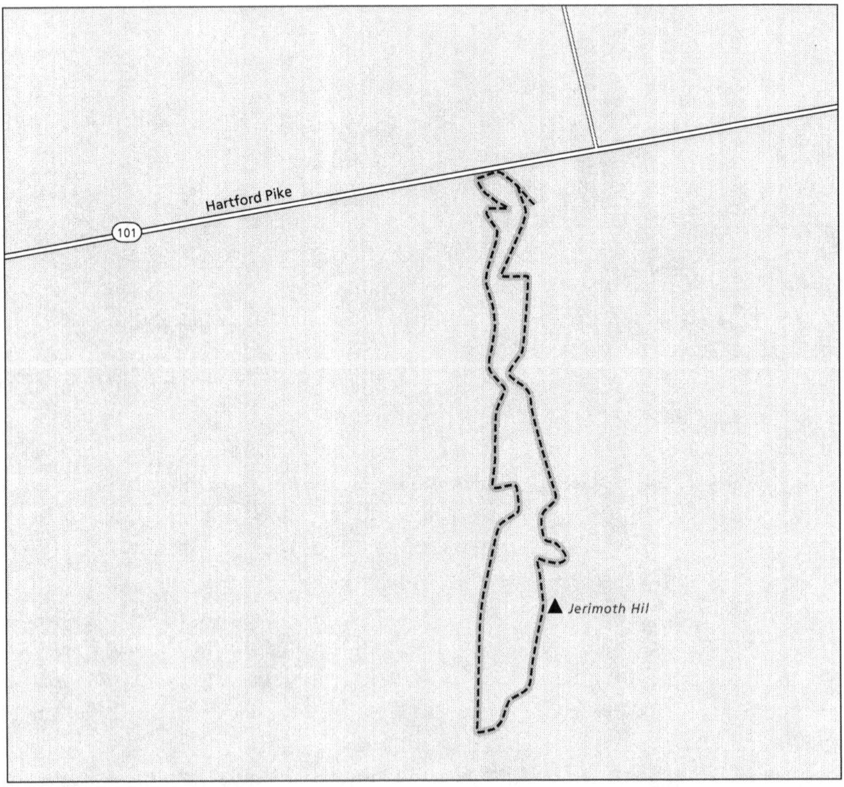

Jerimoth Hill Trail, North Foster, RI

43
South Carolina

Trail name: Boardwalk Loop
Location: Congaree National Park
Distance: 2.7 mi
Duration (active): 1h 9m
Average speed: 2.4 mi/h
Total ascent: 30 ft
Highest point: 127 ft
Difficulty: Easy

I found the recently created (2003) Congaree National Park early in our push-hiking career. Kellisa had just turned seven years old when we spent the Fourth of July weekend in and around the park back in 2006, and we've been going back ever since. I was seeking trails designed for wheelchairs and strollers. I wasn't interested in short, paved paths that start from behind a visitor center and don't go anywhere. If we were going to travel to hike, I wanted to see what other hikers would see. That's when I stumbled upon Congaree National Park and its 2.4-mile-long Boardwalk Loop Trail.

It was by far the longest boardwalk trail that I knew about, and it was only a half day's drive from our house in Jacksonville, Florida. A little more research and I learned that the trail passed through the most extensive tracts of old-growth forest on the East Coast. Congaree is home to many champion trees. Some of the trees reach over 150 feet, and the oldest trees are more than 500 years old. Plus, the park is rich in its biodiversity.

A mosquito meter greets you at the beginning of the Boardwalk Loop Trail, and it ranges from "All Clear" to the ominous "War Zone." We found the mosquitoes to be rated "Moderate" when we arrive in early June 2019 for this book. We knew from living in the southeast how bad the mosquitoes could get, so we did not hesitate to apply strong bug repellent over our entire bodies. I made sure we covered every inch of exposed skin and hair with a liberal overlap onto our clothing.

We arrived after the visitor center had closed. I usually like to stop there first to get a map and ask the ranger a few questions. It wasn't a big deal since we were familiar with the park, and the boardwalk was a simple loop that began and ended just beyond the visitor center. I was surprised and disappointed to see a sign letting visitors know that part of the boardwalk was closed. A tree fell on top of it, creating substantial damage that was waiting to be repaired.

Loaded up with bug spray, we headed down the boardwalk to go as far as we could and enjoy the part of the boardwalk that was open. After going a short distance, you have a choice to make about which direction you want to go. However, with part of the boardwalk closed, visitors could only go left.

At this point, the boardwalk is elevated above the ground. The surrounding bottomlands regularly flood from the nearby Congaree River, but on this afternoon, it was mostly muddy with a few small areas of standing water. Everything was so lush and green; it was apparent recent rains had fallen over the area. The boardwalk takes visitors up close to some of the most towering trees in the park. You feel small when next to such mammoth trees.

I would stop pushing Kellisa whenever we came to one of the areas with standing water. I thought that being near the water would give us the best opportunity to observe some of the local wildlife. On past visits, we've seen turtles and snakes among other little creatures scurrying around the ground, but we came up mostly empty on this trip.

The boardwalk makes a right turn to head toward Weston Lake. We continued following the trail while scanning the surrounding areas. It was late in the afternoon, and we were enjoying having the boardwalk to ourselves. Suddenly, the relative silence was broken by what can only be described as a series of grunts. I stopped pushing Kellisa, and we looked around when a family of feral pigs emerged from some of the lush underbrush and passed directly under us. We quickly maneuvered to observe them on the other side, and they soon disappeared with their grunts eventually fading away too. It was quite the sight to see this family of pigs quickly waddling through the mud on what appeared to be their merry way. I couldn't help but join Kellisa with a few giggles.

The elevated board continued deeper into the forest as the sun was starting to fade. The mosquitoes started coming out as we reached the Weston Lake overlook. I took a few pictures, and we saw a couple of turtles hanging out on the log. I knew the lake was home to a couple of alligators, so I scanned the water but didn't see any. I was taking pictures of Kellisa with the lake as the backdrop when I noticed a mosquito land on Kellisa's arm. Our heavy-duty bug repellent wasn't doing its job, so I quickly applied another thick layer, first on Kellisa and then myself. The new coating seemed to do the trick, and the mosquitoes retreated.

I wanted to linger to enjoy the tranquility but knew the hour was growing late. Usually, we would have continued to complete the boardwalk loop, but since part of the trail was closed, we decided to head back the way we came. We could have continued to the fallen tree for a longer pushike before turning around but didn't want to get caught out after dark when the mosquitoes turn up their frenzy, and no amount of bug spray would prevent brutal attacks.

With the repellent still doing its job, we continued to take our time as we looked for wildlife and appreciated the majesty of the large trees so close that we could almost touch them. As we were nearing the end of our adventure, two toddlers came running toward us with a frantic mother closely behind. The kids didn't know what to do when they came upon Kellisa and her chair, so they stopped and politely stood off to the side of the boardwalk so we could pass. I noticed they were swinging their bare arms wildly while kicking their exposed legs and thrashing their heads. I figured they were out without bug repellent. The mother caught up, and she was wearing pants and a lightweight rain jacket with a full hood and didn't seem too bothered by the hungry raiders. I offered the use of our bug spray, but she refused in a manner that told me not to ask, "Are you sure?"

Our second application of bug repellent was starting to wear off, or maybe the mosquitoes were getting more determined, as we returned to our SUV. I tried to limit the number of mosquitoes entering our vehicle as I quickly got Kellisa in her seat and her chair with our gear in the back. Since I only had to swat four of the little guys and only saw one bite on Kellisa and just a few on my arms, I felt like we made it out unscathed. With proper timing, you can have an enjoyable visit without fighting mosquitoes, and with just a little planning, you can coexist with the biting creatures while having a pleasant visit.

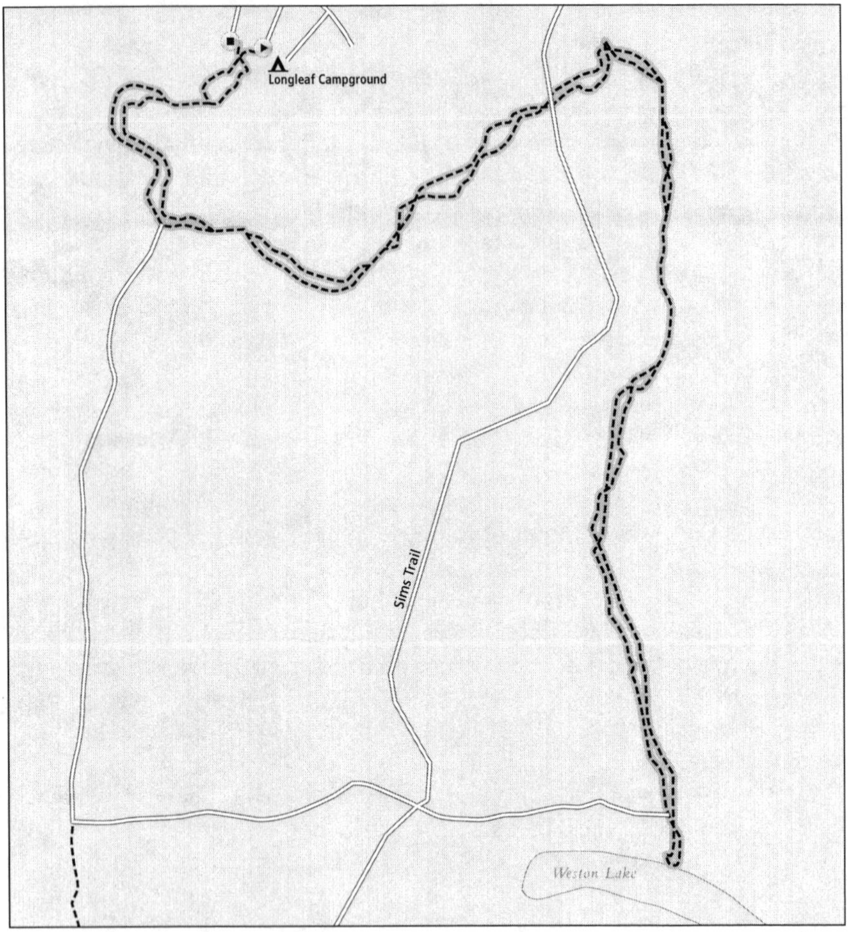

Boardwalk Loop Trail, Gadsden, SC

44

South Dakota

Trail name: Spirit Mound
Location: Spirit Mound Historic Prairie
Distance: 1.5 mi
Duration (active): 48m
Average speed: 1.8 mi/h
Total ascent: 105 ft
Highest point: 1,303 ft
Difficulty: Moderate

I was looking for a trail in South Dakota the old-fashioned way. Kellisa and I canceled our planned pushike in western South Dakota in June 2019 due to inclement weather in Montana earlier in the trip, where we lost a full day and a half. We had a couple of trails picked out in the Black Hills and Badlands National Park. The plan was to finalize the trail as we were driving over from Devils Tower based on how we felt and how much time we had. Since that trip didn't work out, I was looking for a trail in the eastern part of the state to add it on to our Iowa, Nebraska, and Minnesota trip. I pulled out a road atlas and was studying the South Dakota page when I saw a little red dot with Spirit Mound Historic Prairie typed nearby in the same color. I knew we found our pushiking spot before I knew if it even had a trail.

I moved to current technology and started researching Spirit Mound on my computer. I didn't know what I would find online, and the word "Spirit" was mesmerizing since it could have both light and dark meanings. And "Mound" implied an elevation gain with perhaps endless views across the prairie from the top. The initial results were promising as I learned there was a short trail to the summit. A little more digging and I read about the native tribes in the area that believed short people with large heads lived on the mound and would shoot anyone attempting to reach the top.

Perhaps the most interesting fact I would learn was how Lewis and Clark hiked nine miles to reach the mound back in 1804 on their famous expedition across the West. Despite hearing the local stories of certain death, Lewis and Clark reached the top on August 25. Spirit Mound is one of the few places where you can stand, knowing that Lewis and Clark definitively stood in the same spot. The trail was a little shorter than I hoped, but with such a deep history, I knew this trail would be perfect.

I was thankful that Kellisa and I could drive up to the trailhead in the relative comfort of our rental SUV instead of hiking nine miles from the Missouri River. On the other hand, I would have loved to experience the prairie and Spirit Mound the way Lewis and Clark found it, with herds of buffalo and elk roaming along with badgers, coyotes, birds, and edible fruit trees. Outside of a few bugs and maybe a couple of birds, Kellisa and I didn't see any wildlife, but we saw endless agriculture lands.

Spirit Mound was on a privately owned farm until recently, and the surrounding area has been allowed to be reclaimed by native prairie flora. We found large swaying grasses and wildflowers surrounding the parking lot at the trailhead. It was a perfect late-summer afternoon when we arrived. The temperature was comfortable, and there was not a cloud in the sky. Without a single tree to offer protection from the sun, we applied sunscreen before I started pushing Kellisa down the only trail in the small park. We had a perfect view of Spirit Mound rising directly in front of us.

I knew from my research that the trail is approximately a mile and a half round-trip, but Spirit Mound looked a lot farther away than the half-mile it was from our position. The trail curves around and behind Spirit Mound before climbing the last little segment to reach the small summit area. Just before the trail started this curve to the side of the mound, we crossed a small wooden bridge over a crystal-clear creek, which was flowing with a surprisingly swift current. I took a few pictures of Spirit Mound. We looked in the water for creatures but didn't see any.

We passed a college-aged group of four on their way down from the top. They were in a good mood and high-fived Kellisa as they passed while telling her how great it is on top. Kellisa rewarded their kindness by blowing kisses.

The trail had been flat, wide, mostly dry, and free from all obstacles up to this point. I hoped these conditions would prevail for the rest of the pushike as we gained elevation on our way to the summit.

As soon as the trail moved to the western side of the mound, I could tell the trail was starting to get a little steeper. We encountered a few rocks embedded in the trail, but nothing too tricky. We stopped for a couple of minutes once we hit the backside of Spirit Mound to take in the new views to our north and drink some water. I was so busy with my back to the final pitch, I didn't realize there was a steep set of stairs carved into the remaining trail to the summit. It's funny how all the trip reports and pictures failed to mention this one fact, which is a big deal to anyone pushing someone on a trail.

The stairs would not have deterred Kellisa and me from making this pushike, but it would have been nice to know in advance as they might be too much of a barrier for some pushikers. The stairs were steep and not deep enough to rest Kellisa's mobility chair as we went up. Stairs like this are nearly impossible to push someone up because you need to first lift the front tire and set it down before lifting the back tires as you push forward. The problem comes in when the front tire hits the next step before you have room to set the back tires down.

Instead of struggling to push forward, I usually take sections like this with Kellisa going backward. I step up while lifting her mobility chair to the same step. I take a step or two back before going up the next stair. Kellisa's front wheel usually stays in the air during this process. This method isn't my favorite way to gain elevation, but I'm comfortable doing it for short ascents when the trail isn't too muddy and the stairs are mostly clear of rocks or other tripping or slipping obstacles. This trail qualified, but hikers before us had created a small trail to the left side of the stairs. I'm not sure why anyone would do this because it's harder and more dangerous for regular hikers than just using the dozen or so stairs. I'm sure trail crews and park managers hate the user-created path as it's unsightly and creates unnecessary erosion.

When hiking alone, my trail ethics keep me on the established trail whenever possible, but when pushiking with Kellisa, I have a different set of trail ethics. Since other hikers already created the side path, and it would be easier and safer for me to push Kellisa forward past the stairs on this trail, I decided to go that route without a second thought. The path didn't look too muddy or slippery, but you never know. It was steep, so I decided to try a bull rush to make our way to the top in one quick push. I knew I could maneuver Kellisa a couple of feet to the stairs to help stop a sudden slide backward.

My plan worked perfectly, and we were at the summit of Spirit Mound. Lewis and Clark estimated the mound rose about 70 feet above the surrounding prairies while my modern technology indicated we had gained just over 100 feet from the trailhead. Either way, we were the highest two people for as far as we could see in all directions.

The summit had three benches for a rest, but I was afraid to sit down out of fear of not being able to get back up easily. I noticed a military, ammo-type canister in the middle of the benches. I knew from other summits it was likely to hold a logbook and pen. I opened it, and I was correct. I wrote Chris and Kellisa Kain from Roseville, California, and the date. I returned the contents and closed it up for the next visitors.

Kellisa was enjoying the views and mild breeze in her face while I snapped pictures of Kellisa with our stunning views as the background. Out of the blue, Kellisa said, "Hey," while pointing behind me.

I turned around and was surprised to see a man and woman within ten feet of us. The entire trail is free from trees, allowing you to see the whole path back to the trailhead from the summit, and I never noticed anyone else out on the trail. I wasn't thinking about it but figured that we had the trail to ourselves, which is why I was so surprised.

The couple arrived rather abruptly since most hikers would announce their arrival or make some noise to alert you of their presence long before they approached so closely. I was a little concerned because both looked a little out of place and were smoking cigarettes. Many people, usually nonhikers, ask me if I'm afraid of animals when out on a trail, and my usual response is, "I'm more afraid of people."

My answer is brief and mostly accurate. I do worry about animals, but I try to be prepared. Most wild animals are predictable. If you know what to do and how to act, most encounters end with the animal running away. People, on the other hand, can be more unpredictable. I hate to judge people, but when a person looks out of place on a trail, my senses go on heightened alert.

I went from a little uneasy to concerned when my "Hi, beautiful day" comment with a friendly smile went unanswered by both. It didn't concern me that they were ignoring Kellisa's attempts to communicate because that is an all-too-common reaction from strangers.

I resumed taking pictures while trying to keep an eye on them. Kellisa was relentless in her attempts to get the couple to return her greeting. After taking a quick look in all four directions, the couple started back down the trail. The whole encounter lasted less than ninety seconds but left me feeling vulnerable. I don't feel like I overreacted; I was cautious and glad they were just out for a hike like us.

Since I felt safer pushing Kellisa down the stairs, that's how we started our descent. I just kept Kellisa's front wheel in the air as I gently dropped her back wheels down one step at a time. I went slow, but it didn't take long to have the stairs behind us. Even though this was an out-and-back trail, the views on the return were very different from the ascent. It felt like we were on a different trail. On the way up, Spirit Mound always seemed to dominate the view, but now it was behind us, and all we could see was the restored prairies and farmland beyond.

It would have been exciting to see hundreds of buffalo and elk roaming free as Lewis and Clark observed, but Kellisa and I still left satisfied with our unique pushike to the top of Spirit Mound.

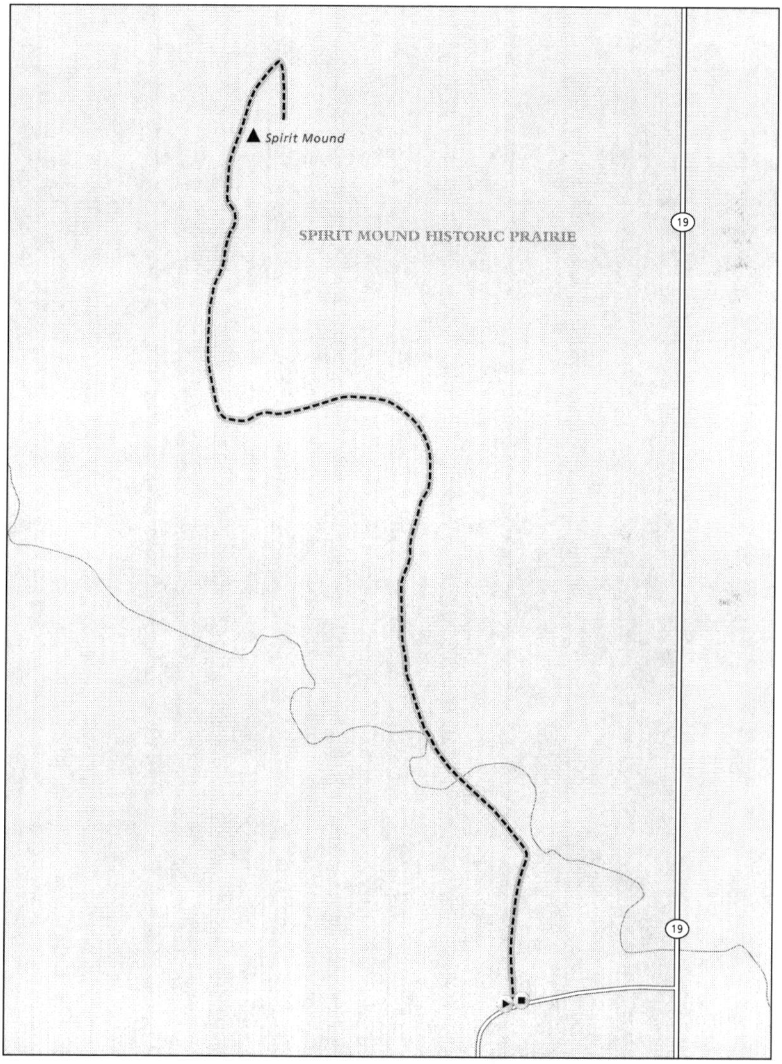

Spirit Mound Trail, Meckling, SD

45
Tennessee

Trail name: Little River
Location: Great Smoky Mountains National Park
Distance: 4.9 mi
Duration (active): 2h 5m
Average speed: 2.3 mi/h
Total ascent: 712 ft
Highest point: 2,520 ft
Difficulty: Challenging

Whenever I'm looking at a map of Tennessee, my eyes are drawn to the dark green oval shape at the bottom left of the pages designating the Great Smoky Mountains National Park, which happens to be visited more than any other national park. I knew from previous trips that finding an excellent pushiking trail would be a challenge. I pushed Kellisa on the very steep and roughly paved trail to Laurel Falls on an earlier visit when we had to make a quick return to our SUV to call 911 because we witnessed a teenage girl slip while climbing the waterfall, which caused her to go over the falls. She fell to the rocks fifteen feet below, where she landed on her back. She also hit her head hard on the rock landing surface. The girl remained conscious but complained about feeling dizzy and said she felt like she had to throw up. The rest of the people in her group helped her to a sitting position then continued climbing the falls themselves. We felt like she needed emergency assistance. When it became apparent no one in her group was going to help, we told her we would get help. Through tears, she thanked us in a whispered tone.

We kept checking for cell service and finally got a bar back at our SUV. We called 911. The dispatcher put us in contact with the national park, and we stayed on the line until the first responders arrived where we were able to fill them in while they got their gear ready. They thanked us before disappearing up the trail. We often wonder what happened to the young girl and hope that she was OK. We've never doubted our decision to call for help since we saw her land hard on her head and would rather be safe than sorry.

Later during the same trip, I pushed Kellisa to Rainbow Falls on a challenging trail that was strewn with large rocks. The frame of her jog stroller broke along this trail. It was almost impossible to push her with the broken chair, and this was the closest we ever came to being stranded on a trail.

I called the manufacturer when we got home about ordering a replacement frame, and I was transferred to their technical director. He told me the model of jog stroller we were using was twenty years old, and this was the first time they ever heard of a frame breaking from regular use. I always knew we were pushing the boundaries of pushiking, and this comment was further proof. It was around this time that I first started thinking it would be nice to have a guidebook for strollers on real wilderness trails.

My initial research didn't reveal any promising trails in the Smoky Mountains that looked ideal for pushiking, so I started looking at other wilderness areas in the state. I found several that looked good, but I kept going back to my desire to find the ultimate pushiking trail deep in the Smoky Mountains.

Just before we left on our trip to Tennessee, I finally found what I was looking for in a trail, and it was in the middle of the Great Smoky Mountains National Park. I read a description of the Little River Trail to Husky Falls. It's rare to find a decent trail to a waterfall that is suitable for pushiking, but the Little River Trail followed an old rocky road. It looked like it would be wide enough, and the rocks along the way seemed like I could navigate our way over and around them. The out-and-back waterfall trail was almost five miles in length and had the right amount of elevation change to make the hike challenging. We arrived in the Smokies on a hot and humid summer morning. As we traveled into the mountains, the temperature dropped several degrees by the time we reached the trailhead. The path started with rocks so compact it almost felt like pushing along a sidewalk while following the Little River. From informative signs, we learned the road was an abandoned railroad bed. The shade provided relief from the summer sun, and the rapidly flowing river created a refreshing breeze adding to the comfort of this early June pushike.

The Little River was filled with large boulders, rapids, and an occasional waterfall. The trail was crowded with tourists of all ages and nationalities near the parking lot. I even saw a tour bus unload dozens of passengers who looked like they were taken from a nearby bingo parlor. I'm sure we looked like we should be walking around our neighborhood on the sidewalk to them, so I'm not going to make any judgments. We saw families on vacation with kids scrambling up rocks and dipping their feet in the water. It was a little too crowded for my liking, but once we were a half-mile from the parking lot, we had the trail to ourselves. We would see an occasional hiker, but they would disappear up or down the path as quickly as they appeared. The trail was nonstop uphill necessitating frequent rest stops to fuel up with water and salty snacks to keep my energy level high.

After a mile or so, the path narrowed slightly, and the rocks weren't as compact. It finally seemed like we were on a trail deep in the mountains. We did pass several people descending the trail, and Kellisa greeted everyone with a loud "Hey."

We interpret Kellisa's "hey" as both a friendly greeting and a shout, meaning "Hey, look at me!" Most of the hikers would say "hi" or "hey" back, which I appreciated because Kellisa would laugh and curl over out of excitement. We made steady progress up the trail as it remained next to the Little River and under the shade of large trees.

Off in the distance, I could see something or someone blocking the trail. Because of the shade, it was hard to tell. Was it a bear? We had seen a mama bear and a couple of cubs playing in the grass just off to the side of the road earlier in the day, so we were on high alert. As we cautiously approached, it became clear that it was just a hiker eating her lunch in the middle of the trail.

I was able to push Kellisa around the lady, but not without spooking her. I doubt she expected to see someone on wheels so far up a trail. She apologized as we went by her. She appeared to be part of a larger group who were taking their break in front of Husky Falls.

The trail continued deeper into the mountains, but this was our turn-around point. I wanted to take a few pictures of the waterfalls and then position Kellisa on the wooden bridge with Husky Falls as the background, but people from the group were in all the prime picture-taking areas. We decided to wait for them to finish. I gave Kellisa an energy bar before enjoying one myself with some water. Everyone around us completed their lunches, but no one was getting up or moving. They were relaxing. I was patiently waiting, but after fifteen minutes, I politely asked a few to move a little so we could take our pictures without strangers in our shots.

They acted a bit put out by my request and moved a minimal amount. I was surprised because most encounters this far on a trail are friendly, and people often take their turn and move along. They will usually offer to take a few pictures while exchanging pleasantries. Not this time. I was disappointed that it was so hard. I started feeling bad for asking, but I waited for them to finish and didn't ask until it became apparent that they weren't moving anytime soon while being oblivious to anyone else around.

Between our arrival and this awkward moment, several other hikers arrived, and I could tell they also wanted clear pictures of the waterfall. I took a few quick photos and moved Kellisa out of the way. I wanted to take a few more to make sure we got a great shot, but I was ready to leave the uncomfortable situation.

I was looking forward to our return hike because I knew it would be all downhill. I was surprised at a few little inclines because I didn't notice any declines while heading out, but for the most part, we flew down the trail. Once I started seeing and hearing little kids running all over along with people using walkers and canes, I knew we were close to the trailhead. I pushed Kellisa while dodging people. It felt good to be back at our rental SUV, but it felt even better to have discovered a quality pushiking trail in the middle of a national park that receives more than eleven million visitors each year.

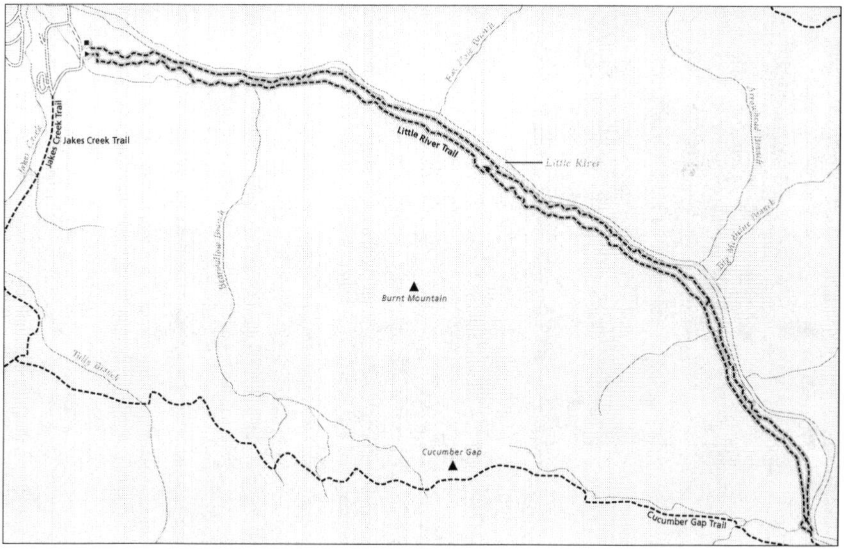

Little River Trail, Elkmont, TN

46
Texas

Trail name: Paluxy River	**Average speed:** 2.5 mi/h
Location: Dinosaur Valley State Park	**Total ascent:** 66 ft
Distance: 1.8 mi	**Highest point:** 674 ft
Duration (active): 43m	**Difficulty:** Easy

We visited Dinosaur Valley State Park, about ninety minutes southwest of Dallas, where we hoped to pushike in the dinosaur tracks. The park has five sets of dinosaur tracks, four of which can be seen by visitors. Dinosaurs left the tracks in the mud millions of years ago. Now the tracks reside under the water of the Paluxy River. We knew it might be tricky to get Kellisa close to the tracks but thought it would be a fun adventure either way. I could have called the park in advance with a few questions, but we usually get a quick yes if it's accessible or a straight no if it's not. Rarely can I convince a ranger there might be a gray area. Rangers just read what I can already see on the park's website.

I selected the Paluxy River Nature Trail because it passed two of the four open track sites, and by all online accounts, I felt confident I would be able to pushike with Kellisa for its entire length. We arrived early on a Sunday morning in October because we knew it was going to be a scorching hot day. Even arriving long before the midday sun, the temperature was 97°F when we started our pushike. Since we lived in a dry climate, the humidity hit us hard. I was concerned because I didn't see any shade near the beginning of the trail.

Kellisa was well hydrated, and I protected her head from the sun with a buff. We usually like to take our time while out on a trail, but I knew we had to move quickly through the sun-exposed areas of the path. We passed the trailhead kiosk without reading any of the information, but I did snap a couple of pictures just in case I needed to reference any information later in our pushike.

I was surprised the trail was paved. My research did not indicate this was a paved trail, and I found it odd that this trail wasn't labeled as ADA compliant. The path skirted the edge of a shallow forest. We could see the low level of the Paluxy River through the trees. On our right side was a large field filled with tall grasses that looked dried out and completely brown. We could see a forest rising on the other side.

I almost regretted my decision to skip the kiosk when I saw the sidewalk approaching an overflow parking lot. I started to think we weren't on an actual trail, but a connector sidewalk. Since we were still under the sun, I didn't want to stop and just hoped the path would lead to a trail. The trail split with one route leading toward the river while the other continued to the overflow lot. I pushed Kellisa into the forest on our way to the river to hopefully see the dinosaur tracks.

It turned out we were on a short spur trail with a few benches placed for a scenic view of the river and cliffs rising on the opposite side. The sidewalk ended abruptly at a fence, forcing us to return to the main path. Before we left the shade, I did consult the pictures on my phone. I concluded the sidewalk was our intended trail. I also checked Kellisa to make sure she was doing OK. No trail is worth getting sick over, and I didn't want to trigger heat-related seizures. Kellisa looked good and told me she wanted to continue. I decided to forge ahead, and if the sidewalk didn't end soon or at least turn into the forest, we would give up our pushike and save Texas for another day.

As the trail continued following above the river past the second parking lot, it turned to a natural surface and entered the forest just before the campground. Soon, the path became hard to follow, and it was difficult to know if we were still on the trail or pushiking through campsites. It was more confusing since all the campsites were vacant. We just followed what looked the most like a path, and after passing several sites, the ground started looking more like a trail.

An ATV was blocking the path just beyond the campground. As we approached, we could see a ranger cutting some of the branches back. He apologized and promptly moved his ATV. It was too hot to stay for small talk, so we were on our way after a quick "Thank you."

I kept looking for a path down to the river, but nothing appeared as a route. Even though we were in the shade, it seemed like the heat and humidity were continually rising with each passing minute, and I understood we would have a long stretch on our return trek where we'd be vulnerable under the relentless Texan sun. With no clear path down to the water, I decided to head back.

We didn't stop and returned to the trailhead in one long push to limit our sun exposure. I kept my eyes on Kellisa, and she seemed to be doing fine, but I knew I made the right decision. Back at the parking lot, I had parked in the closest spot to the trailhead, but I could see what looked like a sidewalk down to the river. I was hoping we could make it down to the water to explore some of the dinosaur tracks before leaving.

The pavement descended toward the water with a couple of places to sit and relax. The view of the rocky river below was serene. We could see many families playing in the water, and from people pointing to the water, we could guess where the tracks were. About halfway down, I was feeling pretty good until I realized it would take going down several steep stairs to reach the river. I couldn't believe the sloping sidewalk just ended short of our intended destination.

There was a path that continued from the end of the pavement, and we followed that a short distance. It didn't look like an official trail, but we thought it might still lead to the river. We were disappointed when it ended at a small clearing, too high above the water to see any tracks. I looked around for an alternative route down but didn't see any. I studied the stairs but did not feel comfortable trying to push Kellisa down and then back up.

I've been known to sling Kellisa over a shoulder and carry her a short distance when needed. We've conquered several stairs using this method, but between the heat and risk of slipping, I didn't think the risk was worth the reward. I would have had to carry Kellisa out in the water for any chance to see the tracks, and there was no way I was going to risk slipping in the river, so we headed back up the paved path in disappointment. I could have left Kellisa in her mobility chair with the brakes on while I went down for a quick view of the dinosaur tracks, but I don't like to do things alone when Kellisa is with me.

There were still two other sets of tracks we could explore, but once we were in our rental SUV with the air conditioning on full blast and water flowing into our bodies, neither one of us was interested in heading back out in the Texas heat for just a chance to see dinosaur tracks. We could wait until the next time we were in the area.

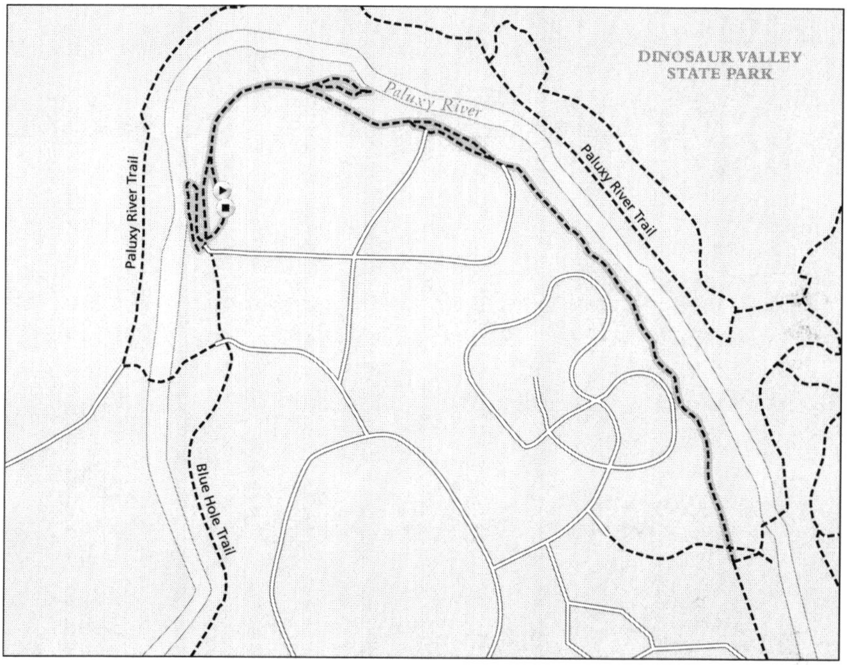

Paluxy River Trail, Glen Rose, TX

47
Utah

Trail name: Goosenecks View	**Average speed:** 1.8 mi
Location: Goosenecks State Park	**Total ascent:** 125 ft
Distance: 2.1 mi	**Highest point:** 4,968 ft
Duration (active): 1h 12m	**Difficulty:** Moderate

Utah is known as an outdoor lover's paradise with five national parks, including two of the most popular, Arches and Zion. Kellisa has been to Zion National Park several times, and one visit each to Arches and Canyonlands National Parks. All three parks are beautiful beyond what words can accurately describe, so it's no surprise they are heavily visited. On each of our visits, we found the roads congested with the parking lots and shuttle buses full and the trails crowded. All the trails we pushiked were magnificent, but it's hard enough traveling and hiking with a jog stroller or mobility chair without all the added crowds. When it takes hours to go a few miles or find an open parking spot, the experience loses something. It's challenging to push Kellisa under the best circumstances, and when you must continuously dodge other people, the quality of the adventure diminishes. I'm sure it's not as crowded during off-peak times, but with kids in school, we tend to visit when most other families can visit too.

While I would highly recommend a visit to all the national parks in Utah, I was looking for a slightly less stressful experience to share in this book. We immediately fell in love with the southeastern section of Utah upon our first visit back in June 2007. Lisa, Kellisa, and I explored the Four Corners region, and in Utah, that meant Monument Valley. It was early in our pushiking career, so I pushed Kellisa along a few trails in her tiny manual travel wheelchair. I found the hard desert soil and rocks made for easy pushing and knew we needed to return to explore beyond Monument Valley.

Kellisa and I would return to the region for a father-daughter spring break trip in 2010. We drove through Monument Valley again and experienced the Moki Dugway in both directions. The Moki Dugway is a road carved into the side of a cliff. The surface is natural, and when approaching the cliff from the bottom, you cannot see the road. It is one of the most unique and beautiful drives we've ever completed. Kellisa and I drove through Valley of the Gods and many other scenic areas.

The weather was unseasonably cold with strong and violent windstorms, which prevented us from doing any pushiking. While we shared a fantastic week, I was disappointed in the lack of time out on trails and vowed to return. Nine and a half years would pass before I needed to select a trail for Utah's chapter in this book. I remember seeing a rough road in Goosenecks State Park following the rim high above the San Juan River and thought that it might double as a trail.

I did a little research, and some consider it a hiking trail. Some of the trip reports even listed the Goosenecks View Trail as stroller and wheelchair friendly. I didn't recall the road looking that accessible, but a lot can change in almost ten years. Either way, I knew it would be a perfect trail to pushike and feature in the Utah chapter.

As you approach Goosenecks State Park, you must stop at a gate to pay an entry fee. Once beyond the entrance station, you can see endless views, including some of the buttes in Monument Valley. What you can't see until you reach the rim is the San Juan River snaking through the canyon far below. There's a viewpoint a short distance from the main parking area. Later in our visit, we noticed that many people come in the evening to watch the sunset from this spot.

We parked in the second parking area near a bathroom and picnic tables. We could see the road extend along the rim and turning to the south before ending at a point. I gave Kellisa some water through her g-tube before lifting her into her mobility chair. The road isn't marked, so I just started pushing Kellisa along the way as we ventured deeper into the state park.

Large rocks and ruts filled the road, but the path is wide enough to push around obstacles without too much of a struggle. I could see several campers set up along the way parked near the edge. I remembered seeing the same thing on our first visit and thinking it would be a great place to camp, even with a tent unless the winds were too violent. With endless views in all directions, it's hard to imagine a better place to witness a sunrise and sunset from the same spot. Goosenecks State Park is also very isolated and far from light pollution. I guess the Milky Way is visible on clear nights. For me, the highlight would be watching a full moon from behind a distant mountain slowly rising above the valleys.

The entire road follows the edge of the rim. While you're never at the edge, there are places where you can easily venture closer for better views down into the canyon. Kellisa and I stayed on the road. It's an out and back with one right turn, which leads out to the point. As we went farther down the road, it got narrower and rockier, but still reasonably easy to navigate. We passed the campers as we made our way toward the point. The trail started to deteriorate, causing me to have to pay closer attention to where I was pushing Kellisa. I was surprised to see some of the campers so far down the road. I don't think I would have attempted to go so far if we had a camper or even a high clearance 4x4 truck.

Shortly after passing the last camper, the road became a scramble of large rocks and boulders. While we could still follow the "road," I would think only highly modified off-road vehicles could continue down this stretch. I was able to navigate the obstacles by pushing Kellisa over and around the rocks and did not have to lift her and the mobility chair. While not extreme, the bumps were constant, and so were Kellisa's laughs. We eventually ran out of trail at the point. The view in all directions took our breath away. The San Juan River didn't look real. It resembled a giant painting. I looked back and could see the parking area where we left our rental SUV, and it looked a lot farther than the mile or so we pushiked.

After taking a few pictures, we started to pushike back to where we started. The sun had been at a wrong angle for photos when we started, but now it was beginning to set, allowing for better picture-taking opportunities. I took advantage of the light and took hundreds of pictures of Kellisa and the surrounding landscapes. As we passed one of the campers, an older man came out and said, "I need to give you guys credit. We've been watching you and didn't think you'd make it out there, but you did. Well done."

I thanked him, and Kellisa blew several kisses before we were on our way. The sun was setting fast, making for dramatic lighting across the valleys. I was tempted to stop every few minutes to take more pictures but wanted to have some time left for the main viewing area. I hoped the views there would reward us by being the best ones in the afternoon. Kellisa was a little confused when we continued past our parked SUV. She started saying "Hey!" while pointing to get my attention.

I told her we would go back to the SUV soon, but we had to watch the sunset first. The park designers picked the right spot for the viewing platform. We were perfectly positioned to watch the sunset while the canyon walls came alive with striking colors as the setting light reflected off at a low angle. I went back and forth between taking landscape pictures and pictures of Kellisa with the breathtaking landscape as the background. With the nightly show nearing its conclusion, I started pushing Kellisa back to our SUV. I wanted to have her and our stuff safely inside before it got pitch black outside.

Our time back in the Four Corners region was short, but our new memories and trail experience will last a lifetime. We started talking about a return trip to spend more time in the area with Lisa and Egypt joining us. Maybe we'll have our own camper or rent one in Phoenix or Albuquerque so we can camp out along the rim in Goosenecks State Park.

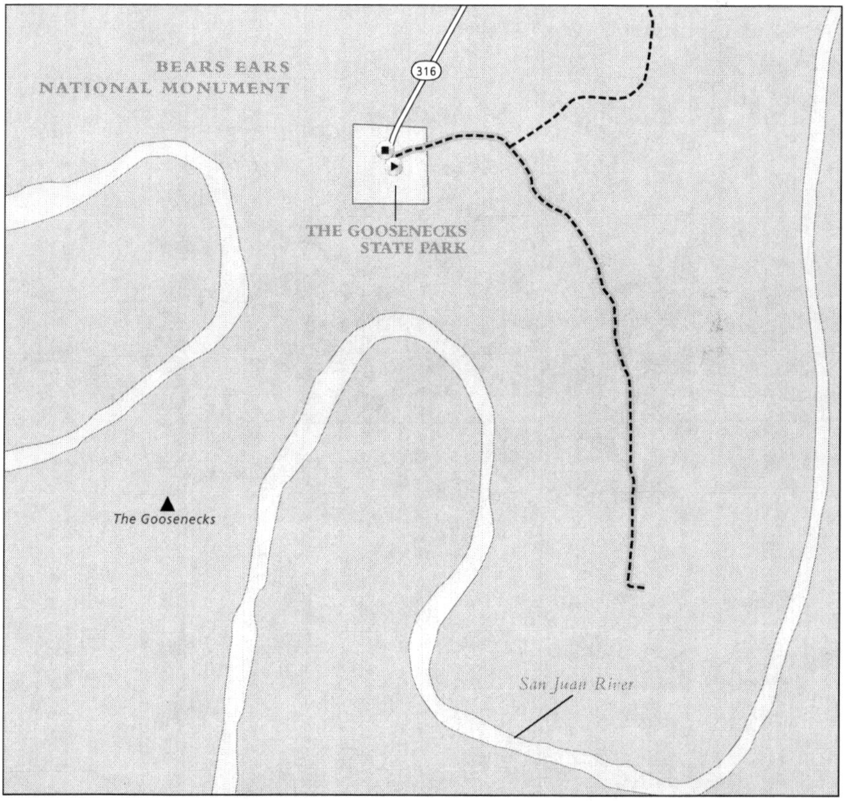

Goosenecks View Trail, Mexican Hat, UT

48
Vermont

Trail name: Old Railroad Passage
Location: Missisquoi National Wildlife Refuge
Distance: 3.0 mi
Duration (active): 1h 28m
Average speed: 2.0 mi/h
Total ascent: 39 ft
Highest point: 133 ft
Difficulty: Moderate

I knew from previous visits and my research that many Vermont trails were too rocky for pushiking. I decided to see if Vermont was home to any national wildlife refuges (NWR). I've had great success over the years finding amazing trails in the NWR system. Vermont has two, and I started with the Missisquoi NWR near the border with Canada. I was drawn to it because of its northern location and it being surrounded by water. I was hoping to find a trail with fewer rocks and flatter terrain. I selected with confidence the three-mile-long Old Railroad Passage trail, which went along a bog and through a forest before reaching Maquam Bay, as our Vermont adventure.

I pulled our rental SUV into the grassy parking lot at the trailhead for our trail. I noticed several other SUVs and a couple of pickups, but nothing out of the ordinary. I didn't have to check for trail conditions, so we started down the trail within a couple of minutes of arriving. While we were on the short stretch of gravel connecting the lot to the kiosk and the trail just beyond, I was startled when a man emerged from the brush dressed in camouflage and holding a shotgun. It was by his side, so I didn't feel too threatened, but still felt some concern.

He smiled and held up his free hand up to signal, "I mean you no harm."

Not entirely convinced, I was still cautious as he approached me and whispered, "We have a deer just off the trail, and I don't want your daughter to see it."

I thanked him for the warning. I pushed Kellisa around three other guys, also in camouflage, blocking a clear view of the dead animal. I distracted Kellisa to look the other way, and we were past them without any further contact. Once we were down the path maybe twenty-five yards, I couldn't help but look back. I saw the four men loading the deer into the back of one of the pickup trucks.

As we continued down the Old Railroad Passage trail, I wondered if hunting was allowed in the refuge. I pulled out my trail map, and there was a note to alert hikers that trails would be closed during the deer firearms season. The trail was open, but we witnessed a deer that had been shot, so I wasn't sure. The path was moving away from the direction where the hunters emerged, and I didn't hear any shotgun blasts, so I thought we would be safe since the trail was open.

Even rail trails seem to have an occasional twist or turn, but the Old Railroad Passage trail was a perfectly straight line. On our left, there was a bog through some trees and bushes. And on our right, a sizeable, open hayfield beyond some bushes. Some of the bushes had bright red leaves to add a splash of color mixed with the usual browns and greens found in the Northwoods.

The trail was a thick grass, which made pushing Kellisa an unexpected challenge for such a flat and level path. I wasn't worried about wildlife encounters or paying close attention to the trail in front of Kellisa's front tire when I saw a large snake scurrying to get off the path before getting run over. I'm not the best at identifying snakes unless they have a distinct rattle for their tail, but I'm mostly sure we saw a four-foot common watersnake. I took a few pictures of the snake hiding in the underbrush, but he was well camouflaged, making identification difficult.

Like most trails in the United States, I knew we could come across snakes in Vermont, including rattlesnakes, but they weren't on my radar until our harmless encounter. The snake was nonaggressive and wanted to get out of our way in peace. From then on, I kept a closer eye on the trail in front of us while pushing Kellisa.

Our route eventually made a little detour through a forest breaking up the straight-line course of the trail. Because I was pushing Kellisa, I detected slight elevation changes during this short section. Most casual hikers probably wouldn't notice when they gain a few feet in altitude, but it's obvious when pushing more than 100 pounds. After the short jaunt through the forest, we were back on the railroad corridor. The trail became narrower, with some of the brush protruding to the edges of the path. I was extra cautious to prevent Kellisa from getting scratched since her elbows can stick out the way she relaxes them on the armrests on her mobility chair. None of the branches were long enough to reach her face, so we continued our pushike to Maquam Bay. We crossed paths with two additional snakes on this section of the trail. Both looked like the first snake we saw, only smaller. They got out of our way before any contact with Kellisa's front wheel.

A swampy area appeared on our left side. It reminded me of trails in the southeastern United States. When I see wet areas like this, I always think alligators and cottonmouth snakes. I was sure we wouldn't see any alligators but wasn't sure about the range of the cottonmouth. I would later learn that the northern edge of their range is in Virginia.

Just ahead, I could see the wide-open waters of the bay through trees void of most of their leaves. The trail made a hard-left turn before reaching the water, leaving us on a piece of land between the swamp and bay. After a short distance, the trail just ended. I would have doubted such an abrupt ending, but there were a few signs alerting hikers that this was indeed the end of the trail. I was curious why the trail builders didn't end the trail at the water. I looked around and saw a few lesser paths heading toward the water, but none of them were wide enough for Kellisa's mobility chair. The lack of full-spreading views across the bay was anticlimactic and a little disappointing.

Our return along the Old Railroad Passage trail was uneventful. Some out-and-back trails look remarkably different from the reverse direction, but not this trail. The views seemed the same, going in both directions. However, it is still a scenic trail well suited for pushiking. We only stopped for a little water and a few pictures.

Once we got to our hotel the evening of our Vermont pushike, I looked up the firearms hunting season for Missisquoi NWR. Deer hunting by archery was open in the area of our pushike, but not firearms. I don't know how the deer was killed, and I can't say I saw any archery equipment, but I didn't look closely at the deer since I was trying to get past the hunters with Kellisa. I'm also not sure if hunters can legally carry firearms while out archery hunting in Vermont. I don't think we were ever in danger, but this incident reminded me to research local hunting seasons before attempting future trails.

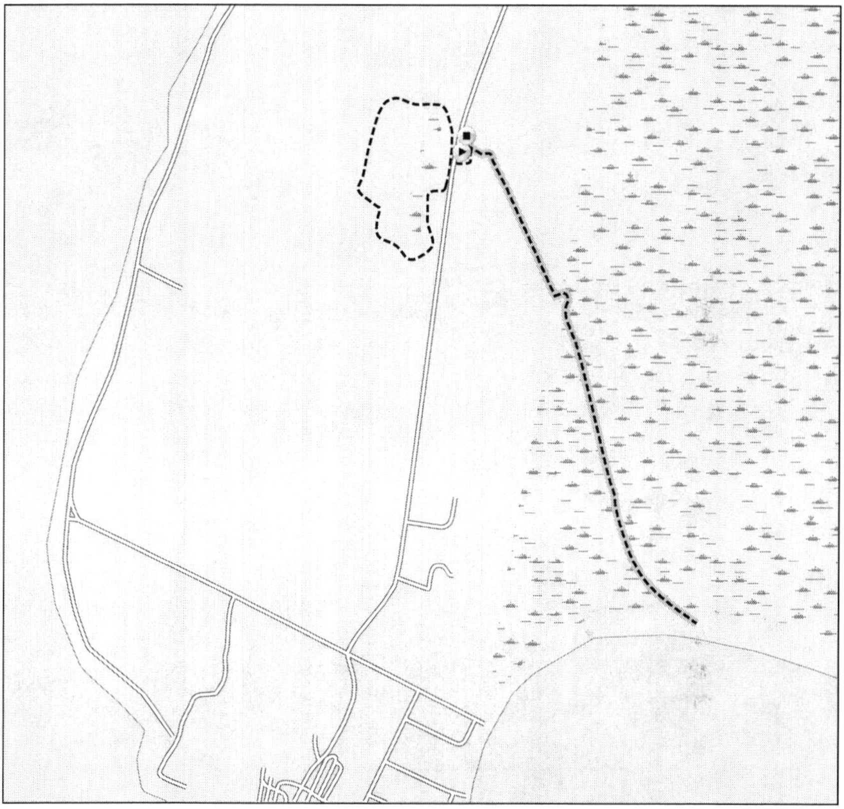

Old Railroad Passage, Franklin County, VT

49

Virginia

Trail name: Virginia Creeper
Location: Mount Rogers National Recreation Area
Distance: 7.3 mi
Duration (active): 2h 13m
Average speed: 3.3 mi/h
Total ascent: -230 ft
Highest point: 2,440 ft
Difficulty: Moderate

Kellisa and I discovered the Virginia Creeper Trail on our first out-of-state father-daughter camping trip back in June 2006. I was driving down a two-lane country road curving around endless bends in a river with mountains rising on both sides. Out of the corner of my eye, I saw what looked like a wide path down by the river's edge. It was hard to get a good look because I had to keep my eyes focused on the road. I eventually passed a small side road on the side with the river. It took about ten minutes before I could safely turn around and backtrack, but I knew I had to investigate this trail.

We were in luck. The road ended at a small parking lot with access to this trail. Signs at the trailhead provided information on the Virginia Creeper Trail. We learned the path followed an abandoned railroad bed for thirty-five miles from Whitetop, Virginia, to Abington, Virginia. I doubt I even knew what a rail-to-trail was at the time, but I didn't hesitate to take Kellisa on a pushike for a few miles following the perfect trail.

When it came time to select a trail in Virginia to pushike for this book, I knew we had to revisit the Virginia Creeper Trail. The early summer skies were threatening rain as we approached Damascus, Virginia, the starting point for our 2019 Virginia Creeper Trail adventure. Since this would be a unique point-to-point pushike, we needed a shuttle service. Fortunately, several companies in Damascus specialize in shuttling bicyclists to Whitetop, where they can cruise mostly downhill back to Damascus or Abington.

I called ahead to one of the outfitters and explained that we would have a mobility chair to transport instead of a bike, and the only question they had for me was, "Can it be strapped down to a bike trailer?"

"I don't see why not," was my answer, and they agreed to provide shuttle service to us.

When I was checking our gear and getting it packed in the parking lot, I realized I forgot our rain gear at home. I knew we would probably need it at some point and was kicking myself for making such a rookie mistake. The bike shuttle company also has a retail store specializing in outdoor equipment and clothing. I knew we could purchase the necessary rain protection, but I wasn't thrilled with the unexpected expense since we already had perfectly good gear at home, and quality outdoor gear can be expensive.

Once inside, I let them know we were there for our shuttle, and they radioed the van driver to meet us out front. I looked at the rain jackets and pants that were on display, and my stomach knotted up. I was on the fence because it was so warm outside, but also knew you could quickly get hypothermia when wet in any condition. I knew we'd be on the trail for at least two hours while being far from help and mostly out of cell coverage. I had to purchase something and started looking for ponchos. The store had high-quality ponchos, and not the type that looks like they're made from clear garbage bags. I bought two and threw them in my backpack to be safe.

As we rolled outside, the van and trailer were waiting. We would be the only two passengers on this trip. I requested a drop-off at the Taylor's Valley trailhead. I lifted Kellisa to a backseat in the large passenger van and put her seat belt on before helping our driver secure her mobility chair to the bike trailer. Once we were satisfied it wasn't going anywhere, I joined Kellisa in the van and we were off. Our van left town and headed up into the mountains. It had been raining off and on for several days, so everything looked alive with fresh greenery. Even with closed windows, you could smell and almost taste the forest around us.

It wasn't long before we found ourselves at Taylor's Valley. I jumped out of the shuttle van to help unload Kellisa's mobility chair. I can be slightly protective of her wheels. I wheeled the chair close to the van's side door and placed Kellisa in her seat, then threw my backpack on. We were ready to go. As the van started to pull away, I waved, and the driver stopped. Since we were joining the Virginia Creeper Trail in the middle, the valley was relatively flat. Feeling all turned around from the winding mountain roads we had just traveled, I wasn't entirely sure which way to go. I pointed in the direction that seemed correct. With a thumbs-up from the driver, we were on our way.

We followed the trail into a tunnel-like opening in the forest where we were greeted by a sign announcing the path was entering Mount Rogers National Recreation Area. Laurel Creek was swiftly flowing to our left, while large boulders and cliffs rose up the mountainside on our right. The trail was damp, wide, and flat as it headed downhill toward Damascus. I tried to stay on the right side of the trail since we might be sharing the path with bikers and even horses. If they came upon us suddenly at a high rate of speed, I wanted them to be able to pass safely.

It wasn't long before we were crossing a refurbished wooden trestle spanning Laurel Creek. Kellisa enjoyed the canyon views while I took a few pictures. With a clear view of the sky directly above us, I looked up to try to assess the possibility of rain. For now, it looked like it might hold off.

The trail continued its mostly downhill descent toward Damascus. Since this was an old railroad bed, the curves following the mountain contours were gentle. When a curve was sharp enough that the engineers couldn't make the turn, a trestle was constructed to span the gap. In total, the Virginia Creeper Trail has forty-seven trestles. Kellisa and I stopped at every trestle for the photo opportunities. The views from the trestles were enhanced by the sounds and aromas coming from the rushing waters far below.

With each crossing, I couldn't help but notice the sky appearing a little grayer, but the rain was still holding off. Other than two mountain bikers, we had the trail to ourselves. That would change around the halfway point of our pushike. I was stopped for a quick sip of water when I had a feeling someone was watching us. I looked around and didn't see or hear anyone. Then I started looking up, and I saw a man standing about a hundred feet above us on the side of the mountain. He was looking in our general direction. When surprised in the outdoors, I usually look to see how the person is dressed. It's not an exact science, but I feel better if they look the part. Between the distance and the deep shade from the trees, I couldn't be sure. It looked like the man was in his fifties, and his clothes indicated he might be a trail runner. I tried not to stare but wanted to keep an eye on him just in case. It seemed like a long time but was probably only about forty-five seconds before he took off running swiftly down what I can only assume was another trail perched high above the Virginia Creeper Trail.

The runner was moving away from us, but I couldn't help looking behind us every couple of minutes until I forgot about our innocent encounter and focused on the trail in front of us. I noticed several campsites set just off the trail in prime locations. The Appalachian Trail follows the Virginia Creeper Trail for a short section, and I could picture thru-hikers stopping here for the night on their march along the famous 2,200-mile scenic trail. I couldn't help but imagine returning someday with Kellisa for a longer pushike on the Virginia Creeper Trail, one where we would have to spend a night or two camping out along Laurel Creek.

The sounds of cars and trucks started penetrating the serene forest when I felt the first raindrops. I knew we were approaching the road leading back to Damascus and would be back to our rental SUV in less than twenty to thirty minutes. The rain was scattered and felt good on my sweaty body, but I was worried about Kellisa, who has more of her body exposed as she sits in her chair. It was still warm out, and I had to balance the potential discomfort from getting wet with the risk of overheating Kellisa under a poncho, which can trigger seizures. I opted to continue in the drizzle.

It wasn't long before the rain intensified to a downpour. I had just pushed Kellisa to the side of the trail under a large tree to help shield us from the rain when just the third mountain biker we would see out on the trail passed us. He was going at a high rate of speed. Considering the wet conditions, I was thankful we were safely off to the side. I pulled out one of our ponchos for Kellisa.

It's always a challenge dressing another person, especially when they're in a sitting position and can't help. There is also a precise science to slipping a poncho over Kellisa. You need to pull it over and under her, so she's completely sitting on it before tugging it over her legs and wrapping it up around her shoes. If I didn't enclose her, she would end up sitting in a puddle that would wick up through her clothes trapping all the moisture under the poncho.

By the time I had Kellisa protected, I was soaked and ready to get moving again. I decided to leave my poncho in the backpack since I knew we were close to the end of our pushike. Kellisa was giggling because the wind was picking up a little making our visibility more of a challenge. I felt relief to see the first building of town just off to our left. A minute later, I could see our SUV parked just outside the outfitters we were using. I was tempted to go right to the SUV, load up Kellisa and our gear, and be on our way, but I wanted Kellisa to get a souvenir T-shirt to commemorate our adventure.

I rolled Kellisa into the store, where I removed her poncho. She was all smiles and giggles. I rolled the poncho up and stuffed it into a side pocket on my backpack. Before we could start shopping, the man who rang up our poncho purchase approached us. "How did you like the trail?"

"It was awesome, and I think you can tell by her smiles and giggles that she had a great time, too," I replied.

The young man thought we'd like to know that just fifteen minutes before our arrival, a mountain biker entered his shop to purchase two ponchos. As he was about to pay, the biker explained that he just passed two people out on the trail stuck in the rain without gear. The man behind the counter asked if it was a father pushing a girl in a crazy-looking blue chair, and the biker said, "That's them."

The man from the store assured the mountain biker that we were okay because he sold us two last-minute ponchos a couple of hours ago just before we were shuttled to our starting point.

Kellisa and I are treated very well by the outdoor community and welcomed without limits most of the time. We left Damascus feeling excellent and eager to return for a backpacking trip.

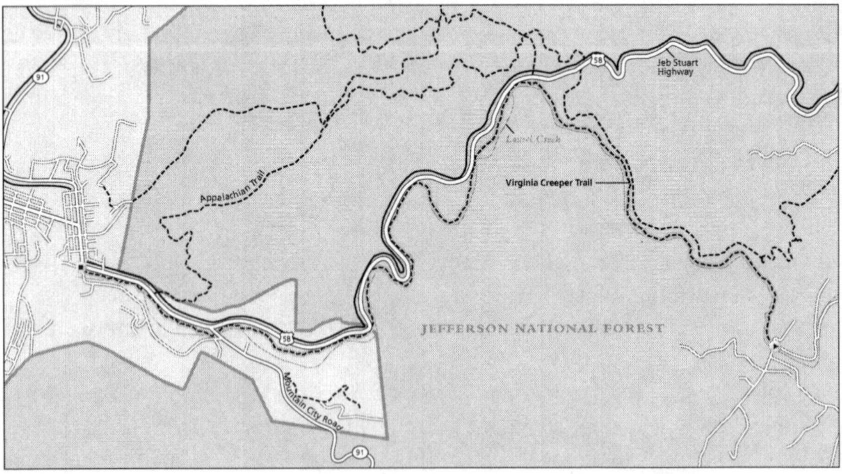

Virginia Creeper Trail, Damascus, VA

50
Washington

Trail name: Old Growth Forest	**Average speed:** 1.0 mi/h
Location: Lewis and Clark State Park	**Total ascent:** 118 ft
Distance: 1.0 mi	**Highest point:** 526 ft
Duration (active): 54m	**Difficulty:** Moderate

Egypt wanted to join her sister on one of her state pushikes so she could be in this book too. I asked her if she had a preference as to which state she pushiked, and not surprising, it didn't matter.

Egypt has been interested in the Lewis and Clark Expedition since she first started learning about them in school a few years ago. When I found an interesting looking trail in Washington in a state park named after the famed expedition, I knew which state to invite Egypt to join us for a pushike. I read the trail and park descriptions to her, and she was on board. We decided to drive up on Labor Day weekend.

It rained hard the day before and the morning of our pushike. By the time we arrived at the park, I was worried about the conditions of the trail. We parked near the trailhead. Egypt was excited to be with her sister out on a trail experience. I think it was bringing back positive memories from traveling around the country for several years on our original fifty states pushiking trips. Egypt takes great pride in that she has visited all fifty states and usually starts conversations with strangers with that fact. Most will look at Lisa or me with doubt, and we must assure them that yes, Egypt has been to all fifty. Most people are surprised and try to figure out how many states they've visited. So far, we haven't met anyone else who's been to all fifty.

I took a few pictures of the girls at the trailhead and still couldn't tell if the trail would be too muddy. I was expecting about 150 feet of elevation gain if we pushiked the entire trail. As soon as we took our first steps, we entered the forest. It was liked stepping and pushing into another world. The old-growth trees towered high above while lush ferns grew in dense clusters on the forest floor. Everything was so alive and fresh from the recent downpours. We could see dozens of shades of green, all vibrant. Egypt noted how nice the forest smelled. I was anxious to pushike, but we stopped for just a few minutes to take in our surroundings.

The beginning of the trail was flat, and we crossed a picturesque wooden bridge to transport us across a small creek. I had read trip reports warning that the path featured several loops, and the intersections are confusing. We found that to be true at the very first intersection. We had already made a couple of turns, and I was disoriented but picked the direction I thought would lead us deeper into the forest.

The trail started to get steeper, and unfortunately, it also was getting muddier. The flatter section was just soggy, but now we were slipping and sliding in the mud. Egypt asked if she could push Kellisa, and I agreed. I felt terrible because I knew she wanted to help her sister, but forward progress was frustratingly slow because of all the mud. It was challenging to get enough traction to push Kellisa up the inclines without sliding back to where you started. I couldn't have been prouder of Egypt, as she was determined and didn't give up.

Kellisa doesn't laugh when Egypt is struggling like she does when I'm behind her mobility chair during challenging sections. She encourages Egypt with kisses and chants of "More."

We slowly made it to another trail junction. It looked like one way descended toward the campground, and I asked Egypt if she wanted to continue on the trail and keep going. I offered to take over with Kellisa for the next section, and Egypt took me up on my suggestion. It was just as hard for me to push Kellisa, and I think Egypt had a harder time hiking without using her sister's mobility chair for leverage.

Egypt and Kellisa have a remarkable relationship. They can get on each other's nerves and fight like any two sisters, but I would argue they have a unique bond stronger than most. Egypt will look out for her big sister and defend her if she feels Kellisa is a victim of discrimination. Egypt is fiercely loyal. She takes great offense if someone ignores Kellisa or accidentally bumps into Kellisa. She will usually say something to the stranger.

Egypt is also what I call a "seizure whisperer." She has a knack of sensing when Kellisa is having a seizure, even if they're in different rooms with a lot of noise in the house. Egypt can't describe it, but I think she has a keen sense of hearing and can detect the change in Kellisa's breathing when she's having a seizure. Egypt doesn't panic and will alert Lisa or me while running to her sister's side. Egypt will start talking to Kellisa in a calm voice: "It's OK, Kellisa. Come on back to me; you're OK. Breathe. Come on, Kellisa, come back to me."

We have never asked Egypt to help take care of Kellisa when they're adults, but she's been talking about "when I'm in charge of Kellisa, I'm going to watch over her and make sure her life is fair."

From a young age, she has assumed on her own that someday she will be Kellisa's guardian when Lisa and I are no longer able to fulfill that responsibility. We never asked or expected for Egypt to have that role, but she's been grooming herself, and I have no doubt she will always be an awesome little sister who watches out for Kellisa.

Kellisa repays Egypt the only way she knows how, she blows kisses of love, encouragement, and thankfulness. Egypt will always acknowledge Kellisa by saying, "Thank you for the kiss, Kellisa. I love you too," before returning the kiss. Kellisa will also give Egypt giant bear hugs.

Kellisa isn't shy in asking for help from Egypt, and most of the time, she's more than happy to help. Egypt will help get Kellisa a snack or meal and prepare it so Kellisa can eat it herself. If it's a food requiring a fork or spoon, Egypt will assist by feeding Kellisa. Another common task is changing the DVDs in Kellisa's room when one is over.

It didn't surprise me when Egypt asked for another turn at pushing Kellisa. I stepped aside as she took over. I was always worried that Kellisa would never go out on a trail once I couldn't push her anymore, but I think she will still get a chance with Egypt. At that moment, we were in the middle of a cathedral of old-growth forest, and I couldn't love my girls more or feel a greater sense of pride.

The trail was now on a constant incline, and the mud was ankle-deep. Without any roots or rocks to gain some traction or stop our slides back, it was becoming almost impossible to push Kellisa. I took over just before the steepest section yet. Egypt offered to go first to test it out for us. She only made it about a quarter of the way up before she came sliding back down. I could tell she was being serious and couldn't go any farther.

I told Egypt, "I'm not going to try; let's start heading back to the SUV."

She was disappointed and asked if I was sure, and I assured her it was alright to stop at this point. I could tell Egypt was worried she was preventing Kellisa and me from finishing the trail. I told her there was no way we could have made it up the hill. I proceeded to attempt to prove it to her, so that she didn't have any doubt or feelings of guilt.

We slipped and slid our way back down to the trailhead. Egypt pushed Kellisa the final stretch along flat ground and the short distance through the park to our SUV. In the end, the trail was 1.7 miles long, with 154 feet of elevation gain according to the trail guide, and we completed precisely 1 mile and gained a respectable 118 feet, considering the harsh conditions.

Egypt was still worried because we usually like to finish a trail, but I explained to her there's more to a path than finishing. Spending quality time with loved ones while experiencing nature is a more fabulous gift than being able to say you completed a trail. I told her how proud I was of her and Kellisa. I also told her how I didn't think most ten-year-olds would have given up a holiday weekend to pushike with their sister on such a demanding trail and do it so happily.

It finally started to make sense when I said, "Egypt, I could tell you were working very hard to get your sister up that trail, and you never gave up. You are very special. I'm so proud of you, and I can't wait to tell mom what a great trail sister you are for Kellisa. I love you."

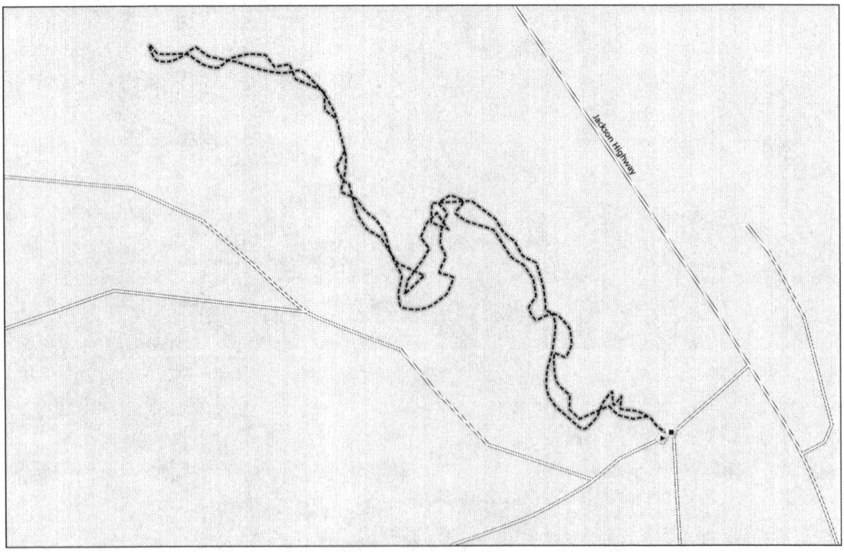

Old Growth Forest Trail, Lewis County, WA

51
West Virginia

Trail name: Overlook
Location: Beech Fork State Park
Distance: 2.8 mi
Duration (active): 1h 22m
Average speed: 2.0 mi/h
Total ascent: 374 ft
Highest point: 877 ft
Difficulty: Challenging

West Virginia is known as the "Mountain State." Selecting a trail with an ascent and view was at the top of my list of trail attributes. Many hours of research revealed most mountainous trails would be too rocky for us to navigate. Eventually, I zeroed in on the Overlook Trail in Beech Fork State Park, just south of Huntington. The trail led to a rock outcrop with the promise of a possible view. From the pictures I could find online, the trail looked steep but clear of most obstacles. I gave us a 70 percent chance of success, just enough for me to feel comfortable making arrangements to make our attempt on the Overlook Trail.

The day we had available was filled with predictions of rain. Kellisa enjoyed swaying from side to side as our rental SUV hugged the edges of the road as we followed a river through the hills and mountains to the park in a rainstorm.

Just as I started having doubts about the weather, the rain stopped as we arrived at the trailhead. We didn't waste time and started our pushike with a bridge crossing over a small creek before passing through a campfire gathering area for park rangers to hold interpretive talks with campers and visitors. Kellisa and I had the park to ourselves on this wet and cold weekday at the end of November.

The trail quickly became demanding as we started the switchbacks portion of our adventure. The trail was covered with wet leaves and a grade just gentle enough to allow for safe pushiking with minimal risk of slipping backward. Like every trail with any elevation changes, I was tethered to Kellisa's chair.

The trail was narrow but just wide enough to allow Kellisa's back wheels to remain on the path, making pushing Kellisa a lot easier. We spied on four deer munching on some lunch just ahead of us after making the turn on the fourth switchback. We watched quietly for several minutes until we were spotted. The deer stared back at us for a minute until Kellisa spooked them with an excited giggle. I'm always amazed at how quickly deer can disappear into the forest.

We continued the constant climb to the rocky overlook. I was trying to keep an eye on the weather through the trees. Even though most of the leaves had fallen, the forest was so dense with overhead clouds and neighboring ridges, it was difficult to predict how much time we had until the next downpour. I had our rain gear but was concerned the trail could become a slippery and dangerous mess too muddy for a safe descent.

We reached the section of the trail where there was a split. To our right was the shortest route to the overlook, and straight ahead was the beginning of a clockwise loop through the forest, eventually leading back to the overlook.

We went for the shorter route because I was thinking we could turn around after reaching the overlook and still consider our pushike a success. The trail became increasingly steep as we approached the top of the ridge. It got to the point where Kellisa's front wheel was probably three feet above my head due to the sharp angle. I knew that stopping wasn't an option. I could see the top where the trail had to level out, and, as always, Kellisa used her wonderful sense of when I need a boost, and she let out a series of giggles and yelled, "More!"

With Kellisa providing the needed energy for my internal drive, we reached the top of the ridge. To our right was the rock outcropping with what promised to be the best view of the entire trail. I had read reports that the view was disappointing for the effort to reach the spot. Summer visitors would have their view limited by the lush green forest rising from the mountainside, but on this late fall day, our view through the bare trees was breathtaking.

I took in the far-reaching views while feeling proud of our accomplishment. After a few minutes, I snapped a few dozen photos of us with the hope that some would be worthy of sharing. We had pushiked approximately three-fourth of a mile and gained close to 300 feet. I had a decision to make: Do we return the way we came and play it safe, or do we continue deeper into the forest to complete the loop? The rain was holding off, and I figured we had already reached the crux of the trail, so the decision was easy. We would continue into the unknown to experience the entire loop.

The trail was narrow with drop-offs on our right while the mountain continued to rise to our left. The path took us farther from the trailhead with noticeable elevation changes as we followed the contours of the mountainside. After making a left turn, which I figured would start pointing us back to complete the loop, the trail descended 200 feet over the next half-mile. I knew we were dropping too fast and would have to make up some of the lost elevation at some point. This can be quite disheartening while out on a challenging pushike, but we continued.

Kellisa enjoyed a couple of low points on the trail where I had to push her through running water. I'm sure these were temporary creeks from the recent rainfall. I paused with Kellisa directly over one of the little streams so she could enjoy the flowing water beneath her chair. Once she started to reach for the water to play, I knew it was time to keep going because it was too cold for both of us to get wet. I felt terrible for denying Kellisa the fun of splashing around but knew it was the responsible decision.

I had difficulty pushing Kellisa up a steep fifty-foot section of the trail due to the slippery leaves covering the path. The trail leveled out as we rounded another bend, and I could tell we were finally on the other side of the mountain.

For some reason, trails always seem longer than they should, but we eventually completed the loop. I proudly looked up at the steep trail to the rock overlook and was thankful we had that section already on our pushiking resume.

After a short water break, we followed the trail down the switchbacks. Because going downhill is so much easier with gravity on our side, it seemed like we were down in a fraction of the time it took to ascend. The rain started to fall just as we were crossing the wooden bridge near the parking lot.

As I drove slowly through a raging rainstorm, I was thankful we avoided getting drenched out on the trail while feeling satisfied with our trail experience in the "Mountain State."

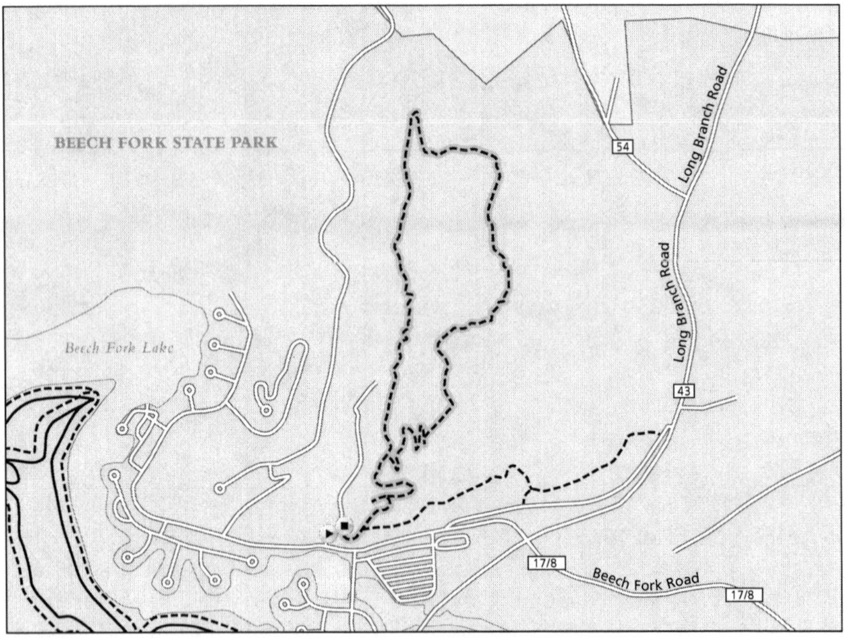

Overlook Trail, Barboursville, WV

52
Wisconsin

Trail name: Dry Lake Trail Loop
Location: Chippewa Moraine State Recreation Area
Distance: 2.1 mi
Duration (active): 1h 19m
Average speed: 1.6 mi/h
Total ascent: 233 ft
Highest point: 1,239 ft
Difficulty: Challenging

Kellisa and I have pushiked trails from beaches to swamps to mountains to forests to deserts under blazing heat and across frozen lakes. We've pushiked trails from less than a mile in length to our longest day of twenty miles across the desert in New Mexico. We've been out on a trail for less than an hour to three days pushiking around Grand Island in Lake Superior. The one thing we haven't done is a thru-hike. A thru-hike is a long trail that requires many days to several months to complete. Some hikers complete a thru-hike in one continuous push, while others hike partial segments over several, or even many, years. Many people ask me the question, "What's next?" and while I don't have a definite answer, I would like to complete a thru-hike someday with Kellisa.

Even if we never attempt to complete a long trail from start to finish, I would like to plan a one-to-two-week backpacking trip. While researching and planning day hikes, I often come across trails with possibilities for multiday pushikes. One trail that makes this list is the Ice Age Trail stretching for 1,200 miles across Wisconsin. I'm not sure the entire length is possible with a mobility chair, but I'm confident we could find a multiday route.

For this book, I selected a 2.1-mile loop trail in the Northwoods, which shares a small segment of the Ice Age Trail. The United States is a vast country with every kind of outdoor environment imaginable, and if I had to pick a favorite, it just might be the Northwoods, especially Minnesota through Wisconsin to the upper peninsula of Michigan.

Usually, I'd be full of excitement while driving to a trail in northern Wisconsin. However, I spent the four-hour approach drive feeling nervous due to the consistent downpour of rain. I was worried the rain wouldn't stop, and even if it did, the trail would be too muddy to attempt our pushike. I like to have a plan B, but I must admit I didn't have one for Wisconsin, and we were on a tight schedule.

I always pack rain gear or ponchos on our pushikes, but I hope we never need them. I don't like starting a pushike in the rain. I'd rather delay the pushike or wait for another day with better conditions. However, I was afraid we'd have no choice but to start our Wisconsin trail in a downpour.

We were driving over from Minnesota, where we pushiked in Myre-Big Island State Park earlier in the day. I stopped at a store near the border between Minnesota and Wisconsin to pick up a few supplies. We got soaked while quickly running into the store and were surprised to see it finally let up to a mild drizzle when we left the store only a few minutes later. I was filled with hope as we drove the last hour or so to the trailhead under gray skies and scattered light rain.

It was still drizzling as I pulled into the Interpretive Center's parking lot, which doubles as the trailhead for our pushike. I would have loved to take Kellisa inside to see the displays, including live native reptiles and snakes, but we couldn't afford the time. I wanted to start the trail while it was only drizzling since the skies looked like they could still produce a torrential downpour at any moment. I couldn't have scripted the weather any better, but it stopped raining as I was getting Kellisa's mobility chair and our gear out of the rental SUV. With excitement and hope, Kellisa and I blazed a trail through a grassy area toward the trailhead sign. We would soon find out if the trail was too muddy for our adventure.

After just a few steps, we felt utterly absorbed by the forest as it closed in from all sides. It wasn't raining, but rainwater was continually dripping from the leaves and branches high above, which helped against the intense humidity. We had to decide to start our loop to our right or left. For no real reason, I decided to go right, making this a counterclockwise loop. The trail was muddy, but not too deep as we continued on a narrow trail with drop-offs to our left. There were a few slight elevation changes and roots, but nothing too worrisome. We crossed a short wooden bridge before dropping out of the forest with a large field to our right. Wildflowers were blowing in the post-rain wind filling the air with their vibrant scent. Kellisa's wheels sunk in the soggy grass through this section with mild elevation changes making the pushing a little more challenging. I'm sure the trail is firm when it's dry.

Around 0.7 miles in, the Dry Lake Trail Loop merges with the Ice Age Trail. We continued to our left following both trails as they skirted several lakes created after the last glacial period when this area was covered by hundreds of feet of ice. The trail crossed another wooden bridge before disappearing back into the forest. We were now at the bottom of the steep drop-off we saw at the beginning of the trail. I couldn't help but be a little concerned that we had a lot of elevation to gain at some point, and I was hoping it wouldn't be too muddy. I didn't want to backtrack.

At one point, lakes were on both sides of the trail surrounded by the forest, now fully displaying its vibrant greens from the recent rains. It was late in the afternoon, and I was pleasantly surprised by the lack of mosquitoes considering so much water surrounded us. The trail was following a slow, steady incline when we came to another intersection. We could go left on the Mammoth Nature Trail, which would be a shortcut back to the trailhead, or we could continue our loop.

The weather conditions remained favorable, so we decided to proceed with the Dry Lake Loop. (I will note the Mammoth Nature Trail looked a little steep.) The trail curved around another lake and eventually dropped down to the very edge of the water. I hated giving up any elevation, knowing we would have to make it up again, but I was more worried about the deep mud. It looked like a short, but difficult section. The wheels sunk deep in the mud, making progress painstakingly slow. My hiking boots were also sinking in the mud. I was looking for roots or rocks to gain traction, but we were surrounded by mud and water.

As the trail moved away from the edge of the lake, it started up a hill, creating the steepest ascent of the afternoon. I was relieved to be past the mud but wasn't looking forward to a climb so soon after struggling. It didn't take the trail long to lessen the incline returning our progress to a steady speed. It seemed like we were going farther away from the trailhead when I felt like we already made the turn toward the end. I checked the map and was confident we were still on the correct trail, but once I have any doubt, I always like to check and double-check my map. I prefer to take a few extra minutes figuring everything out than make a wrong decision because it usually leads to more bad choices.

An intersection appeared, and it was clearly labeled with directions. The long Ice Age Trail continued one way, and the other direction led back to our trailhead. It was reassuring to know exactly where we were, and we were on the correct path. We were going slower than usual, which probably added to my thinking we were out on the trail too long.

I thought we were on the home stretch, but I was wrong. The trail dropped down again to the edge of another lake. At the bottom was a mud pit that required another slog across. I shouldn't have looked ahead, but I did and saw the trail rise again just beyond the mud. I kicked it up a gear to push through this section and up the incline. I needed to stop to rest for a minute and drink some water once we reached the top. My little break didn't last long because someone rang the bell, and it was feeding time for the mosquitoes. They came out of nowhere with a kamikaze method of dive-bombing us.

I knew we were close to the end, but decided I needed to get us protected from the biting pests. I sprayed Kellisa first before turning the repellent on myself. A few got through and bit us before the repellent was applied. The bug spray did its job, and we were left alone except for some buzzing sounds near our ears as they attempted to attack but pulled back before making a landing.

The trail followed a gentle ridge the last 0.2 of a mile back to the trailhead where we emerged on the grassy field with our SUV in sight. The Interpretive Center had closed for the day, and we would have to be content knowing we will most likely return someday in the dry season for a multiday pushike on the Ice Age Trail, and Kellisa could enjoy the displays and local wildlife exhibits at that time.

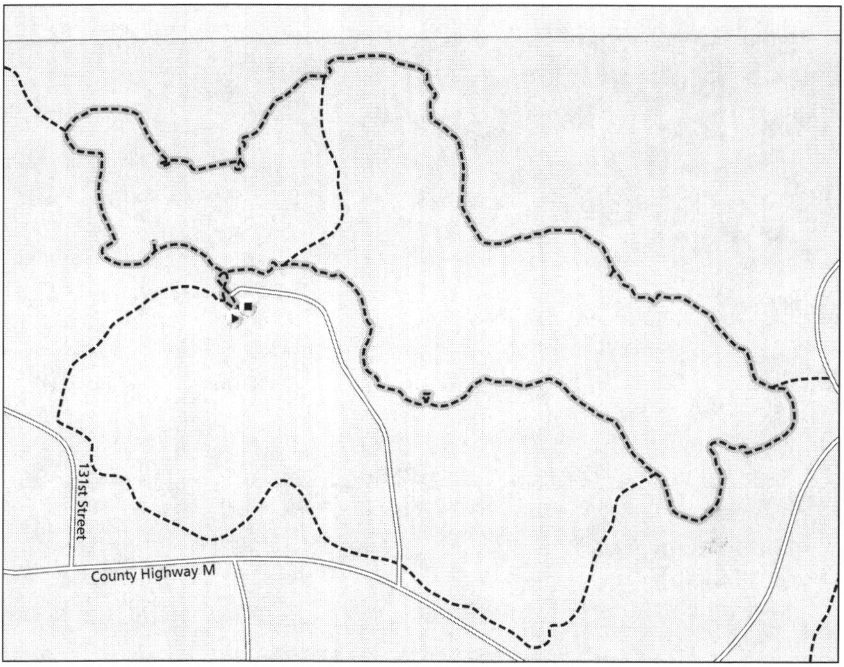

Dry Lake Trail Loop, Chippewa County, WI

53
Wyoming

Trail name: Devils Tower
Location: Devils Tower National Monument
Distance: 1.7 mi
Duration (active): 1h 7m
Average speed: 1.5 mi/h
Total ascent: 299 ft
Highest point: 4,414 ft
Difficulty: Moderate

Wyoming is home to the world-famous Grand Teton and Yellowstone National Parks. But when it came time to select a trail for this book, I had an image in my mind of Devils Tower, a mammoth rock rising 1,267 feet straight up from the ground above the Belle Fourche River in the far northeastern corner of the state. This mental picture of Devils Tower is from the movie *Close Encounters of the Third Kind*. I was too young to watch the film when it was first released, but I vividly remember being scared by the commercials and movie posters. The dramatic image of the tower lit up by spaceship lights under a night sky has been firmly embedded in my mind ever since.

In 1906, President Theodore Roosevelt established Devils Tower as the first national monument in the United States. (Following the geographic naming standard, Devils Tower omits the otherwise necessary apostrophe.) The monument has several trails circling the tower. I was immediately able to eliminate one because it was paved. If you've read this book in order, you realize I don't often select paved trails. I like to say, "If we wanted pavement, we'd take a walk around the block."

My attention turned to the 2.8-mile Red Beds Trail, although I was concerned it would be a little too rocky. After reviewing as many pictures as I could find from trip reports with the understanding that none of them were from people using wheels, I had to rely on my instinct. I gave us a better-than-average chance of completing the trail.

It was an unusually hot June afternoon when we arrived at Devils Tower National Monument for our pushike. It was also a little later in the day than I planned. As we entered the park, I could see some of the Red Beds Trail, and it looked too rocky for us. It was also out in the open, meaning there was no protection from the sun. These conditions concerned me. I continued the drive circling the tower to the end in a large parking lot filled with vehicles and people looking up. While I filled our water bottles outside the visitor center, I regretted not having a backup trail in the area.

Returning to our parked rental SUV, I saw the beginning of the paved trail, and something immediately caught my eye. It was the disabled blue sign with a white wheelchair and rider with a circle around it and a line drawn diagonally with the words "Not Accessible" below. A sidewalk trail, and they couldn't even make it accessible? Most people would walk away, but I saw this sign as an invitation for us to investigate further. I knew we might not be able to complete enough of the trail to use for the book. If that happened, we would have to return to Wyoming for a trail to write about, but it was worth the risk.

The Devils Tower Trail is a shorter trail because it circles closer to the base. The path started nicely paved and wide enough to maneuver around the many tourists loitering close to the trailhead. I appreciated the shade offered by the towering Ponderosa Pines over our heads. We noticed that most visitors weren't hiking this trail; they were looking for quick photo opportunities. After maybe

200 yards, we had the path to ourselves. I thought if it was this easy all the way around, it could probably be considered "accessible" for all to enjoy.

In front of us, Devils Tower rose to dizzying heights straight up from the rubble of giant boulders. We were following the trail in a counterclockwise direction. After the first hard-right turn, it was immediately apparent why this paved trail wasn't considered accessible. It had steep sections along with narrow portions between car-sized rocks, and a few tight turns. The pavement also had some significant cracks and broken areas due to harsh freeze/thaw weather cycles. Water can get in the smallest crack and will expand when it drops below freezing, which widens the crack farther. If the span from one side to the other of a crack is too far and/or one side is higher than the other, it becomes difficult and possibly impossible to push a wheelchair safely over it. A jog stroller or mobility chair can navigate these cracks with relative ease. Cracks can be dangerous because they can cause a wheelchair to come to a sudden stop, but the momentum may continue with the occupant falling forward. If the user doesn't have full upper-body control or the instinct to brace against a fall, he or she will land on his or her face.

Because Kellisa never learned to crawl and walk, she never developed the instinct to brace a fall with her hands. Since she can propel herself in her wheelchair, we usually don't limit what she can do or where she can go. Our primary concern is curbs, stairs, and cracks. Over the years, Kellisa has landed on her face and has a few scars from road rash to prove it.

Kellisa's worst fall happened in October 2006 when she was seven years old. Kellisa was outside on the playground during recess at school and just happened to be chasing a boy she was crushing on at the time. He was on a tricycle, and she was determined to catch him. He made a sudden turn. When Kellisa attempted the same turn, one of her front wheels cut the corner just short and briefly left the pavement into wood chips. The wheel was now lower than the adjacent sidewalk, which caused her wheelchair to come to a sudden stop. The forward momentum flipped the chair forward, and Kellisa landed on her nose and forehead without the benefit of any bracing.

The school nurse was called and immediately attended to Kellisa. The school staff called 911 and Lisa. Kellisa was bleeding, and they were concerned about the trauma to her head. When Lisa arrived at the school, she could hear Kellisa giggling from inside the nurse's office. Once inside, the source of the giggles was obvious; Kellisa was surrounded by six male first responders from the local firehouse, and she was soaking up all the attention. Even though Kellisa was happy, she was still transported to the hospital for further testing and observation to play it safe.

In the end, she "wheeled" away with just some missing skin on her nose and forehead that looked far worse than it was for several months. Kellisa was very proud of her scars and loved showing them off to anyone within twenty feet when they were still fresh. To this day, you can still see marks from this fall on her face.

We would never want to see Kellisa hurt, but there was a part of us that felt thankful she was being included with regular kids at school and was doing what everyone else was doing. We were horrified when the school informed us the following day that they would keep Kellisa inside. They felt it was too dangerous for her to be on the playground and wanted to make sure she would never fall on her face again. We understood how scary the situation was for the staff that worked with Kellisa, but we protested this new safety measure without a second of hesitation. Limiting Kellisa's activities to prevent her from doing something she loved in the name of safety seemed more harmful than anything that could happen out on the playground. On that October afternoon, Kellisa was just a normal kid on the playground with her friends. If she could run, it would have been her knees and palms with the road rash. Since the school knew we were the type of parents to dig in, they allowed her to continue playing on the playground after we gave written permission.

The Devils Tower Trail didn't pose any significant risk to Kellisa since we could safely negotiate the uneven sidewalk. Still, I could understand why wheelchairs would be prohibited from using this trail, or, as I like to think of it, not advised to use it. That said, they could have easily made this trail wheelchair friendly when it was first designed. Sadly, they did not. The only real concern for us was on some of the steeper sections. Since I'm always tethered to Kellisa's chair, her well-being was never in any additional danger. She was probably the safest kid in the park since she wouldn't be scrambling on any of the boulders or tripping over the cracks.

There was enough of a challenge on this trail for me to consider this a pushike instead of just a walk down a sidewalk. Having Devils Tower rising to our left with drop-away views to a faraway horizon on the right helped the trail to feel more like a wilderness experience. If we didn't count the large crowd of people near the trailhead, we could count the number of other hikers encountered on our combined hands, and I'm not sure we would have needed Kellisa's hands. The trail never went in a straight line, which added to the experience. If it wasn't cutting through boulders, it was winding its way around the tower through strands of Ponderosa Pine trees. Benches were scattered along the trail, usually placed at scenic overlooks. You could always see some part of Devils Tower, but views from the base directly up to the summit were limited to the areas free of the pines.

We could tell we were nearing the end of our loop when we started to see tourists milling around the trail. There were a couple of beautiful viewing areas surrounded by large rocks near the base of Devils Tower. I had to strain my neck to look straight up toward the summit. I took a few beautiful pictures of Kellisa before moving on our way. We had to navigate through kids running around and several retired couples huffing and puffing before reaching the mass of visitors just before the trailhead.

The parking lot was free from shade, so I didn't waste time getting Kellisa and myself inside our SUV to cool off with the air conditioning turned to full blast. As I sat there looking up through the trees at Devils Tower, I reflected on how I was wrong about the paved trails. The Devils Tower Trail is a worthy pushiking destination because it breaks the stereotype that all paved wilderness trails are short, boring, and lack challenge. I couldn't help but wonder what other trails were out there for Kellisa, both rugged and paved.

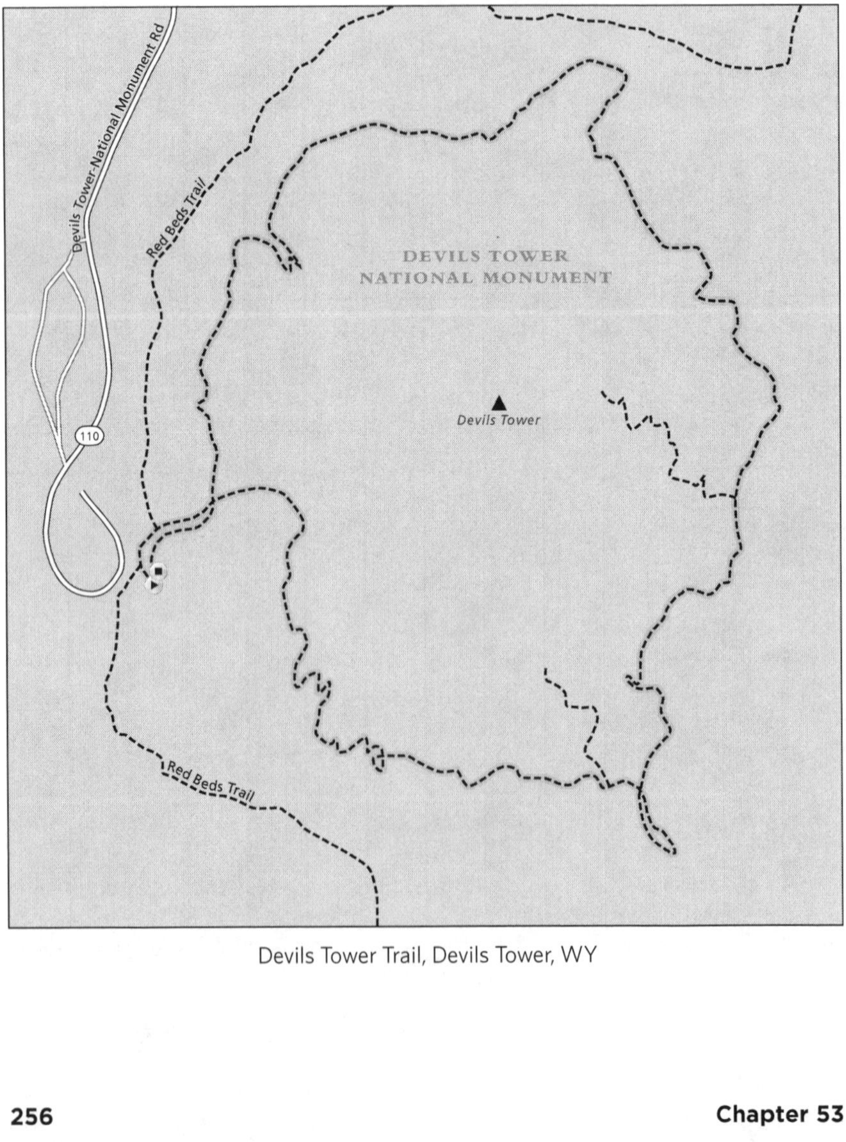

Devils Tower Trail, Devils Tower, WY

54
Washington, DC

Trail name: Outer Loop
Location: Theodore Roosevelt Island National Memorial
Distance: 1.9 mi
Duration (active): 52m
Average speed: 2.2 mi/h
Total ascent: 72 ft
Highest point: 49 ft
Difficulty: Moderate

Theodore Roosevelt is known as the conservation president and is responsible for creating five national parks, 18 national monuments, and ultimately protecting 230 million acres. It only fits that Roosevelt's memorial in Washington, DC, is a forested island in the Potomac River. Trails lead to a plaza with fountains and a giant statue of Roosevelt in the island's interior. Other paths circle the island with shorter connecting trails between them. It is interesting to note that if you arrive by car, you park it in a lot located in the state of Virginia. That is what we did on a Monday morning in early October. Once we were ready, I pushed Kellisa over a footbridge connecting the parking lot to Theodore Roosevelt Island in Washington, DC.

We decided to take the short trail to visit the plaza and statue where I took a picture of Kellisa in the same spot as our first trip to the island back in June 2010. I enjoy looking at photographs of Kellisa taken at the same location years apart to document her growth. After exploring the memorial area, it was time to pushike. I knew we would pushike on Theodore Roosevelt Island, but I didn't have specific trails selected to explore, so I consulted a trail map on a kiosk. I noticed a boardwalk through a swamp area along the backside of the island. I didn't remember this from our first visit, so we decided to pushike the perimeter loop, which included the swamp boardwalk section.

If you're looking for a trail with seclusion, peace, and quiet, you will not find it on Theodore Roosevelt Island. We encountered a steady flow of hikers and joggers, many with dogs. Kellisa was excited to see so many dogs out on the trail. She said "Hey" to all of them as they passed, followed by a giggle. Besides joggers, we saw many people just out for a walk, including many in the forest dressed for business. We even saw three people hiking barefoot. One man was hiking dressed as a pilgrim. The diversity of the people enjoying the island was unmatched on any of our other trails.

Since the island is adjacent to an expressway and highway bridge connecting Virginia to the nation's capital, there was a constant sound of traffic. The island is also close to Reagan National Airport. Planes landing at the airport fly directly over the island every ninety seconds. Most of the island is heavily wooded. Every time we were in a small clearing, Kellisa would get excited and point to the sky for each approaching plane and yell, "Plane!"

We pushiked the perimeter in a counterclockwise direction. The trail was damp from recent rains, but not at all muddy. The path was wide and mostly free from roots and rocks. As we headed toward the southern end of the island, there was a short descent, yet nothing too hard. It was difficult to hear anything but the traffic above us as the trail ran next to the highway bridge.

With a little distance and trees between us and the bridge, the noise died down slightly once we reached the swamp at the backside of the memorial. The boardwalk ran along the edge of the swamp, with the forest rising on the opposite side of the water. This section reminded me of Georgia and South

Carolina. I caught myself looking in the water and on logs for alligators. The boardwalk was in excellent condition. So often, boards are missing, or sections have shifted, causing height variances from one area to the next, which makes pushing a challenge, but this boardwalk was well kept. There were several areas to sit and reflect at the edge of the swamp. I was also surprised at how long the boardwalk stretched. Overall, we were very impressed with the high quality of this trail.

As we neared the northern section of the island, we left the boardwalk behind and started along the natural surface trail again with some slight elevation changes. At this point, we started hearing and eventually seeing several helicopters flying low over the Potomac River. Kellisa thought these loud machines were funny, but I couldn't hear her laughs. To our surprise, there was a water fountain placed next to the trail, and it was refreshing to get a drink of cold water before hitting the final stretch of trail. As the trail turned back toward the pedestrian bridge to the parking lot, we saw a sign announcing the section up ahead was closed due to mud. It was just a sign, and nothing was placed across the trail to block forward progress. We could have backtracked to take an interior trail back to the plaza area and then the spur trail to the bridge, but we decided to continue with the thought of turning back if we encountered extreme mud. There was only one short section that I would describe as damp, but not muddy. It was easy enough to push Kellisa through this area, and just beyond it, we were back at the pedestrian bridge with the parking lot on the other side. I'm guessing the sign was placed several days before our visit when the trail conditions were worse from recent rains.

We paused for maybe ten minutes on the bridge so that Kellisa could watch the landing planes fly over her head. In between planes, she would greet everyone crossing the bridge. It was like Kellisa was the ambassador for Theodore Roosevelt Island National Memorial for the morning. Most of the hikers, joggers, and businesspeople acknowledged Kellisa with a smile or quick "Hi," which made both of us feel good. I plan on writing the National Park Service to see if they will offer a paying job to Kellisa!

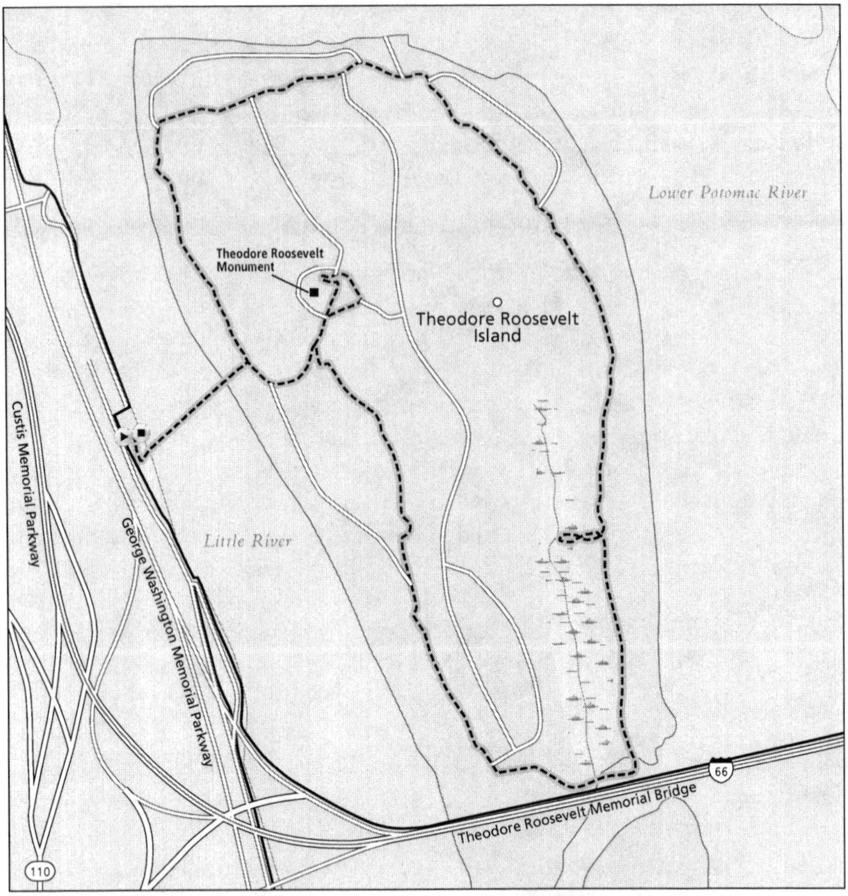

Outer Loop, Theodore Roosevelt Island, Washington, DC

Appendix: Trail Websites

Alabama: https://www.fs.usda.gov/recarea/alabama/recarea/?recid=30113
Alaska: https://www.fs.usda.gov/detail/chugach/learning/?cid=stelprdb5058790
Arizona: https://www.nps.gov/grca/index.htm
Arkansas: https://www.arkansasstateparks.com/parks/mount-nebo-state-park
California, Northern: https://www.parks.ca.gov/?page_id=425
California, Southern: https://www.nps.gov/deva/index.htm
Colorado: https://www.nps.gov/romo/index.htm
Connecticut: https://www.wyndhamlandtrust.org/project/bull-hill/
Delaware: https://www.destateparks.com/BrandywineCreek
Florida: https://www.nps.gov/timu/index.htm
Georgia: https://www.fws.gov/refuge/okefenokee/
Hawaii, Difficult: https://www.maui-hikes.com/ohai-trail
Hawaii, Easy: https://www.fws.gov/refuge/kealia_pond/
Idaho: https://www.cityofboise.org/departments/parks-and-recreation/parks/oregon-trail-reserve/
Illinois: https://www.dnr.illinois.gov/Parks/Pages/VoloBog.aspx
Indiana: https://eaglecreekpark.org/
Iowa: https://www.mycountyparks.com/county/dubuque/Park/Whitewater-Canyon-Wildlife-Area.aspx
Kansas: https://www.nps.gov/tapr/index.htm
Kentucky: https://www.nps.gov/cuga/index.htm
Louisiana: https://www.crt.state.la.us/louisiana-state-parks/parks/fontainebleau-state-park/
Maine: https://www.fws.gov/refuge/rachel_carson/
Maryland: https://www.aacounty.org/departments/recreation-parks/parks/beverly-triton/index.html
Massachusetts: https://www.mass.gov/locations/walden-pond-state-reservation
Michigan, Lower Peninsula: http://www.michigandnr.com/parksandtrails/Details.aspx?type=SPRK&id=453
Michigan, Upper Peninsula: https://www.nps.gov/piro/index.htm
Minnesota: https://www.dnr.state.mn.us/state_parks/park.html?id=spk00175#homepage

Mississippi: https://www.fws.gov/refuge/Mississippi_Sandhill_Crane/
Missouri: https://mostateparks.com/park/prairie-state-park
Montana: http://stateparks.mt.gov/medicine-rocks/
Nebraska: http://outdoornebraska.gov/ponca/
Nevada: https://www.fs.usda.gov/recarea/htnf/recarea/?recid=65818
New Hampshire: https://www.wildlife.state.nh.us/merrimack/sewallsfalls.html
New Jersey: https://www.fws.gov/refuge/supawna_meadows/
New Mexico: https://www.losalamosnm.us/government/departments/community_services/parks_recreation_and_open_spaces/openspaceandtrails/canyon_rim_trails
New York: https://wildadirondacks.org/bloomingdale-bog-trail.html
North Carolina: https://www.fs.usda.gov/recarea/nfsnc/recarea/?recid=48620
North Dakota: https://www.nps.gov/thro/index.htm
Ohio: https://naturepreserves.ohiodnr.gov/sheldonmarsh
Oklahoma: https://www.nps.gov/chic/index.htm
Oregon: https://www.nps.gov/crla/index.htm
Pennsylvania: https://www.fws.gov/refuge/cherry_valley/
Rhode Island: https://www.summitpost.org/jerimoth-hill/152342
South Carolina: https://www.nps.gov/cong/index.htm
South Dakota: https://www.nps.gov/lecl/learn/historyculture/spirit-mound.htm
Tennessee: https://www.nps.gov/grsm/index.htm
Texas: https://tpwd.texas.gov/state-parks/dinosaur-valley
Utah: https://stateparks.utah.gov/parks/goosenecks/
Vermont: https://www.fws.gov/refuge/missisquoi/
Virginia: https://www.vacreepertrail.org/
Washington: https://parks.state.wa.us/538/Lewis-Clark
West Virginia: https://wvstateparks.com/park/beech-fork-state-park/
Wisconsin: https://dnr.wi.gov/topic/parks/name/chipmoraine
Wyoming: https://www.nps.gov/deto/index.htm
Washington, DC: https://www.nps.gov/this/index.htm

Index

About the Author

Christopher Kain has been defining pushiking for more than fifteen years. With his daughter Kellisa, they've traveled to all fifty states at least twice and have pushiked at least two trails in every state. Chris and Kellisa are often found "where wheels weren't meant to go," and they have pushiked twenty miles across the desert in New Mexico and across frozen Rainy Lake in Minnesota. They've summited twenty-two state highpoints. Together, they've been featured in newspapers, cable news websites, and local news programs across the country.

Chris shares his family's adventures on his blog (www.kellisaspath.com) and maintains an author website (www.christopherkain.com).

When not on a trail, Chris is the western area technical manager and social media representative for H. B. Fuller Construction Products.

Chris resides in Roseville, California, with his wife, Lisa, and daughters, Kellisa and Egypt.

Egypt has joined Chris and Kellisa in all fifty states and has pushiked at least one trail in each state.